FOOD or WAR

Ours is the *Age of Food*. Food is a central obsession in all cultures, nations, the media and society. Our future supply of food is filled with risk, and history tells us that lack of food leads to war. But it also presents us with spectacular opportunities for fresh human creativity and technological prowess. Julian Cribb describes a new food system capable of meeting all humans' needs on our hot, overcrowded planet. The book is for anyone concerned about the health, safety, affordability, diversity and sustainability of their food – and the peace of our planet. This book is not just timely – its message is of the greatest urgency. Audiences include consumers, 'foodies', policymakers, researchers, cooks, chefs and farmers. Indeed, anyone who cares about their food, where it comes from and what it means for them, their children and grandchildren.

Julian Cribb FRSA FTSE is an Australian author and science communicator. His career includes appointments as scientific editor for *The Australian* newspaper, director of national awareness for the Australian Commonwealth Scientific and Industrial Research Organisation (CSIRO), editor of several newspapers, member of numerous scientific boards and advisory panels, and president of national professional bodies for agricultural journalism and science communication. His published work includes over 9000 articles, 3000 science media releases and ten books. He has received 32 awards for journalism. His previous books include *The Coming Famine* (2010), *Poisoned Planet* (2014), and *Surviving the 21st Century* (2017). As a science writer and a grandparent, Julian Cribb is deeply concerned at the existential emergency facing humanity, the mounting scientific evidence for it and the deficit of clear thinking about how to overcome it.

'Food, like air, water, soil and biodiversity, is one of humankind's most fundamental needs, a source of joy and creator of community. The eco-crises of climate change and loss of biodiversity reveal the total unsustainability of the current global food system. This book is an urgent call for recognition that the inescapable need for change also brings enormous opportunities.'

David Suzuki

'Food or War targets an issue that touches every human life, every day: food. And that, without it, people fight. It shows that our "jawprint" is the heaviest of all our impacts on our finite planet – and that, for civilisation to survive, how we produce food must change . . . Anyone with an interest in either the human future or food should read this clear, authoritative, scary book. So should all first-year college classes.'

Paul R. Ehrlich, co-author of Jaws: The Story of a Hidden Epidemic; Bing Professor of Population Studies, Emeritus; President, Center for Conservation Biology; Department of Biology, Stanford University

'Throughout history, food has been both a tool and a consequence of conflict and migration, which continues today exacerbated by arable land lost to cities, unreliable climate and excess consumption in rich nations while millions remain malnourished elsewhere. Cribb's analysis is urgently apposite, as is his practical call for a sustainable, nourishing and resilient global food system.'

Professor Lindsay Falvey FTSE, FAIAS, University of Melbourne, and Life Member of Clare Hall, University of Cambridge

'Wars rage on in Syria, Yemen and elsewhere, in part driven by food shortages. What to do? . . . We can turn this imbalance around. Cribb points the way in this must-read book.'

Tim Fischer, AC, former Deputy Prime Minister of Australia, and Chair of the Global Crop Trust with Seed Vault in Svalbard and HQ in Bonn, Germany

'Julian Cribb's comprehensive and thoughtful plan to deal with an impending global food security disaster deserves coordinated and urgent consideration by the UN FAO and all national governments.'

Major General Michael Jeffery, former Governor General of Australia

'Access to this book will enrich deliberations on critical issues of global food supply, dealing with refugees and poverty, and the food/land/water nexus. The evidence-based approach, integration across issues, and presentation of opportunities for the future make this text stand out from the crowd. It is highly recommended.'

Kath Bowmer, former Deputy Chief of CSIRO Land and Water and Deputy Vice Chancellor of Charles Sturt University

'On an increasingly crowded planet that is itself subject to an existential threat, Julian focuses this book on the "Food Challenge", its magnitude and urgency. We have much to think about and prepare.'

John Hewson, Crawford School of Public Policy, Australian National University, and former Federal Liberal and Opposition Leader

'Food or War details the consequences for the global food supply that humanity faces due to the cascading impacts of climate, resource scarcity, toxicity and other threats – and provides workable solutions. I am convinced that this is going to be one of the most cited books and will be an important source of guidance for future generations. I recommend this book to every single person who loves the planet they live on and cares for the future of their grandkids.'

Razia Shaik, Charles Sturt University

'Drawing on his extensive scientific and historical knowledge, Cribb takes us on a grim and tightly argued odyssey to the edge of the Earth. He holds our hand while we stare into the abyss. Frightening. Having outlined the reality of our tenuous hold on the supports of life, he offers creative and imaginative solutions. A must-read for anyone who cares about the future of humanity.'

Bruce Haigh, former Australian diplomat and refugee advocate

'In a time when we are absorbed in populist, political nonsense, Julian brings us to heel with the existential threat we face, in simple language; he joins all the dots.'

The Hon. John Kerin, former Australian Minister for
Primary Industry

'Unputdownable. Dealing with the multiple threats to humanity's most basic need – food – it unceremoniously pulls your head from the sand – but empowers you with the knowledge to do something. An absolutely essential read. This masterful work articulates clearly humanity's future and may just be warning enough for globally connected communities to avert the avalanche of existential threats bearing down.'

Brad Collis, Editorial Director, Coretext; CSIRO, Australia;
author of Fields of Discovery

'Human nature meets human need when the red and black horsemen ride in the ultimate existential food fight. At once perceptive and persuasive, Julian Cribb delivers another science-based study of the human condition at its most basic. Food or War is exceptional.'

David Hulme, Publisher, Vision.org

'A compelling case for turning swords into ploughshares and building a sustainable global food supply in this century of existential climate risks.'

David Spratt, Washington College of Law, and author of
Climate Code Red

'Food or War is a provocative title for a book that delves into the depths of the relationship between global peace and our future capacity to produce and distribute food that is healthy, efficiently produced and equitably enjoyed. An urgent lesson we must all learn before it is too late to do so.'

Ms. Christiana Figueres, Founding Partner, Global Optimism and
Former Executive Secretary, UN Climate Convention (2010-2016)

'Cribb argues that a fair and equitable global food system based on ecological principles is the key to peace and future prosperity in an era of multiple environmental crises and growing population.'

Stephen Leahy

FOOD or WAR

JULIAN CRIBB

CAMBRIDGE
UNIVERSITY PRESS

CAMBRIDGE
UNIVERSITY PRESS

University Printing House, Cambridge CB2 8BS, United Kingdom

One Liberty Plaza, 20th Floor, New York, NY 10006, USA

477 Williamstown Road, Port Melbourne, VIC 3207, Australia

314–321, 3rd Floor, Plot 3, Splendor Forum, Jasola District Centre, New Delhi – 110025, India

79 Anson Road, #06-04/06, Singapore 079906

Cambridge University Press is part of the University of Cambridge.

It furthers the University's mission by disseminating knowledge in the pursuit of education, learning, and research at the highest international levels of excellence.

www.cambridge.org
Information on this title: www.cambridge.org/9781108712903
DOI: 10.1017/9781108690126

First published 2019

Printed in the United Kingdom by TJ International Ltd. Padstow Cornwall

A catalogue record for this publication is available from the British Library.

ISBN 978-1-108-71290-3 Paperback

DEDICATION

This book is dedicated to Emeritus Professor Paul Ehrlich, Major General Michael Jeffery and Emeritus Professor Bob Douglas, whose wisdom enables them to see further into the human destiny than most of us.

CONTENTS

PREFACE

For as long as humans have fought one another, food has been a pivotal element in their struggles, yet one that is often ignored – or else footnoted in histories and reportage. In recent centuries, more people have perished during wars from hunger than have died through direct military action. And more wars have originated in the fear and hatred which lack of fair access to food, land and water generates among contending cultures, creeds, classes, tribes and nations, than from other causes.

Despite these well-evidenced facts people, scholars and the media have a tendency to focus on the political, religious or nationalistic differences between warring factions – seldom on the underlying drivers that thrust them into conflict with one another in the first place. This book presents evidence that food – or fear of its lack – plays a central role in the genesis of human conflict, and that the opposite is also true: that ensuring a reliable, sustainable and nutritious food supply is a sure way to lower the tensions that lead to conflict. Indeed, it argues that food is one of the greatest, least recognised and most affordable 'weapons of peace' available to humanity.

Ours are perilous times. As human numbers lurch towards 10 billion, all expecting highly varied diets rich in protein, today's farming systems are starting to crumble. For reasons that will be made clear, the modern food system has never been more vulnerable or at greater risk of compound failure.

If we humans truly want a peaceful world, free from warfare and vast refugee tsunamis, it follows that we must eliminate, one by one, the factors that are conducive to war. And hunger, or the fear of it, is among the greatest.

This book is the fourth in a science-based series I have written on the existential emergency facing humanity in the present and coming generations, and what we need to do to avoid it:

- *The Coming Famine* (UCP 2010) explored the drivers behind growing global food insecurity amid the illusion of plenty, and what should be done about them;
- *Poisoned Planet* (A&U 2014) assessed the human chemical impact on the planet and our health, finding it far larger than most people imagine. It offered solutions;
- *Surviving the 21st Century* (Springer 2017) surveyed the scientific evidence for the ten great existential threats to humanity, their integrated nature, and what we can do about them both as a species and as individuals.

This book, *Food or War*, zeroes in on an issue that touches every single human life, every single day: food. And the fact that, without it, we usually fight.

If issues such as climate change, mass extinction, weapons of mass destruction (WMD) or pandemic disease sometimes seem a bit large and intractable to the average citizen as they go about their daily life, food most definitely isn't. Its lack, or fear of its lack, are a frequent cause of alarm – but even its abundance, and the poor quality of the world diet that accompanies it, are disturbing in other ways. Our 'jawprint' is, of all the human impacts, by far the heaviest on our finite planet.

Furthermore, food is one way that individuals can have a powerful impact on global issues such as climate, conflict, extinction and mass toxicity. Choosing carefully how and what we eat empowers every one of us to decide the kind of world we want our children to inherit: one that is verdant, resilient and abundant with life – or a smouldering toxic slagheap, devastated by wars and ruinous technologies.

My main purpose in writing this book is not only to document the intimate connectivity between food and war so that people appreciate it better, but also to help further the essential understanding that our fate is in our own hands – not merely those of the politicians, plutocrats and potentates who claim to rule over us. We get to decide what sort of world we want – not they. And a key part of the decision lies in our food choices.

This book is intended to empower each and every one of us to make wiser, more informed, decisions, so we may together survive to fulfil our destiny as a wise species, wherever that may take us.

I wish to acknowledge, with my sincere thanks, the advice, inspiration, criticism, feedback, ideas and wisdom of: Paul Ehrlich, Lindsay Falvey, Robyn Alders, Bruce French, John Kerin, Bob Douglas, Ravi Naidu, Terry Hughes, Michael Jeffery, John Hartley, Bill D'Arcy, Brad Collis, David Hulme, Pennie Scott, Lars Charas, Sue Radd, Mark Bittman, Shenggen Fan, Robyn Williams, Ian Chambers, Suzette Searle, Bruce Haigh, Karalyn Hingston, John Schmidt, Michael Brown, Ta-Yan Leong, Richard Davies, Oscar Rodriguez, Will Steffen, Sister Corrie Evidente, Martha Mundy, Virginia Gorsevski, Cynthia Gharios, Peter Robinson, Félix Pharand-Deschênes, Danielle Nierenberg, Jon Foley, Ken Drummond, Paulie Higgison and Tilly's Devine Café Gallery. In particular, I wish to express my gratitude and appreciation to Matt Lloyd and the team at Cambridge University Press, including Zoë Pruce, 'Raj' Rajmohan, Charlotte Porter and Beverley Lawrence, for their skill and professionalism in helping to arouse a sleeping world to one of the many perils it faces.

Julian Cribb, Canberra 2019

Albrecht Dürer's famous woodcut of the Four Horsemen of the Apocalypse, 1498. Left to right: Pestilence and Death; Famine; War; and False Saviours. Metropolitan Museum of Art, NY.

1 FOOD AND CONFLICT: PREMONITIONS

The Crimson Thread – Food Empires – Here Come the
Long Ships – Food and the Rise of China – Food and
India – Food and War – Fear of Famine

'Homo homini lupus: Man is the Wolf of Man'

Latin proverb

The Crimson Thread

For thousands of years, famine and conflict have united
in the human mind and destiny. And they will rule its future,
also.

In Albrecht Dürer's famous woodcut of the Four Horsemen of
the Apocalypse (opposite), drawn from the Biblical book of Reve-
lation, Famine is the central figure, astride a black horse and
with empty food scales in hand, riding down the hapless multi-
tudes of citizens, along with his grim allies: False Ideologies (or
Saviours); War; and Pestilence and Death.[1]

Most people who die in wars perish from hunger, as their food
stocks are plundered and devoured by marauding armies,
farming is disrupted by military recruitment, food requisitions
and scorched earth policies, and the food and trading systems
that sustain their society collapse. Contrary to the popular
imagery of war, hunger is a far greater killer than military
action or disease, though it interacts with both.

The earliest-known battle painting of all, a vivid piece of
Australian Aboriginal rock art (Figure 1.1) dating from perhaps
17,000 years ago depicts two battlelines of combatants exchan-
ging volleys of multi-barbed harpoons and boomerangs – which
are primarily hunting implements rather than weapons. The

Figure 1.1. The 17,000 year old Gwion Gwion rock art from Australia depicting a battle between two groups of warriors, hurling multi-barbed harpoons and boomerangs. Credit: Bradshaw Foundation & G. L. Walsh.

leader of one side has charged his enemies and fallen before their missiles. The painting is from an enigmatic phase of art in the Kimberley (northwestern Australia) known as Gwion Gwion, which was strangely different to other, later, Aboriginal art forms and was contemporary with the peak of the last Ice Age.[2] The fact that the combatants are using hunting tools, rather than purpose-made man-killing weapons, hints that the origins of their dispute lie in access to food in the form of hunting rights, territory or water (which amount to the same thing, as animals were often hunted when they came to drink at water holes in the parched Australian landscape).

The figures depicted in the Australian battle scene are from the later 'clothes peg' period of Gwion Gwion, which is thought to coincide with a time when sea levels were rising rapidly, by an astonishing 53 metres (174 feet), as the great ice sheets covering the continents melted and collapsed. The flood they unleashed inundated a quarter of the Australian landmass (over 2.12 million square kilometres) drowning beneath the sea an area larger than France, Spain, Germany, Britain and Italy combined. Prehistorians have calculated this flooding would have halved the area of good coastal land available to support each inhabitant of the continent at the time, thrusting overwhelming stresses onto populations which had expanded over the previous 20,000 years with the largesse of a far greater area. On the fertile, well-watered coastal plains where most of these hunter-gatherer people subsisted, the pressure on resources would have become intense as the existing population was compressed into a rapidly dwindling area, or else driven into the harsh interior Australian deserts.[3] At the end of this period the Gwion Gwion art ceases abruptly and is replaced by the Wandjina tradition. It may be no coincidence that this was also about the same time that Australia's Ice Age megafauna – giant kangaroos, emus and wombats – also vanished entirely and forever. Thus, it is also probably no mere coincidence that the world's first battle painting appears at this time of stress, extinction and possible genocide. Those ancient warriors were in all likelihood fighting over food and the shrinking territory that supplied it – as a direct consequence of a rapidly warming world.

Conflict over scarce resources of food, land and water is a crimson thread that runs through the entirety of human history. In every inhabited continent periods of scarcity have ignited conflict, insurrection and war – and wars have been followed in turn by prolonged hunger and hardship, sometimes giving rise to new wars in a horrible, almost interminable cycle.

Food Empires

Food has played a dynamic role in the genesis of human conflict since the dawn of civilisation – and not merely its lack. Also its abundance. The world's great civilisations almost all arose in fertile river valleys such as the Nile, the Tigris–Euphrates, the Indus, the Ganges, the Yangtse and Yellow, the Mekong, the Rhine, the Danube, the Tiber and lake systems such as those of Switzerland, Scandinavia and Mexico for a good reason: to build and maintain an army you need two things – a surplus of young males to use as warriors and a surplus of food to breed and feed them. With the advent and spread of agriculture, 5000–7000 years ago, in the fertile bottomlands of the great rivers and lakes, a comparatively stable food surplus became possible for the first time in the human experience. With pottery and basketry came the ability to store and preserve nutrients through the lean times of the year, leading to declines in infant and maternal mortality. This in turn bred steady expansion in human populations – which soon began to exceed, or even to exhaust, the resources within their traditional boundaries. Since farming makes it possible for one person to support many, there were soon plenty of spare, fit young males to go a-roving – and this coincided with the advent of the age of metals. These raids, like those of the later Vikings and Mongolian tribes, soon developed into organised warfare. Time and again, the fertile regions of the world have spewed out great armies, bent on conquest, plunder and, often, on the acquisition of fresh lands in which their people can flourish. But first they must displace or absorb the conquered.

It is likely that the Tiber Valley, in Italy, provided sufficient reliable sustenance to support a primitive Roman army, originally organised into legions on family clan lines, that was able to subdue many of its neighbouring tribes, like the Sabines, Latins, Volscians and Etruscans, who inhabited hillier, less-fertile regions. However, this amateur force was nowhere near powerful enough to resist the military might of the Gauls, who had crossed the Alps and subjugated the fertile Po Valley in northern Italy, flourishing as a consequence. In 390 BC, a well-fed Gallic warband under King Brennus broke out of the Po Valley, smashed the early Roman army at the battle of the Allia and then went on to sack and occupy the little city of Rome – though legend insists the citadel on the Capitoline Hill held out, thanks to the geese who warned the sleeping guards of an attempt by the invaders to storm their hilltop fortress. The Romans fled in all directions, taking shelter with their frightened neighbours. Eventually these scattered Romans managed to raise enough cash to ransom their city and induce the Gauls to depart, and the invaders made their way into southern Italy.[4] Their departure left a power vacuum which the Romans, having rebuilt their city and army more strongly, gradually filled over the next two centuries, asserting hegemony over the whole of Italy.

During this period, Rome faced another invasion, led by the Carthaginian general Hannibal who, in 216 BC, after the prodigious feat of crossing the Alps from southern France with his army, its horses and elephants, inflicted several crushing military defeats on the Roman army – but failed to capture the city, which was, by then, ringed with a formidable stone wall. The Romans and the Carthaginians had been scrapping with one another on and off for almost half a century, as their growing spheres of trade, colonial and political interest collided. To begin with, Carthage, chief city of the Phoenicians in North Africa, had the upper hand because theirs was a 'thalassocracy' – an empire founded on the wealth garnered from its sea-borne trade and its maritime strike power. However, this perspective overlooks one of the chief dynamics in its rise: the ability to grow crops and supply its largely mercenary armies through access to the great grain bowl of the Mediterranean, the North African coastline, stretching from Egypt to Morocco, including its own Libyan hinterland. Access to reliable food supplies thus fed the growth of both the Roman and Carthaginian empires and their war machines, bringing forward the inevitable head-clash over colliding spheres of interest in the form of the three devastating Punic Wars. These ended only when the Romans, spurred by the vitriolic cries of the Elder Cato that '*Cartago delenda est* ' ('Carthage must be destroyed') provoked the third war by demanding the Carthaginians surrender all their children, then used their refusal as a pretext to besiege, starve and eventually take the city and enslave its inhabitants. To make sure that Carthage never arose to trouble them again they razed the city and its defences utterly, cursed the rubble and sowed the surrounding fields with salt, so they could not grow crops. This ancient Roman 'Agent Orange' tactic is nowadays questioned by some scholars, but the *Cambridge Ancient History* asserts 'Buildings and walls were razed to the ground; the plough passed over the site, and salt was sown in the furrow made... A solemn curse was pronounced that neither house, nor crops, should ever rise again'. [5] Logically, if you curse a place, you might wish to make sure the curse will stick – and salt, which is freely available from desert lakebeds in North Africa, was an effective way to discourage wheat production, for a time at least.

If they indeed salted the Carthaginian farmland, then the Romans clearly understood the importance of a sustainable local food supply as the springboard for the growth of both a city and a military power (although it was not a permanent solution, as the salt would eventually leach out of the soil after a few years of rain). The Romans' most important gains from the conquest of Carthage and their consequent acquisition of its overseas territories in Spain and Africa were a navy, which they used to suppress piracy and encourage peaceful trade across the entire Mediterranean, and access to the priceless grain belt of Egypt and North Africa. This both fed and enriched the subsequent expansion of Rome and its imperial dominions, supplying the vital bread that accompanied the circuses that various Emperors used to placate the mob and manage local urban politics. More importantly, the grain trade generated a large part of the mercantile wealth that was taxed to pay the 55 legions that guarded the Empire's frontiers, from Britain and Spain to the Black Sea and Persia. The importance of this industrial-scale grain trade to Rome's life and economy can still be seen in the vast ruins of the harbour at Ostia.

Besides being competent warriors, the Romans were excellent farmers themselves and their agricultural system, from the huge *latifundia* (large slave-worked estates) to the diversity of smallholder agriculture supplied most of their needs for grains, olives, vegetables, meat and grapes. Indeed, our global food supply today is still essentially patterned on the Roman system of broadacre single-crop agriculture in favoured regions, exporting grain and other produce to distant cities – except that today, industrial technology has substituted machinery and chemicals for agricultural slavery and draft animals. This point needs to be borne in mind as we explore the frailties of the modern food system in later chapters (Chapters 3 and 4). Ominously, when its food system failed in the early centuries of the Christian Era, the Roman Empire collapsed.

There are numerous popular theories as to why Rome fell, starting with the obvious proximate cause – the invasion of Goths, Huns and other barbarian tribes – imperial overreach (the favoured view of the historian Gibbon) and the economic mismanagement of the Empire itself. However, history is seldom quite so simple.

In 165 AD, Roman legionaries returning from the Middle East brought with them a horrible plague, whose symptoms were fever, diarrhoea and boils. Known as the Antonine Plague (165–180 AD) it was probably smallpox. It slew an estimated seven million people throughout the Roman Empire before subsiding. Plagues, classically, are thought of as largely urban contagions stemming from overcrowding and bad public hygiene – but their effects among country dwellers and farmers, whose immune systems have never been 'vaccinated' by previous exposure to city diseases, can be even more devastating (as the Black Death subsequently demonstrated in the fourteenth century). The Antonine Plague was followed in 251–266 AD by the Cyprian Plague, possibly also smallpox or maybe a virulent form of measles – which was then a killer, not a 'childhood disease'. These two events made a massive hole in the Roman agricultural workforce, as well as in the cities and trading fleets of the Empire and its economy. Between 482 AD and 535 AD, a third pandemic, the Plague of Justinian, cut another swathe through the population.

Simultaneously, the climate changed. Between about 150 AD and 400 AD weather conditions cooled and deteriorated with temperatures reaching unprecedented lows in what became known as the 'Late Antique Little Ice Age'. This climatic switch, combined with short-term weather events such as the failure in 244 AD of the Nile River to rise and flood the grain farms along its banks, created a time of hunger which interacted with the incoming plagues to make them even more lethal, according to epidemiologist and historian Tony McMichael.[6] This had a compounding effect on the Roman food supply and economy, and especially on the ability of Rome to pay and feed its legions. Many of these legions were made up largely of local recruits who then mutinied, becoming independent war bands, some of which even joined forces with the raiding Goths who devoured the Western Empire.[7] Scholars have also found that periods of drought correlate strongly with the assassinations of 25 Roman Emperors and unrest among Germanic tribes between 27 BC and 476 AD.[8]

If the pathway to war, government failure or the collapse of a civilisation can be thought of as a series of dominoes, collapsing one upon another, the fall of the food domino and the climate domino lie very early in the sequence and have irresistible impact and consequences. Despite our technological mastery, these dominoes are no less deadly in a twentyfirst century world which, typically, has only about 10–12 weeks' surplus of grain in store at any time – a surplus that depends for its renewal on the succession of harvests round the planet. A major crop failure in any of the great grain bowls would reduce this to zero and send world bread prices rocketing through the roof for everybody, thanks to the globalised trading system and world grain prices that now exist. Since our population is now straining at the very limits of the Earth itself (Chapters 3 and 4), this risk is more pronounced than ever. Indeed, food insecurity represents as direct an existential threat to our civilisation in the event of major disruption – such as a worldwide conflict, a nuclear war or a climate catastrophe – as it did to the ancient Romans. We ignore the lesson of their experience at our peril.

Here Come the Long Ships

In 789 AD, a sheriff called Beaduheard who worked for the King of Wessex in southern England went to greet three Norwegian ships that had been observed pulling into Portland Bay. Naively assuming they were merchants, he invited the Viking crews to meet with the King in Dorchester to discuss trade, which they, having other ideas, refused to do. In the ensuing dispute and scuffle they cut him down, and Beaduheard became the first named victim in three centuries of violence, plunder and exploitation that was visited on the countries of Western Europe from the North.[9] But who were the Vikings? And why did they come?

The Vikings were not, as they are sometimes considered, a separate race of people. They were a violent and rapacious minority of an otherwise largely peaceful and prosperous community of farming settlements extending across Norway, Denmark, Sweden and Jutland. Outcasts, adventurers, terrorists and religious fanatics, Vikings were a product of a long, slow improvement in farming methods from the Iron Age onward that had brought about a steady expansion in Nordic populations. This pastoral progress was then rudely disrupted by the same climatic blow that brought down the Roman Empire – a sudden cold spell when crop yields, especially in Northern climes where growing seasons are short and cool, fell below subsistence and communities that had hitherto had ample sustenance found their wooden trenchers empty. The situation was especially dire in countries such as Norway, where level farmland was in scant supply along the towering walls of the fjords. Over the next few centuries this period is marked archaeologically by a proliferation in fortified homesteads, villages and towns across Scandinavia, whose sturdy defences testify to the unsettled nature of the times.

What began as petty raids among local Scandinavian tribes, probably with food, slaves and farmland as the chief aims,

steadily grew with experience into a more formalised kind of
warfare, especially with the development of the Viking long
ship, which could cover thousands of miles of open sea or major
European river systems as far afield as Russia and Turkey in one
direction and Greenland and America in the other. Armed initially with the weaponry of the failing Roman Empire and lured
on by its riches – silver, gold, iron, food and slaves – from weakly
defended Roman centres which presented easy targets to a ruthless, unexpected adversary – the Viking raiding tradition was
born. In countries such as Iceland, Ireland, Normandy and
northeast England the raiders soon settled down and began to
farm again, once they had taken suitable lands. This farming
had two aims – to sustain those who wished to settle perman-
ently, a form of eighth-century agrarian colonialism or
Lebensraum[10], and to feed up the Viking raiding forces for the
next season's depredation. Particular targets were the rich monasteries, fortified towns and cities which the post-Roman Euro-
peans could no longer protect, places such as London, York,
Paris, Rouen, Cologne, Aachen and Bonn. Eventually the Vikings,
raiding, trading and settling along the Dneipr/Volga river
system – where they founded Kiev – teamed up with the local
Rus to assault Constantinople (Istanbul) in 907 AD.

Then as now, most Scandinavians were peaceable people with a
strong social ethos and an attachment to their land. But when
ample food increased their populations and climate-induced
famine followed, the young, the strong and the ruthless among
them of necessity became wolves – *homo homini lupus*[11] as the
chroniclers put it. Like the Gauls who had raided Italy in the fourth
century BC, the source of their manpower was a reliable food
supply, the trigger for their outward movement was lack of it –
and the aim of further settlement was to feed their military might.

Thanks to vivid accounts left by quaking mediaeval chroniclers, especially in the monasteries, the Vikings are usually
remembered as merciless, bloodthirsty pirates roving and
butchering at will. However, historian John Hayward argues
they were also civilised traders, farmers, craftsmen, artists and
sailors – the settlement of Iceland, which boasted the world's

first Parliament, the founding of the first towns in Ireland and the establishment of the Danelaw in England being cases in point. Over time these settlements mostly assimilated with the local culture.

Thus, the Vikings were probably no more piratical than many folk during this turbulent period of world history. Such a view is supported by evidence that in the nineteenth and twentieth centuries, when the introduction of modern farming methods caused the Nordic population once again to expand rapidly, outgrowing the local capacity to support it, there was a second huge wave of Scandinavian out-migration, this time mostly to North America, and entirely peaceful.

The interaction of food surpluses and shortages with Scandinavian population, emigration and warfare is another vivid instance of how food, in subtle ways, interweaves with the greater weft and warp of human history, occasionally surfacing as a crimson, bloody thread.

Food and the Rise of China

Food has played a pivotal role in the rise of the greatest nation to emerge in the modern era: the story of China is intimately interwoven with food and its development. The Yangtse River marks the climatic boundary between Chinese wheat culture, to the north, and rice culture to the south. When China was unified under powerful dynastic rulers from 200 BC onwards, these together furnished a year-round food supply and the basis for sustained population growth, punctuated by occasional climatic disasters. Wheat is not native to China but is thought to have arrived from the Middle East along the Silk Road around 4500 years before the present.[12] Rice culture has been traced by modern science to a single domestication event in the Pearl River basin some 8500 years ago,[13] but may have originated as long ago as 12,000 or even 15,000 years (in Korea), according to some sources. Together, the rice and wheat cultures built and sustained early China to a population approaching 100 million (Figure 1.2).[14]

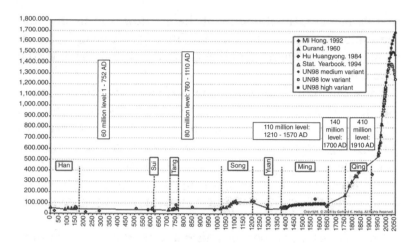

Figure 1.2. China's population, 0 AD to 2050 AD. Source: IIASA, 1999.

However, with agriculture also comes crop failure. Chroniclers recount that famine stamped its brutal footprints on Chinese history – coupled with ensuing revolts, conflicts and refugee tides – for over 3600 years. Northern China, in particular, is susceptible to drought when the seasonal rains which are the tail end of the Indian monsoon sometimes fail to penetrate to wheat-growing regions. More than seventeen major droughts have been recorded in the past two millennia, including: the famine of 1630–31, which led to a revolt culminating in the collapse of the Ming Dynasty; the drought and Taiping rebellion, which claimed around 20–30 million lives in the mid nineteenth century; and the famine and Boxer rebellion of the 1890s. The Japanese invasion in the 1930s unleashed war and famine that killed 35 million. Between 1958 and 1962, Mao Zedong's ill-conceived Great Leap Forward combined with drought to create the 'Three Years of Difficulty', which took 15 million lives – some scholars say as many as 50 million. When local community leaders protested there was no food, they were told 'That's right-deviationist thinking. You're viewing the problem in an overly simplistic matter'.[15]

As far back as 500 BC, China's arch codifier of military platitudes, Sun-Tzu, saw a red-hot connection between food and war, advocating the use of sustenance as a military weapon: 'Steal food from the enemy so that you have enough food to eat as well' and 'Maintaining an army is difficult as the common people will suffer due to lack of resources and higher prices... Forage on the enemy's resources', he counselled. And generations of military commanders have taken his advice.

Despite such occasional setbacks, food was nevertheless the mainspring of the vast population surge which has taken place in China since the 1950s. For most of the previous 3000 years, the teetering balance between abundance and famine held the Chinese population at between 60–140 million people – less than a tenth of its present level.

The Green Revolution, which rapidly doubled and redoubled farming yields through the introduction of superior crop varieties, fertilisers, pest control and machinery leading to better diets, in combination with vaccine prevention of infectious disease and improved public health – lit the fuse for an unanticipated explosion in numbers from the 1950s onward, potentially peopling the Chinese landmass way beyond its natural capacity to sustain in the longer term.

The Chinese population explosion was chiefly the result of the zeal of the Agriculture and Health Ministries of the People's Republic of China (PRC), which had ensured that the new knowledge about how to increase food production and how to reduce infectious disease was widely and efficiently disseminated among hundreds of millions of people with the resulting broad-scale industrialisation of food production and decline in infant death rates. India underwent a similar explosion, and for much the same reasons – whereas in Africa, where the Green Revolution was slower to take hold, owing to less effective farm extension services and poorer healthcare, the main population surge did not begin until the 1990s.

Agriculture played a second key role in the rise of modern China – it helped ignite the economic miracle. After the death of Mao Zedong, Deng Xiaoping began the huge task of transitioning China from a state retarded by ideology-driven central planning to a more liberal 'socialist market economy'. One of the first places he began was on the farm, dismantling the inefficient state-run enterprises in favour of individual farms and allowing China's peasant farmers to sell their produce on the open market instead of to the government because, as he is said to have put it, 'wealth is glorious'. The Chinese economic miracle thus began, ingloriously but highly effectively, with cabbages and carrots and with erstwhile peasants getting rich. This food revolution laid a stable foundation for the industrial, mercantile, financial and IT revolutions to follow. Also, with the population already exceeding a billion, it came in the nick of time.

In the mid 1980s, when China was first opening up, I interviewed a number of eminent professors at the Chinese Academy of Sciences who were experts in farming, soil, water, food and population. Their considered and scientific view – contrary to then Communist Party doctrine – was that the long-term 'carrying capacity' of China, based on its soils, water and contemporary technology, was a maximum of about 645 million people. This is less than half the present-day population of 1.4+ billion, and barely a third of the UN's high-growth scenario, where it peaks at 1.7 billion or above.

Throughout recent Chinese history periodic famine has been one of the principle drivers of emigration, first into South East Asia but subsequently all around the world. To begin with, the communist PRC Government frowned on emigration and discouraged it – but from the 1980s onward it rapidly began to relax restrictions and issue passports for study, business and tourism. This led to a sharp rise in emigration culminating in the modern-day Chinese diaspora in which, it is estimated, some 50–60 million ethnic Chinese now reside outside of China.[16]

Whether this is the result of a deliberate policy of the Chinese Government to relieve population pressures, expand its sphere of influence globally or the natural outward impulses of businesses, individuals and families – or all three combined – is debatable. Foreign policy expert Howard French, for example, argues that more than a million Chinese 'are building a second Empire in Africa' (although Chinese migration to the USA is thought to be double that to Africa).[17] The claim that China as a whole has colonial ambitions in Africa, however, is rejected by scholars such as Deborah Brautigam, of John Hopkins University. 'There is no evidence to support the notion that Chinese firms in rural Africa are the beachhead of a rising imperial power…' nor of 'a state-sponsored quest to lock up vast tracts of African land', she states.[18] No evidence does not, however, equate with no intention.

The Chinese Government is plainly alert to the risks of famine, based on the nation's historical experience and particularly on the growing scarcity of water in the bread basket of the north as the great aquifers that supply agriculture on the North China Plain run dry in the face of gargantuan demand from China's northern megacities. In 2014, the PRC Ministry of Agriculture, excited by the success of Chinese investment in global oil resources, blurted out that it had a similar plan to acquire farmland in other countries around the world. Oil is one thing – but foreign acquisition of land often provokes howls of anger from local farmers and the subsequent international media debacle resulted in a red-faced backdown by the Ministry, which then declared it never had any such intent. Subsequent history suggests otherwise: Chinese agricultural and food acquisitions now span the globe, embracing millions of hectares in Africa, Latin America, Southeast Asia, Australia and New Zealand, the Russian Far East, Central Asia and Europe – wherever, in fact, farm land or agribusiness enterprises are up for easy sale to foreign buyers.

There appear to be five main approaches to the contemporary risk of famine faced by China:

- to buy up large tracts of farm land and food processing companies overseas and feed itself from other countries;
- to improve domestic water supplies, conserve soil and recycle more water and nutrients;
- to invest heavily in new technologies such as biotechnology and biocultures and improve the efficiency of agricultural markets;
- to develop high-intensity urban farms to help feed the swollen megacities; and

- to ease domestic population pressures by encouraging
  its own people, especially surplus males, to re-settle
  overseas.

Population control, as once practised in the PRC under the one-child policy, has gone out the window. Owing to urbanisation, rising household incomes and education levels, birth rates have fallen well below replacement. While measures to further limit population growth could be reintroduced, it is now far too late for them to have any but a marginal effect on the trajectory of Chinese population growth, at least in the coming 50 years.

However, it appears China is implementing all five of the above measures. These are probably thought of as its insurance policy against future food shortages. Whether they will succeed in a time of acute and growing water scarcity and increasingly severe climatic impacts is discussed in Chapter 5.

At the same time, thanks to the combination of its former one-child policy and pregnancy ultrasound tests – which enabled parents to selectively abort female foetuses – China has a growing disparity of males over females, roughly 118 males being born for every 100 females. By 2020 males are expected to outnumber females by some 35 million.[19] The implications of this bachelor army – or 'bare branches' as they are known within China – for Chinese military aspirations are not yet clear. However, throughout human history, male surpluses have frequently led to a heightened risk of conflict, both internal and external.

If China cannot feed itself through the twentyfirst century, it follows that others, whether willingly or unwillingly, will have to do so – or else face the prospect of a tsunami of Chinese out-migration potentially totalling hundreds of millions. The Chinese Government has been anxious to represent its agricultural investments as benign, as business partnerships, or as aid to help African and other countries (such as the Philippines) to develop their own agricultural resources along the highly successful (until now) Chinese model. However, at some point, the issue will inevitably arise whether the food so produced will be used to feed local people or Chinese people in China. Who will take priority? Almost certainly this will occur as a result of water- or climate-induced food scarcity in both regions, or globally. Almost certainly, too, it will lead to tensions and to conflict. Whatever happens in the twentyfirst century, food will rule the fate of China – and hence, the whole world.

Food and India

Like China, India is blessed with mighty rivers. These are filled with water from the snowmelt in the girdling northern mountain chains of the Pamirs, Hindu Kush, Karakorum and Himalaya. These form vast, fertile floodplains where agriculture has thriven for more than 7000 years and, until recent times, furnished an inexhaustible supply of fresh water for the growing of food. Like China too, an abundance of food bred steady Indian population growth in historic times (Figure 1.3), the rise of great cities and an almost endless succession of wars between the various Indian states and principalities, as well as attracting the attention of land-hungry invaders like the Mughals. With an agricultural system highly dependent on the monsoon rains, India has faced famine time and again and these events are recorded as far back as 2000 years. During the eighteenth, nineteenth and twentieth centuries, when its population averaged 200 million, it is estimated that more than 60 million Indians died of hunger. Today, with a population exceeding 1.3 billion, for all of its high technology-fuelled advancement and economic miracles, Indian poverty and malnutrition remain among the gravest on the planet, giving rise to the phenomenon known as 'hunger in a time of plenty'.[20]

The remarkable feature of all this is that India, from being in a condition of repeated famine and constant food deficits, managed through a prodigious effort by its farmers, the Indian Agriculture Department and the scientists of the Green Revolution to become self-sufficient in cereal production from the 1980s on. This miracle was accomplished in barely six years, through the introduction of high-yielding varieties of rice,

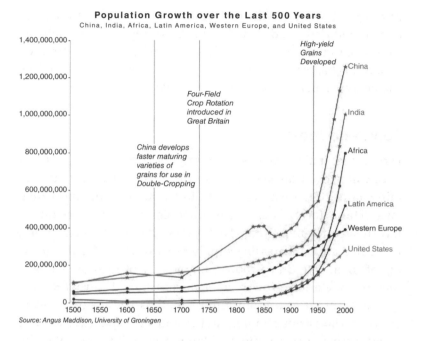

Population Growth over the Last 500 Years

China, India, Africa, Latin America, Western Europe, and United States

Source: Angus Maddison, University of Groningen

Figure 1.3. Indian and other population growth, 1500–2000. Source: Angus Maddison, 2003 (http://www.wrsc.org/attach_image/population-growth-over-last-500-years).

wheat and pulses and modern agricultural techniques under the inspiration of scientists like M S Swaminathan, especially in northern India. However, today, though living in one of the world's largest and most efficient grain-producing nations, an estimated one quarter of India's population still goes to bed hungry, and 800 million receive government-subsidised food – a condition variously attributed to inefficient food distribution and waste, endemic corruption, poverty and lack of land tenure.

Climate change, the spread of irrigation and the burgeoning of its megacities are devouring India's water resources – surface and groundwater – at an alarming rate, while soil erosion remains widespread. Together these raise the spectre of future food insecurity. The consequences of this for India and the world are discussed in Chapter 5.

Food and War

Of the 200+ million people who have perished in wars between nation states since the 1850s, it is estimated that over half – 105 million – have died of hunger. This makes food by far the deadliest of all the weapons deployed by governments, against their own people or others (Figure 1.4).

The World Peace Foundation 'has compiled a catalogue of every case of famine or forced mass starvation since 1870 that killed at least 100,000 people. There are 61 entries on the list, responsible for the deaths of at least 105 million people', writes WPF executive director Alex de Waal.[21] He continues:

About two thirds of the famine deaths in this period were in Asia, about 20 per cent in Europe and the USSR, just under 10 per cent in Africa. The biggest killers were famines that resulted from political decisions, among them the Gilded Age famines, the Great War famines in the Middle East, including the forced starvation of a million Armenians, the Russian Civil War famine, Stalin's starvation

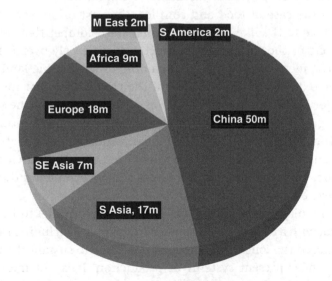

Figure 1.4. World famine deaths by region, 1870–2010. Source: World Peace Foundation, 2017.

of Ukraine from 1932 until 1934 (now known as the Holodomor*),
the Nazi "hunger plan" for the Soviet Union, the famines during the
Chinese Civil War, the starvation inflicted by the Japanese during the
Second World War, and by Mao's Great Leap Forward of 1958–62,
the largest famine on record, which killed at least 25 million.*

In his book *Mass Starvation*[22], de Waal states that the worldwide death toll from famine had declined markedly since 1980 –
although this may be an exception since, from the 2010s, it
showed signs of increasing again. De Waal argues that famines
in recent times have tended to be the result of deliberate political crimes rather than climatic factors alone, as was the case in
earlier centuries.

The American philosopher George Santayana is famed for his
aphorism 'Those who cannot remember the past are con-
demned to repeat it'. (This is often misquoted as 'Those who
do not learn from the lessons of history are doomed to repeat
it'.) Strictly speaking, history – or the past – does not actually
repeat itself, at least in detail, but its patterns, which are
defined by certain basic elements of human nature, certainly
do. In the case of food and conflict, the past offers very clear
guidance to the likely future. Humans are competitive beings,
and one of the things they compete most fiercely over is food
and the means to produce it, including especially the land and
water required to grow it. One of the things they fear most is
hunger – and this is often taken as a justification for the mass
killing of others. It follows that, in the twentyfirst century, a
significant disruption to either global, regional or even national
food supplies will generate the kind of tensions that can lead to
conflict on a scale ranging from riots and government failure to
nuclear exchange (Table 1.1).

Humanity as a whole is now in a position parallel to that of
China, with a total population whose demands – including food –
far exceed the long-term ability of the Earth to sustain them, at
least under present systems of production. It is not merely a
matter of population: today each human consumes around ten

Table 1.1 Catastrophic food conflicts and famines in recent history

Date	Place	Death toll (millions)	Cause
1618–48	Germany	7	Religious war
1769–73	Bengal, India	10	Drought/war
1795–1815	Europe	5	Napoleonic wars
1845–49	Ireland	1.5	Potato famine
1876–9	China	20–30	El Niño drought/civil war
1876	India	6	El Niño drought/ maladministration
1888	Sudan	2	Drought/civil war
1895	India	5.5	Drought/maladministration
1896	Brazil	1	Drought/economic crisis
1914–18	Germany	>1	Wartime starvation
1917–19	Persia	>10	Drought/wartime starvation
1921–2	Russia	5–10	Civil war
1928–30	China	5–10	Drought/civil war
1932–4	USSR	11	War on farmers/resulting famine
1941–4	USSR/E Europe	8.7	German 'Hunger Plan'/war
1943	India	2.1	War/drought/ maladministration
1942–5	China	20–35	War/Japanese occupation
1942–5	SE Asia	4–5	War/Japanese occupation
1947	India	2–3	Religious war/partition
1958–62	China	>43	Great Leap Forward/Cultural Revolution
1970	Nigeria (Biafra)	1	Civil war
1974	Bangladesh	1.5	Climate/maladministration
1975	Cambodia	>2	Civil war/government policy
1996	North Korea	>3	Drought/maladministration
1992–2018	Africa	10–11	Numerous droughts/civil wars

times more material goods (water, soil, timber, metals, energy, food, etc.) than did their great grandparents a century ago, while those living in the richest countries consume six to ten times more resources than those in the poorest. Factoring in a quadrupling in our numbers over the same period of time, this means humans presently devour 40 times more stuff than we did in the early twentieth century. The combined volume of this consumption is now so vast, and so great is our general ignorance of the long industrial chains that produce these goods, that many people have difficulty in envisioning them.

We do not perceive the unavoidable nexus between food and conflict now bearing down on us at a shocking pace.

Fear of Famine

Hunger is among the most feared of human afflictions – and not without reason. Death by starvation is one of the most lingering, painful and psychologically traumatic ways to die. It gives rise to a great sense of helplessness and impotence – and this in turn can fuel the rage and aggression that lead to conflict when food resources become scarce.

Starvation has two components – a lack of the energy needed by the body to perform its normal tasks and a lack of key nutrients, essential in a balanced diet, which maintain certain vital bodily systems and keep particular diseases at bay. Thus, it is possible to eat food containing ample energy – and still starve, because of the lack of vitamins, minerals and other important nutrients.

A starving person undergoes a whole range of body system breakdowns. To begin with they lack energy, may experience chronic diarrhoea and become anaemic. The legs often swell as the blood loses its protein content and fluids build up beneath the skin. Their sex drive dissipates. Wounds may not heal. It becomes harder to digest normal food because the stomach is not producing enough digestive acid. The victim may become irritable, have difficulty in concentrating and experience periods of great lassitude. The body's fat deposits shrink away and, when these are depleted, the muscles begin to waste as the body consumes itself: the victim becomes increasingly weak. Vital organs such as the heart, lungs, ovaries or testes, begin to shrink and their functions to fail. The immune system breaks down, exposing the sufferer to a range of opportunistic infections by microbes, many of which are harmless to a healthy person. Riboflavin (vitamin B2) deficiency makes the mouth and throat sore, producing skin rashes and anaemia and may cause the heart to fail and the brain to swell. Niacin (vitamin B3) deficiency produces diarrhoea, skin rashes, brain dysfunction, tongue, mouth and vaginal irritation and trouble swallowing. Lack of vitamin C causes hair to fall out, bleeding under the skin, in muscles and joints, gum disease and poor wound healing. In severe cases it causes convulsions, fever, loss of blood pressure and death. Lack of vitamin A may lead to blindness. Lack of vitamin D may cause rickets and bone weakening. Lack of vitamin K prevents blood from clotting, leading to increased risk of bleeding.[23]

In adults, total starvation brings death within eight to twelve weeks. In its final stages, the victim may suffer hallucinations and convulsions, along with severe muscle pain and fluctuations in heart rhythm. In children, prolonged starvation retards growth and mental development in ways from which they may never recover, even if sound nutrition is restored.

In short, starvation is one of the most excruciating ways to die, both physically and mentally – far worse, indeed, than most tortures invented by cruel people, because it takes so long and involves the destruction of virtually every system in the human body. In turn, the body becomes focussed on trying to obtain the nutrients indispensable to life – and it is this subconscious awareness in all people of the risks of hunger that drives our desire to contest food resources so fiercely, to challenge, displace and even kill those who compete for them. It is one of the fundamental motives for the mass flight of refugees from famine and war-torn regions – and for genocide, when one group seeks to eliminate others whom it regards as rivals for scarce local food resources. Fear of hunger is the deep motive in establishing tribal territories, feudal fiefdoms, kingdoms, national borders, even maritime boundaries – to secure their food production assets against outsiders.

Fear of hunger exists in all societies – not just those on the brink of starvation. Of the 68.5 million refugees worldwide in 2018,[24] the vast majority were fleeing hunger. Of the 258 million economic migrants in 2017,[25] most were educated, thoughtful people trying to escape what they regarded as the probable disintegration of their home society and build a better future for themselves and their families, primarily in countries which were more food-secure.

These deeper motivations will define the nature of, and set the scene for, conflict in the overcrowded world of the twentyfirst century as much, or more, than in any previous human epoch. They confront humanity at large, and each of us as individuals, with a stark choice: food... or war.

2 WAR AND HUNGER

The Thirty Years' War – Food and Revolution – Killing
Farmers – Rice Catastrophe – World War I – World
War II – India and Partition – Categories of Food
Conflict

'Lo que separa la civilización de la anarquía son solo siete comidas.'
Spanish proverb

As Albrecht Dürer warns us, hunger is the ineluctable compan-
ion of conflict. In this chapter we examine historical instances of
the nexus between food and war – famine resulting from conflict, conflict from famine and the two combined. The food
system is thus cause, instrument and victim of conflict.

The Thirty Years' War

Now largely forgotten except by scholars and in parts of Europe,
the Thirty Years' War (1618–48) could be described as the first
truly international conflict. Though it took place mainly within
200 or so small German principalities it also embroiled, to a
greater or lesser degree, the Great Powers of Sweden, France,
Austria and Spain as well as Holland, Norway–Denmark, Italy,
England, Scotland, Turkey and Russia. As a consequence, ill-
disciplined foreign armies ravaged, raped, burned and plundered their way mercilessly across the bountiful German countryside (Figure 2.1), turning it to a hellish devastation
resembling a painting by Pieter Breughel.

The spark that lit the fuse was religious – after decades of
simmering tensions, the Hapsburg Ferdinand II of Bohemia
attempted to suppress Protestantism throughout the Holy
Roman Empire, which was then suzerain to almost a thousand
minor states and principalities. The Protestant states fought
back and the war escalated as, one by one, the Great Powers sent

Figure 2.1. Mass executions of peasants were a common feature of the Thirty Years' War. Jacques Callot, 1632.

armies to join the fray, each taking sides according to their religious or political interests. The Protestant cause, ably led by Gustavus Adolphus of Sweden, was successful for a time, re-taking most of Germany and prompting the Catholics to appeal for help to Spain, which in turn sent armies that expelled the Swedes from southern Germany. Fearing Spanish encirclement of its borders, France – though Catholic – sided with the Protestant cause, gradually forcing a stalemate that ended in the Peace of Westphalia.[1]

Meanwhile the war had proven by far the most destructive event to befall Germany until World War II. An estimated one quarter of the entire population perished, and in a swathe from the Baltic to the Black Forest casualties reached more than half of the population. In all, it is thought around seven million people died, mostly civilians, and mostly from hunger and disease as brutal mercenary armies ploughed their way across the countryside like hordes of locusts, devouring grain supplies, stealing cattle and horses, burning farmsteads, slaughtering or conscripting farm workers. The Swedish armies alone are thought to have destroyed 18,000 villages and 1500 towns – a third of all German towns – and the Catholic side was as bad, or worse. If alerted in time to the approach of an army, farmers and villagers usually fled, depopulating entire regions and causing food production to collapse.

The war was noted for its atrocities, such as the destruction of the Protestant city of Magdeburg in 1631, in which five people out of every six perished when the unpaid Catholic soldiery went berserk. The victorious General, von Pappenheim, wrote 'I believe that over twenty thousand souls were lost. It is certain that no more terrible work and divine punishment has been seen since the Destruction of Jerusalem. All of our soldiers became rich. God with us!'. Pope Urban VIII rejoiced that 'this nest of heretics' was destroyed. However, its real consequence was only to stiffen Protestant resistance, harden Protestant hearts in favour of retribution, and prolong both the war and the suffering.

Less spectacular, but more punitive in terms of famine, were the 500 or more garrisoned fortresses that were spread across Germany by the war's end. Unsupplied by their leaders, each of these could exist only by plundering the surrounding lands and this became the standing policy of their local commanders. At the same time, they pursued a 'scorched earth' policy, destroying all they could not themselves consume or carry off, in order to deny sustenance to the enemy. Local farming populations were forced to flee the pillaged regions, and no new crops were sown.

The lack of discipline in both armies and their commanders gave rise to a sinister transition in which the purpose of military action was often less about defeating the enemy than it was about amassing wealth by plundering anyone and everyone. Writes Pascal Daudin of the International Red Cross, 'In some ways, war became an industry in its own right. Profiteers plundered resources at every opportunity to sustain their business model, leaving entire regions devastated with no chance of a quick recovery'.[2]

Also, as with the Roman Empire, the climate domino fell. 'All this came against the backdrop of the "Little Ice Age", which blighted agriculture and left food in short supply', Daudin adds. The coldest phase, which coincided with the third decade of the war, produced a climate one to two degrees colder than today. 'Winters were bitterly cold and summers were often cool and wet. These conditions led to widespread crop failure, famine, and population decline. The tree line and snowline dropped and glaciers advanced, overrunning towns and farms in the process. There were increased levels of social unrest as large portions of the population were reduced to starvation and poverty.'[3]

With its fertile river valleys, such as the Rhine, the Elbe and Danube, Germany/Austria is one of the richest regions, agriculturally, in the world. Over time this has led to constant and steady population growth, a high degree of prosperity and the periodic eruption of large armies from the time of the Baltic Crusades in the twelfth century. In the first half of the seventeenth century however, owing to the Thirty Years' War, the German population actually declined sharply – from 14 million to 7.9 million.[4]

The Black Rider, Famine, had much to do with it. It took Germany a hundred years to recover.

Food and Revolution

Between 1700 and 1789, the population of France grew from 20 million to 28 million. At the time agriculture was the mainspring of the French economy, generating three quarters of all production: despite this it was a backward industry, reliant mainly on small holdings and peasant labour and poorly run aristocratic estates, which had not yet caught up with the advances of the Agricultural Revolution being made in Britain and elsewhere. In the previous century, France's population and food supply had remained in reasonable balance, but the steady growth in human numbers combined with a succession of bad harvests in 1769, 1770, 1775 and 1776 – which some historians connect in part to the peak of the 'Little Ice Age' (described above), a global cooling cycle between 1350 and 1850[5] – led to sudden shortages and sky-high bread prices which shocked the populace.[6] This, along with government attempts to reform the grain trade, ignited conspiracy theories that bread was deliberately being withheld from the people by wealthy merchants and aristocrats in order to starve them out – the so-called *Pacte de*

Famine. It was in this belief that the seeds of the Revolution were sown.[7] The 1775 shortages brought on a string of riots, known as 'La Guerre des Farines' (the Flour Wars).

Then, on top of the Little Ice Age, in 1783–4 the Laki volcanic fissure on Iceland erupted violently, chilling the climate still further and spoiling harvests across the whole of Europe. In 1788, this misfortune was followed in France by severe drought which finally broke in the form of hailstorms with stones 'as large as a quart bottle' that killed people and destroyed fruit and vegetable crops in a wide area around Paris. This was followed by floods and a freezing winter, which added to the misery of a populace already overtaxed to pay for King Louis XVI's war in America. Food shortages became critical and bread prices nearly doubled from 8 sous a loaf to 14.5 sous – equal to nine tenths of the daily wage of a Parisian labourer.

This discontent, originating once again in food insecurity and climatic impacts, was the fuel for widespread urban unrest culminating in the storming of the Bastille, which ushered in the Revolution. This swept away the monarchy and old aristocracy and, under the Jacobins, unleashed the Reign of Terror in which 17,000 perceived enemies of the new order, including Louis himself and his Queen, Marie Antoinette, were tried and guillotined, and 23,000 more were murdered or died in prison. Marie Antoinette herself may have been an early victim of 'fake news', having been widely and wrongly quoted for the contemptuous phrase 'Let them eat cake' ('Qu'ils mangent de la brioche') when allegedly told the people were starving. In fact, the phrase probably originated a hundred years earlier with Queen Maria Theresa, as it was cited by Rousseau in his Confessions in 1765 – which was published when Marie herself was only nine years old and living outside France: 'At length I remembered the last resort of a great princess who, when told that the peasants had no bread, replied: "Then let them eat brioches"'. The tale is told here to illustrate the powerful impulse on the popular imagination of rumour, however baseless, about food scarcity and its causes.

In the French Revolution and civil war itself, the final toll was about 160,000, but there is no record of the numbers who died of starvation in this period. The Napoleonic Wars, which were an outgrowth of the Revolution, claimed more than five million lives across Europe. Of these, about three million were combat deaths but of the remainder many starved as a consequence of the depredations of vast armies that supplied themselves from the lands they passed through. And out of the Napoleonic Wars arose the greatest threat to peace in the modern world: the nation state.

Thus, the crimson thread which began as a series of poor harvests fuelled by popular rumour in one country, expanded into regime change, continental-scale political, social and economic upheaval, civil and ultimately an international war that was global in scale, being fought in places as remote as the Indian Ocean and Southeast Asia as well as the Americas. Its most significant legacy, the rise of the nation state and the nationalistic madness that so often accompanies it, remains with us to this day, an ominous and omnipresent threat to the survival of humanity in the era of state-owned nuclear weapons. With the benefit of historical hindsight, it is easy to see how this process could perhaps have been arrested at the outset through the application of advanced (even by eighteenth-century standards) agricultural methods and a government that properly attended to food distribution and pricing. It prompts tantalising questions such as: would modern nations and their nuclear panoply exist today, had the French not gone hungry then?

Revolution in France inspired Revolution in Russia. French thought had long fostered revolutionary ideation. Paris was home to Karl Marx during his most fertile period as a revolutionary writer, and a Mecca to Lenin and other leading Bolsheviks, some of whom witnessed the short-lived uprising of the workers in the Paris Commune (1871). Nevertheless, the true seeds of Revolution in Russia lay, again, in hunger.

As in pre-Revolutionary France, Russian agriculture had failed to move with the times, being largely locked into traditional manual labour by the peasantry. Emancipation of the serfs in 1861 had failed to ignite the hoped-for lift in productivity, as those peasants who were allotted small areas of communal land could neither sell it, nor borrow against it, nor grow enough food on it to meet their own needs, buy food or pay the taxes due. However, as in France, the population of Russian peasants had quietly doubled over the nineteenth century, while the area of land being farmed had failed to keep pace. This ratcheted up the stresses on an unstable and unproductive system, leading to a Malthusian crisis. Famine broke out in 1892–3 in the Volga region following a cold, dry winter in which crop losses from 'winterkill' (caused by low snow cover and hard frosts), were huge.

Thus, famine stoked the revolutionary sentiment that had been rising in Russia throughout the nineteenth century. The great novelist Tolstoy, working as a famine-relief volunteer, blamed the Tsar and Orthodox Church – for which offence he was excommunicated. Famine and discontent again erupted in 1902 in the region around Kharkov and Poltava, leading to widespread looting of the homes of the nobility. Subsequent government inquiries concluded 'no part of the countryside was prosperous; some parts, especially the fertile areas known as "black-soil region", were in decline'.[8] These crop failures produced not only hunger, but also precipitated a collapse in Russian trade and an economic crisis which was then aggravated by the worldwide bank crash of 1896. This in turn affected Russian city workers who lost their jobs or saw their wages cut, while food prices soared.

Simmering discontent, urban and rural, burst into open rebellion on Bloody Sunday of 1905, when the Tsar's troops shot down demonstrators in St Petersburg. This launched the First Russian Revolution, which compelled Tsar Nicholas II to appoint Russia's first 'parliament', a consultative body called the Duma, and draw up a new constitution. More significantly, these events cemented the rise in influence of Bolshevik revolutionaries and at the same time made the food situation for Russians in general worse. Prior to the outbreak of World War I, droughts and famines were reported in key parts of the Russian foodbowl in 1901, 1906 and 1911. Food was by no means the only factor in the Russian Revolution of 1917, although the necessity of feeding the armies and rampant inflation had led to a collapse in farm production, with disgruntled peasants growing enough for themselves – but not for the cities or the war effort. Growing political radicalism, the failure of Russian arms, lingering disaffection over the treatment of ethnic minorities and appalling pay and industrial conditions for workers, along with loss of confidence in the Tsarist regime all contributed to the potent brew.

However, one of the germinal events leading up to the October Revolution that toppled Nicholas II was a women's protest in St Petersburg on International Women's Day, February 23, 1917. Tens of thousands of people, mainly women, paraded along Nevsky Prospekt with banners demanding 'Feed the children of the defenders of the motherland' and 'Supplement the ration of soldiers' families, defenders of freedom and the people's peace', indicating food was very much a live issue in the complex of triggers for the bloodshed that was to follow (Figure 2.2).[9]

Figure 2.2. Women protesting food scarcity in St Petersburg, 1917. Credit: Central State Archive, St Petersburg.

Between 1917 and 1922 an estimated 6.7 million people perished in the Russian civil war – and far worse was to come.

The lesson from both of these celebrated historic revolutions in France and Russia – and a number since, including Darfur and Syria – is that hunger is often the spark that ignites the powder keg of popular outrage and precipitates the fall of government. Radicalism, industrial strikes and street riots are one thing – but it takes a food shortage to turn the larger population militant to the point where they align in sympathy with radicals and revolutionaries, where anger is incandescent to the point that ordinary citizens will risk their lives in confronting the military and their rulers. In Spain, where famine, rebellion and harsh repression are an oft-told historic tale, there is a famous saying:

> 'There are only seven meals between civilisation and anarchy'.[10]

Killing Farmers

In one of history's darkest ironies, famine became the engine for the further destruction of the food supply and the very people who produced it, in the post-Revolutionary Soviet Union.

In his Tolstoyan epic, *The House of Government*, Russian writer Yuri Slezkine recounts the stories, and ultimate fates, of the true believers, leaders, theoreticians and administrators of the Bolshevik Revolution, many of whom dwelt in a vast and privileged apartment complex on the south bank of the Moskva River opposite the Kremlin.[11] The story traces an extraordinary arc from the zeal of the young revolutionaries exiled to Siberia or scattered across Europe who were seized with the vision of building a brighter, fairer world – only to become the blood-stained practitioners of the Revolution, the brutal and uncaring tyrants who built the 'Workers Paradise', the self-centred and greedy new elite of the USSR – before mostly falling, disgraced, tortured, bloody and shot through the skull to the floor of the NKVD (People's Commissariat for Internal Affairs) gaols, victims of the overwhelming suspicion, cynicism and cruelty of Josef Stalin. While the story of the Soviet show-trials and periodic purges is well-documented, rather than being about politics, Slezkine recasts Bolshevism in the light of a failed millenarian cult, turning inwards and devouring itself when its long-awaited Utopia failed to materialise. Part of this cannibalistic process involved the destruction of Russian food production.

In a brutal regime, this was one of the Soviet Union's most mindless episodes – the slaughter and dispossession of the farming class, the kulaks. In Russian the world 'kulak' means 'tight-fisted'. The word is an insult, intended to characterise the class of small- and medium-scale farmers who sometimes withheld their produce from market in defiance of the authorities, whether tsarist or communist. The Bolshevik rulers defined a kulak as anyone having a couple of cows, or a few acres of land, more than the average peasant's marginal holding. They were, in short, the professional farmers of Russia, the ones who grew most of the food surplus that fed the cities.

Although the programme of 'de-kulakisation' of agriculture implemented in the USSR between 1929 and 1933 is seldom treated by historians as a war, it was in fact a ruthless class war, comparable in human cost with Nazi Germany's Final Solution for Europe's Jews and gypsies. Its toll, direct and indirect, was even greater – larger, indeed, than that of most wars in human history.

In the mid 1920s, with Lenin sliding into his long, last illness and Stalin slyly consolidating his hold on power, easing it out from under his fellow revolutionaries with masterful stealth, after a decade of heady triumphalism, Bolshevism was pitching into a crisis of self-belief. Consequently, Marxism–Leninism was being abandoned in favour of a command economy and centralised control. Somehow, the idyll of the workers' paradise had failed to materialise – despite all the zeal and idealism, the blood and the violence, the five-year plans, all the windy dialectic, hortatory proletarian art and turgid literature, all the self-criticism and personal sacrifices, all the restructuring of industry and society. The communist dream of re-making the world, its social and economic orders, was proving a massive disappointment. Its failure was underscored by inability to feed its

Figure 2.3. Down with the Private Peasants! Soviet propaganda poster, 1930s. Wikimedia Commons.

own citizens: droughts and famines in 1920, 1921 and 1924/5 indicated that climate and harvest needed more than political dogma to repair them (Figure 2.3).

Stalin announced the 'liquidation of the kulaks as a class' on 27 December 1929.[12] The kulaks 'were to have their backs broken once and for all'.[13] The process involved dividing them into three groups, the first of which were either to be immediately imprisoned in concentration camps 'not hesitating to use the death penalty' where thought appropriate, the second was to be exiled to remote regions of the USSR and the third to be moved off their land and forcibly resettled somewhere within their native region. Regardless of the kulaks' innocence or guilt, the Commissars of the various Soviet regions were given quotas: in the Ukraine, for example, 49,000–60,000 were initially to be executed or gaoled and 129,000–154,000 exiled. Family members of Category One kulaks automatically fell into Category Two, and so on. The matter proceeded with ruthless zeal, as local Party bosses vied with one another to please the master and demonstrate 'Bolshevik firmness' by filing the longest lists of shootings and displacements.

It was indiscriminate. In the village of Galtsova, a railway worker named Mishin found himself declared a kulak and de-kulakised because 'he spoke out against collective farms at a village meeting'. At nearby Ust-Inza, the Imagulov family was driven from their home into the snow where the two-day-old baby died and her mother was badly frostbitten. Kulaks attempting to flee the kolkhozes (collective farms) or take back their livestock were adjudged 'anti-Soviet' elements. In an orgy of accusation, farmers were branded 'White Guardists' and sabo-teurs of the grain supply. And, having got rid of most of the people who actually knew how to farm, gradually the state-run farms began themselves to starve, while grain supplies reaching the cities fell to crisis levels.

Josef Stalin was the son of a drunken cobbler, 'the best but also the naughtiest' student in his Church school, and a restless young seminarian who imbibed widely of the revolutionary literature of the day, and drew his nickname, 'Koba', from it. The only real job he ever held was a brief spell as a meteorolo-gist, before becoming a full-time revolutionary, strike organiser and gangster, which led to his arrest and exile in 1902. In common with many politicians who grow up in towns and cities, it is doubtful if Stalin had even the haziest appreciation of what is involved in the struggle with nature that is farming – the forethought, the intuitive caution, the accumulated practical wisdom of generations. When he declared war on the farmers of the USSR, Stalin probably had no idea what he was unleash-ing. Also, he did not much care. This led, at the height of the kulak purges, to the bizarre situation in which regional Com-munist Party bosses, while ruthlessly demolishing the farming skills of their region, also began writing hand-wringing personal appeals to Stalin, Molotov, Kaganovich and other Politburo chief-tains to end the madness. They were bluntly told to get on with it and 'fulfil their grain procurement plan by any means'. So they increased the expropriations of grain from the countryside to

feed the cities – and at the same time raised the quotas of
farmers, whom they blamed for the shortages, to be killed or
exiled. Lesser bosses who failed to fulfil their targets were sum-
marily dismissed. The more ruthless floated to the top. Unsurprisingly, the more farmers who were removed, the harder it
became to fill grain delivery quotas – and the blame game
intensified up and down the chain of command.

As both country and city began to starve, reports of
cannibalism began to filter up the communist chain of command, adding fresh humiliation to the unravelling ideology of
the worker's paradise. In the areas of resettlement, former
kulaks, swollen with hunger, ate soup made from nettles and
forgot the taste of bread. Villages stood abandoned. Along country roads, bodies were sometimes found 'stacked like cordwood'.

> Hungry peasants tried to stay alive by eating grass, straw, and their
> draft animals. Then came the dogs and cats, and finally, in some
> instances, even the children of the village. Some peasants, driven by
> hunger, fell into temporary insanity and began to feed on the dead
> bodies of their own and their neighbor's children. This cannibalism
> reached a point where the Soviet government – instead of stopping the
> mad exportation of grain – began to print posters with the following
> warning: "To eat your own children is a barbarian act"

record historians Steven and Agnes Vardy.[14]

Meanwhile the Party elite somehow still managed to gorge
itself on suckling pig, pheasants, grapes, melons, oranges and ice
cream.[15]

In all, it is thought, some four million died in the process of de-
kulakisation and collectivisation, either executed or starved to
death while being moved to their places of exile. The survivors
were then dumped in places like the Arctic, Urals, Siberia or Far
East where farming was next to impossible, without tools or food,
and told to build new lives. Many more perished. In the famine
that erupted out of this ruthless process, a further seven million
Soviet citizens starved to death, bringing the awful toll of Stalin's
war on farmers to 11 million. This Great Famine affected most

parts of the Soviet Union, and was known especially in the Ukraine as *Holodomor*, the Terror Famine or Famine Genocide. The population of Kazakhstan was thought to have halved. Throughout the USSR, birth rates dropped alarmingly as mothers starved. The three chief architects of the famine were Stalin, Khrushchev (as Commissar for the Ukraine) and Kaganovich.

There are several schools of thought as to the motivation behind the Great Famine. In the Ukraine it is still viewed as a purposeful act of genocide on the part of ethnic Russian communists against Ukrainians. Historians such as Robert Conquest concluded that Stalin had, simply and cynically, put ideology before bread. And, of course, Soviet propaganda consistently blamed the kulaks, for resisting collectivisation and withholding grain. An important understanding for future history of the human food supply is that Stalin, as an urban politician, had scant grasp of the likely consequences of his actions. As hunger spiralled out of control, his only answer was to unleash more terror, which made matters worse. De-kulakisation was, in effect, a process of weeding out the competent farmers, and then placing the full weight of responsibility for food production on the shoulders of the least-educated and least-competent ones, who had been drafted into huge State-run collective farms where, more often than not, an urban commissar devoid of farming experience called the shots. It was a victory for denial and wilful human ignorance, from the top down – which has unsettling echoes in contemporary climate-change denialism.

The shockwaves from Stalin's incomprehension and poor decisions about food continued long after his own death in 1953, reaching well into the mid 1970s when the USSR, despite its extensive farmlands and rich soils, was still short of grain. Desperate to overcome the persistent failure of Soviet agriculture, in 1940 Stalin had appointed an eccentric plant breeder, Trofim Lysenko, who held pseudoscientific views and was promising to revolutionise food production along the lines of Lamarckian theory rather than Mendelian genetics, as head of agricultural science. Lysenko promptly initiated a ruthless purge of the USSR's leading agricultural scientists by staging conferences at which they were invited to deliver their views on how best to overcome the low productivity of Soviet agriculture. Those whose views departed from Lysenko's were then shot or exiled.[16] As a consequence, Soviet agricultural technology was thrust into a dark age by being, for decades, deprived of a vital branch of science – genetics – which, through improved crop varieties and seeds, was revolutionising food production in the west and was soon to power the Green Revolution worldwide.

Rice Catastrophe

A second instance of an ideological 'war on farmers' resulting in national famine was the murderous regime of Cambodian dictator Pol Pot and the Khmer Rouge from 1975 to 1979. Pol Pot, who preached a sick mixture of Marxism and nationalism, drew his inspiration for savage agrarian reforms from the (failed) examples of the USSR and People's Republic of China. While much of the focus was on forcibly relocating urban middle-class Cambodians into the countryside for slave labour as peasants, and on the dispossession of ethnic minorities, it also involved the widespread murder of existing farmers and agricultural specialists in the so-called 'Killing Fields' who, like the kulaks, had stubbornly resisted the trend (Figure 2.4).

Cambodia is a rice culture, and growing rice involves a deep knowledge of irrigation, seasons, varieties, growing techniques and other complex farming practices. From the fifteenth century on, the Khmer people had pioneered Asia's most sophisticated irrigation and water distribution system. By the 1960s the country was one of Asia's leading rice exporters. Under the Khmer Rouge regime, however, in barely four years the Cambodian harvest collapsed by 84 per cent – from four million tonnes to barely half a million tonnes. The local seed rice, carefully conserved over generations to suit the local climate, soils and conditions and to resist pests, was devoured by the starving populace. The loss of farming knowhow along with its practitioners thus ignited a famine that is estimated to have killed a quarter of all Cambodians, around two million people

Figure 2.4. The Killing Fields. Painting by Vann Nath, from Tuol Sleng Genocide Museum.

(Figure 2.5). The effect of the loss of farming knowledge and skills, and the setback to its agricultural development, was still being felt in Cambodia in the late 1990s.

In 1988, almost ten years after the Pol Pot regime fell, things had barely improved. Two Australian agricultural scientists, Harry Nesbitt and Glenn Denning, were sent in by their country's aid programme to try to turn the killing fields back into rice fields.

> *Almost all the knowledge of traditional rice varieties and their traits, of the different soils, of irrigation and drainage, of plant breeding, cultivation, and pest management, was gone. The country's trained agriculturists had either been murdered or forced to flee, farmers had been relocated to unfamiliar soils and terrain, and to cap it off, most of the traditional Cambodian seed had been eaten. Many farmers were now struggling with unsuitable Chinese rice varieties introduced by the Khmer Rouge*

author Bradley Collis recounts.[17]

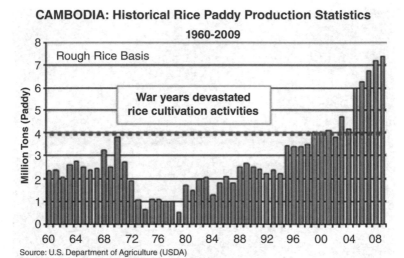

CAMBODIA: Historical Rice Paddy Production Statistics
1960-2009

Rough Rice Basis

War years devastated rice cultivation activities

Source: U.S. Department of Agriculture (USDA)

Figure 2.5. The collapse in the Cambodian rice harvest during the genocide. Source: USDA.

What Nesbitt found, as he examined the scale of their task, was nutritional ground zero:

> It wasn't until a few days later when we started to look around that we realised what we had got ourselves into. Villages had been razed and traditional village life all but extinguished. You'd drive down narrow dirt tracks past rows of cement steps rising from the jungle to empty sky; the houses all gone. People were dying from hunger, and what they had been through was still staring them in the face; human bones were stacked in the centre of most of the major towns. A quarter of the population, anyone educated, skilled or who had worked with westerners, were killed by the Khmer Rouge under Pol Pot.

To restore production they had to re-import Cambodian rice seed, which had fortunately been safely stored in the seed bank of the International Rice Research Institute (IRRI) in the Philippines, because all the local varieties were gone. They had to rebuild entire networks of irrigation channels: the Khmer

Rouge's rough attempts, constructed by slave labour and over-
seen by incompetents, were useless: 'The agricultural engineers
who might have made them functional, had been murdered in
the purge of the professional classes'. In the end, they had to re-
create an entire rice system, one which employed modern technology, from top to bottom – from the smallest farm, to the
entire irrigation system, to a national science effort that ensured
rice production adapted to the Cambodian climate, soils and
conditions.

The abiding lesson of both the Soviet and Cambodian experiences is that making war on farmers – especially the imposition
of uncomprehending ideologies conceived by urban politicians –
is a very foolish and counterproductive measure if your intention is to satisfy the food needs of the people or maintain a stable
government.

World War I

World War I did much to shape the modern impression of how
food and war affect one another – incorrectly, as it turns out. In
the main theatre of war, the Western Front – a line of trenches
extending from Switzerland to the North Sea – there was utter
devastation of farming and the towns and villages that supported it. A few miles beyond the immediate conflict zone,
however, production progressed more or less as normal, except
for the gargantuan appetites of the competing armies for both
food and men. In the end this far outran the simple industrial
farming methods of the time. As a result, both combatants and
non-combatants went hungry, and sometimes starved.

Just one of the combatants, Great Britain, supplied a total of
3.2 million tonnes of food to its soldiers in France and Belgium
over the course of the war and employed a separate 'army' of
300,000 cooks, storemen and drivers to supply it.[18] Australian
Corps commander General John Monash explained: 'It takes a
couple of thousand men and horses with hundreds of wagons,
and 118 huge motor lorries, to supply the daily wants of my
population of 20,000. With reference to food we have to see that

Figure 2.6. Even in the USA, people were urged to save wheat to help ease European hunger. Source: US Library of Congress.

all the men in the front lines regularly get hot food – coffee, oxo, porridge, stews'.

Nonetheless, British soldiers saw their meat rations halved and the bread ration also cut over the course of the war, as agriculture failed to keep pace, even though supplemented by grain imports from America, Australia and Canada – and grumbled constantly about their food (Figure 2.6). At home, matters were even worse. In the winter of 1916, during the 'flour crisis', Britons at home were asked by their Government to eat less bread in order to keep the British Fleet at sea and the army fed. What bread was available was rough, made from turnips and often caused diarrhoea. Stories abounded of butchers selling cat and dog meat – and while this may or may not have been true, they certainly served horse meat.[19] The women of Britain were bluntly told:

> The British fighting line extends and shifts and now you are in it. The struggle is not only on the land and sea, it is in your larder, your kitchen and your dining room. Every meal you serve is now literally a battle. Every well-cooked meal that saves bread and wastes no food is

a victory. Our soldiers are beating the Germans on land. Our sailors are beating them at sea. You can beat them in the larder and the kitchen. Victory in the food-fight will turn the scale. . .

By 1918 the domestic food shortage was so severe that nationwide rationing was introduced for the first time. Even King George and Queen Mary had ration books restricting what they could eat. Women were told to make sausages from rice and fish, rather than meat and bread. The shortages were due in part to the success of the German U-boat campaign in World War I which, in pursuit of Sun Tzu's dictum about depriving the enemy of sustenance, opened unrestricted warfare on Britain's merchant shipping on 4 February 1915. This was suspended briefly following the world outcry that arose over the sinking of the ocean passenger liner *Lusitania* but was then resumed in early 1917 after Imperial Germany failed to gain command of the seas at the battle of Jutland. Ultimately the Imperial German Navy sank almost 5000 British merchant ships for a loss of 178 submarines. Both Britain and France were highly dependent on imported grain – at the start of the war in 1914, for example, Britain was importing nearly 60 per cent of its total food needs – so the German submarine campaign had a punishing effect on food availability and compelled the introduction of rationing, but failed to ignite a British civil uprising, as the German High Command had vainly hoped.

Hunger stalked the civilian populations of all the combatant nations. Agriculture and food distribution suffered from strains imposed by the war and naval blockades reduced food imports. Some countries met this threat more successfully than others. The war took men and horses away from farm work. Imports of nitrate fertilizers were hit. Reduced agricultural output forced up prices and encouraged hoarding. Governments responded by putting price controls on staple foodstuffs. Food queues formed of women and children became a common sight in cities across Europe

writes historian Paul Cornish.[20]

Food distribution in Russia and Turkey broke down completely and many starved in both countries. In Russia the food crisis, following a number of pre-war famines, was one of the impelling factors in the outbreak of revolution, as the Women's March of 1917, where the main issue was food for the army and the home front, so clearly shows.

German attempts to starve Britain into civil disorder were themselves but a *riposte* to the British blockade of Germany, administered by the Royal Navy, which was even more effective. Here the starvation of Germany – which imported about a third of its food – was a deliberate Allied policy, advocated by politicians such as Winston Churchill, who was at the time First Lord of the Admiralty, and thus in an ideal position to enforce it. Churchill is said to have admitted the aim of the policy was to 'starve the whole population – men, women, and children, old and young, wounded and sound – into submission'.[21]

German food supplies were also drained away by the necessity of supplying huge field armies that eventually totalled 11 million men, fighting on two fronts, often with extended lines of supply over difficult country such as the marshy regions of the Eastern Front, where much food was spoiled or lost *en route*. As the war proceeded, Germany found itself impaled on a growing, self-inflicted dilemma: it could not both feed its armies and its civilian population without taking men from the armies to grow more food. It was literally a case of win or starve – and, in the end, the latter proved the case.

'Germany introduced numerous government controls on food production and sale, but these proved to be badly thought out and worsened the effects of the British naval blockade. Substitute foodstuffs were produced from a variety of unappetising ingredients, but their nutritional value was negligible and Germans became increasingly malnourished from 1916 onwards', Cornish writes.

Britain's naval blockade cut German imports of all goods, but especially food, to a trickle, as the War Cabinet noted with some satisfaction on 1 January 1917.[22] Germany's total food imports, by land and sea, fell by a third. 'Staple foodstuffs such as grain, potatoes, meat and dairy products became so scarce by the winter of 1916 that many people subsisted on a diet of ersatz products that ranged from so-called "war bread"[23] to powdered milk. The shortages caused looting and food riots, not only in Germany, but also in the Habsburg cities of Vienna and Budapest, where wartime privations were felt equally acutely.'[24] The winter of 1916–17 was known in Germany as the 'turnip winter' because of food shortages exacerbated by poor grain and potato harvests, which left turnips and beets as the main subsistence of the nation. By mid 1917, the official German diet was 1500 calories a day, two thirds of the needs of a healthy adult. According to a prominent Berlin physician, 80,000 German children perished of starvation in 1916 alone.[25]

Civilian morale and confidence in the Imperial regime were shaken. It must be remembered that Germany, with its fertile plains and river valleys, was one of the most bountiful countries in the world in terms of food production, and its military potency over centuries stemmed directly from it. Now, a German woman lamented 'We are all growing thinner every day, and the rounded contours of the German nation have become a legend of the past. We are all gaunt and bony now, and have dark shadows round our eyes, and our thoughts are chiefly taken up with wondering what our next meal will be – and dreaming of the good things that once existed'.[26]

Reflecting the privation, a British officer, Captain Jim Perry MC, who was interned in Rastatt, Baden, in late 1918 records that POWs were fed on 'barley porridge or *griessuppe* which looked very uninviting and rather like the bill (poster) stickers paste one knew in England' and an anonymous 'brown stew', and would have starved had it not been for their Red Cross parcels and the occasional raid on the guards' potato patch.[27]

Historians still debate the role of hunger in the collapse of Imperial Germany, the ending of World War I, the dethroning of the Kaiser and the introduction of a German Republic. The whole process took barely ten days, beginning with a mutiny by sailors of the Imperial German Navy at Wilhelmshaven – where hunger was a key factor in the discontent. Sailors who had volunteered for the U-boat service continued to receive full rations – but the majority, whose warships had been tied up, useless, at the dock since the Battle of Jutland in 1916, were placed on part-rations. The discontent fomented protests, which were met with harsh punishment and executions, and the formation in secret of Sailors Councils (called Soviets, in emulation of events in Russia the previous year). It was also a striking herald of events in Russia three years later in 1921, when sailors in the starving city of Leningrad (St Petersburg) revolted against the new Bolshevik government in the Kronstadt mutiny. In the first case, however, mutiny driven by hunger eclipsed an Empire; in the second it was brutally suppressed and led to the consolidation of Bolshevik control – including increased grain requisitions to feed the starving cities, which spiralled eventually into the War on the Kulaks and thence into the mass death of Soviet citizenry known as *Holodomor*, described above.

An irony of the initially successful German offensive on the Western Front in the Spring of 1918, was that when the hungry German armies, after capturing more territory than in all the war so far, broke into Allied rear-echelon depots, they found them bursting with food for the armies. They had been told by their High Command that the Allies were starving due to the U-boat campaign – and this highly edible evidence to the contrary was one more factor in the disillusion that led to the German military's decision to lay down its arms in early November 1918.[28]

Another irony was that Britain, which began the war importing two thirds of its food, became significantly more efficient at producing food as the war progressed. Indeed, the British response to hunger was to pull soldiers with agricultural skills out of the front line and put them to work back on the farm. Germany did the opposite: a warrior culture, it valued soldiers above farmers and by the war's end was even less capable of meeting its own food needs than at its start. Thus Germany starved – but by the will of its own government, as well as the Allied blockade.

Hunger in Germany did not end with the war itself. To keep pressure on the new Republic of Germany until the Treaty of

Versailles was signed and sealed, the British Navy maintained the blockade of German sea trade and food imports up until July of 1919. Additionally, Germany lost all its overseas colonies, along with border regions such as the Saar/Rhineland and Danzig corridor, which had previously contributed to the national food supply. Consequently, a German representative at Versailles, the Count von Brockdorf-Rantzau, claimed 'The hundreds of thousands of noncombatants who have perished since November 11, 1918, as a result of the blockade, were killed with cold deliberation, after our enemies had been assured of their complete victory'. In reality the guilt fell equally on both sides: hunger had become a weapon of war by other means and civilians were now squarely in the gunsight.

For most of history commanders had observed Sun Tzu's dictum about depriving the enemy army of its sources of sustenance. Now this extended to entire civilian populations, as they were regarded as 'supporting the war effort' (whether they were or not). For the future of humanity, the larger significance of World War I was the formal weaponisation of food.

The effects of hunger, and the fear it generated, lasted for years. According to the economist John Maynard Keynes, a US observer visiting a German kindergarten in the 1920s said:

> You think [this] is a kindergarten for the little ones. No, these are children of seven and eight years. Tiny faces, with large, dull eyes, overshadowed by huge puffed, rickety foreheads, their small arms just skin and bones, and above the crooked legs with their dislocated joints the swollen, pointed stomachs of the hunger edema... "You see this child here," the physician in charge explained, "it consumed an incredible amount of bread, and yet it did not get any stronger. I found out that it hid all the bread it received underneath its straw mattress. The fear of hunger was so deeply rooted in the child that it collected the stores instead of eating the food: a misguided animal instinct made the dread of hunger worse than the actual pangs.[29]

Thus, it was the *fear of hunger* that was to provide the main-spring for even more terrible events to follow. Official statistics

Figure 2.7. Hunger Map of Europe. Source: US Food Administration, 1918.

attribute the deaths of more than three quarters of a million Germans to starvation in World War I and a further 150,000 to epidemics of diseases such as typhus and influenza which interacted with it. However, owing to the unpalatability of the message to official ears and the German government's own responsibility in the matter, these are almost certainly underestimates, not including the many infants, children and elderly who perished from malnutrition and its associated diseases, but whose deaths were discreetly attributed to other causes.

In December 1918, a telling US 'Hunger Map' of Europe (Figure 2.7) shows how widespread were the famine consequences of the conflict beyond Germany itself. To a greater or lesser degree, the entire continent had suffered. (The map was created to bolster US domestic support for food aid efforts.) Even in the abundant USA itself, as a consequence of the diversion of food to its armed services and as foreign aid, citizens were being asked to eat less meat and sugar, to plant food gardens, and to clean their plates.[30] This illustrates the planetary ripple-effect of conflict-induced hunger, even in 1918, the drain on civilian food supplies to sustain the war effort, and its consequences even in far-off lands. In the modern era of globalisation, the impact of food scarcity – in any key region and for any cause – will be felt almost everywhere in the space of a few days, thanks to the speed-of-light reflexes of world commodity and money markets.

Just as Pestilence – in this case the 1918 'Spanish flu' – had galloped across the globe, seeded by the universal movement of millions of soldiers and refugees and battening on hunger-weakened populations, so Famine too rode down millions world-wide as a consequence of World War I. This established the prevailing image of war as a cause of hunger – but not its reciprocal, of hunger as a cause of war.

This was soon to come.

World War II

It is an almost forgotten fact of history that World War II – in Europe especially – was originally fought mainly over food and the means to produce it.

The military philosopher Clausewitz is credited with the observation that 'War is the continuation of politics by other means' and, in the case of 1920s' Weimar Republic Germany, the politics were very much about securing sufficient new land for the nation to thrive and to avoid a repetition of the horrors of World War I starvation, which were fresh in everyone's minds and still scarred their bodies. While he carried no particular brief for farmers as a class, an ambitious politician like Adolf Hitler knew hunger personally, understood its power over the minds of his fellow Germans and the importance of aligning himself with populist causes in order to pursue his more extreme agenda. At the time, few causes were more popular than *Lebensraum* (space for living), a racially tinged German ideology that had been circulating in the national discourse since the 1890s.

Lebensraum as a concept originated with a German ethnographer, Friedrich Ratzel, but its deep roots lay in successive German eastwards settler movements since the time of the Teutonic Knights and Baltic 'crusades' in the thirteenth century, which had conquered, settled and farmed the lands that became East Prussia and the contested Baltic coast. In World War I, the annexation of lands belonging to Poland in the Danzig corridor, by military conquest and for settlement purposes was an official German war aim. In the Treaty of Brest–Litovsk (March 1917) between Germany and Soviet Russia, whereby the Russians withdrew from the war, the Germans fleetingly acquired rich lands as far afield as parts of European Russia, the Baltic states, Belarus, Ukraine and the Caucasus – which they promptly lost again 15 months later in the Treaty of Versailles (June 1919).

Hitler knew that, short of outbuilding and outgunning the Royal Navy, Germany was never going to get back its former African and Pacific colonies to feed it, and his mind became more and more focussed around the acquisition of *Lebensraum* to the east: Poland, Czechoslovakia and Russia. Incredibly, he even believed the British would back him: in 1922 he confided to a sympathetic newspaper editor 'The destruction of Russia, with the help of England, would have to be attempted. Russia would give Germany sufficient land for German settlers and a wide field of activity for German industry'.[31]

In 1924, for his part in staging the failed Beer Hall Putsch in Munich, Hitler was gaoled in Landsberg Prison. Here, his dreams about acquiring vast lands for a new Germany began to take shape, encouraged and fed by his adoring deputy and fellow gaolbird, Rudolph Hess – who held mystical views on soil and German blood – while he wrote *Mein Kampf* (1925/6). In it, Hitler tipped his hand by enunciating his three main aims:

- to demolish the Treaty of Versailles and its 'unfair' effects on Germany;
- to unify the German-speaking peoples, i.e. form them into a much larger, more powerful and cohesive racial and cultural unit; and
- to expand eastwards to create sufficient living space (*Lebensraum*) for the new, enlarged Reich.

Evoking German mediaeval history from the time of the crusading Teutonic Knights as his precedent, Hitler explained 'And so, we National Socialists consciously draw a line beneath the foreign policy tendency of our pre-War period. We take up where we broke off six hundred years ago. We stop the endless German movement to the south and west, and turn our gaze toward the land in the East. At long last, we break off the colonial and commercial policy of the pre-War period and shift to the soil policy of the future'. Thus, the USSR had a good 16 years' forward notice of German intentions, which Stalin wilfully ignored. And soil, with its atavistic call to patriot sentiment, became the potent symbol for Nazi racial and territorial ambitions.

Nazi philosophy was grounded in already widely held popular notions of German racial superiority. Thus, the idea of taking land from 'racial inferiors' – Poles, Slavs, Balts, Jews, etc. – was not short of public or private support. Indeed, it struck a similar nationalistic chord with Germans as did the imperial conquests of Victoria's reign with Britons, the destruction of the plains Indians with Americans or the dispossession of the Aborigines with Australian settlers: to make way for the great and powerful, the indigenes must go. The fact that, in the case of the USSR, many leading lights were 'Jewish Bolsheviks' appealed to politically right-wing Germans, augmenting the rationale for taking their land. Furthermore, defeat in World War I had not diminished German confidence in its military prowess and the dream of a colonial expansion for agricultural settlers to the east, enforced at the point of the sword or bayonet, was still strong. Equally goading were the bitter memories of the starvation in Germany – almost every household had lost someone – for which the Allied blockade, rightly or wrongly, was blamed. This brew of popular resentment, nationalist fantasy and prejudice lay ripe for exploitation by a cunning politician, the visionary leader who could give it voice.

Propelled by the memory of hunger, *Lebensraum* thus became the central pillar and objective of German foreign policy under Hitler in the 1930s and 40s, and hence Germany's chief war aim, historian Manfred Messerschmidt states.[32] Just before the invasion of Poland in 1939 – and while he was still, on paper, an ally of the USSR – Hitler himself declared that Germany needed 'the

Ukraine, in order that no one is able to starve us again, as in the last war'.[33]

Thus, European World War II was first and foremost about soil – and the overarching objective was to take it from the USSR, resettle and manage it on solid German agrarian principles. What was to be done with the displaced populations was not, at first, clearly spelt out.

As they mapped out Operation Barbarossa, the invasion of the USSR, it became increasingly clear to German war planners that the tenuous Soviet road and railway network would not be able to resupply their armies, which would therefore be forced, like Napoleon's army, to a large extent, to live off the land. A meeting of the responsible German ministries in May 1941, a month before the panzers rolled into Russia, concluded:

- 'The war can only be continued if the entire Wehrmacht is fed from Russia in the third year of the war.'
- 'If we take what we need out of the country, there can be no doubt that tens of millions of people will die of starvation.'[34]

In charge of this horror was a mild-looking technocrat, Herbert Backe, who had actually been born in Georgia to German parents and studied in Tbilisi (like Stalin) before returning to Germany to study agronomy. His thesis (which was rejected) was on Soviet grain production and its relationship to the Soviet economy. Backe was by now an SS officer and the second highest Nazi official in the food administration responsible, among other things, for domestic rationing. His solution, known as The Hunger Plan (der Hungerplan) plotted methodically the death by starvation of millions of Soviet citizens[35] and was the true weaponisation of hunger. The resulting death toll from starvation of Ukrainians, Byelorussians and Jews, has been placed at 4.2 million. In addition, around 3.5 million captured Russian soldiers died of starvation in German POW camps, and a further million Soviet citizens are said to have perished of hunger in the siege of Leningrad.

While not so explicit a war aim for Japan as for Germany, the acquisition of new lands to stave off hunger at home was nevertheless a potent driver in the origins of World War II in the East.

Japan had suffered from the Great Depression as deeply, or more so, than most western nations and this was compounded by famine: 'Around 1931, rural impoverishment became severe. Moreover in 1934, rural communities were hit by famine. Especially in Tohoku (north eastern) Region of Japan, rural poverty generated many undernourished children and some farmers were forced to sell their daughters for prostitution. This rural disaster caused much anger and popular criticism against the government and big businesses'.[36]

Contrary to many western histories, the roots of World War II began in the East with the Japanese occupation of Manchuria in north eastern China in June 1931, when some military officers, acting without the approval of their commanders or government, staged an invasion in the so-called Mukden Incident. However, their deeds were endorsed retrospectively when the Seiyukai party, representing rich industrialists and rural landlords, took power in December 1931 and began to pursue a policy of foreign expansion in order to secure more territory and resources, including food, in order to overcome the effects of the Depression. The occupation of Manchukuo – as the puppet state became known – with its rich natural and agricultural resources, thus found wide public support in Japan where it became known as the 'Manchurian lifeline'. Partly as a solution to rural depression at home, partly to develop offshore food supplies and partly to satisfy dreams of Imperial conquest, Japanese farmers were then transferred *en masse* to Manchuria as settlers, in an uncanny echo of German *Lebensraum* thinking.[37] By 1936, the Japanese Government's '*Millions to Manchuria*' migration programme was deluging rural Japan with leaflets and posters extolling the need to resettle a million Japanese farmers in Manchuria over the coming 20 years (Figure 2.8). Around 380,000 answered the call – and were joined by a further 600,000 Korean agrarian resettlers.[38]

China and Japan continued to skirmish until the 1937 Marco Polo Bridge Incident, where both sides mobilised in an inconsequential dispute over a missing Japanese soldier – and the actual fighting in World War II began. In the ensuing Second

Figure 2.8. Japanese Government poster urging farmer resettlement of Manchuria, 1930s.

Sino-Japanese War, the Japanese army took both Shanghai and the Chinese capital Nanking, before the Chinese managed to stabilise the front. The conflict lasted until 1945 and claimed between 20 million and 35 million lives, only three million of whom were military casualties (on both sides). The war was a direct cause of the Chinese famine of 1942–43: in Henan Province alone, three million perished.

Food scarcity was a universal feature of World War II as, once again, fields and warehouses were emptied to feed the massive armies and farms stripped of their manpower. Britain again found itself dangerously short of food as the German U-boat offensive began to choke off its maritime trade. Rationing within the combatant countries was universal, even in those, such as the United States, whose domestic food supply was under no real threat from enemy action.

Then starvation again began to take its toll, as hunger – once again – was deployed as a weapon of war, worse even than the strategic bombing that levelled cities across Europe and Asia. According to nutrition historian Lizzie Collingham, more than 20 million people died of hunger in World War II, compared with 19.5 million deaths resulting from combat. The actual total may be far higher, if the estimates of starvation in China are correct. Many of these deaths were the result of purposeful policies intended to weaken opposition, control occupied peoples or starve locals to feed armies.[39] These famines present a series of separate, yet intimately connected, food crimes.

- In Holland, a non-combatant country caught up in the tides of war whose food supplies were cut off by the Germans in reprisal for Dutch support of the Allied invasion, the ensuing 'Hongerwinter' of 1944–45 affected 4.5 million people, causing an estimated 22,000 deaths due to starvation, mainly among the elderly.
- In Henan, China, where as many as three million died, 'a woman boiled her baby for food, pleading that it was already dead when it went in the pot, while others skimmed the algae off fetid pools to eat'.[40]
- From 1941 to 1944, Axis-occupied Greece suffered an event remembered as the 'Great Famine' due to German looting and the Allied blockade. An estimated 300,000 civilians perished in Athens and the major cities, while death rates on some islands rose as much as ninefold.
- A major famine in British-controlled Bengal in 1943 is thought to have claimed 2.1 million lives. The famine was attributed to poor agricultural practices, overpopulation, weather disasters, corruption, maladministration and grain restrictions imposed by the British War Cabinet.
- In Japanese-occupied Vietnam a major famine in 1945 caused 600,000 (French estimate) to 1–2 million deaths (Vietnamese estimate). There were multiple causes, including weather, Japanese Army food seizures, French maladministration, and the general effects of the wider conflict.
- In the USSR, most people faced hunger after the invading Germans captured the Ukrainian grain bowl and

appropriated its food in line with the German 'Hunger Plan', while many in besieged cities such as Leningrad and Kharkov died of starvation. In all, about 8.7 million Soviet citizens perished of hunger during the war. The recapture of the Ukraine by the Soviets, along with a drought, precipitated a second mass famine from 1945 to 1947 in which about 1.5 million died, and reports of cannibalism were widespread.

- In Poland, deliberate starvation was an extensive cause of death among inhabitants of the Warsaw, Lodz and other Jewish ghettoes, who were denied food by the German Army of Occupation. In total it is thought about one third of ghetto inhabitants died of hunger, the remainder being shot or gassed in concentration camps.

- Germany itself paid in full the price of using food as a weapon following the Soviet invasion of 1944 and the shortages that accompanied the war in the west. Starvation was rampant. James Bacque estimates the ultimate cost of hunger alone was nine million German lives, which he claims were mostly lost as a result of intentional Allied policies.[41]

- In Japan, hunger gripped most of the population by the end of the war, but was probably not a cause of mortality on the same scale as in Europe, China or Southeast Asia. The bluntly named American 'Operation Starvation', initiated by Admiral Nimitz, was a deliberate policy to deprive Japan of both food and war material by aerial mining of its ports to destroy shipping. However, General MacArthur, when he took over Japan after its surrender, was quick to supply food aid to ease the hunger situation.

India and Partition

The partition of India in 1947 took place in the early days of Indian Independence, under British supervision, and was brought about by the growing incompatibility between the Moslem and Hindu populations and the demands of the Moslem League for a separate state. It is included here as an example of

mass starvation occasioned by a fundamentally religious conflict. Around 14 million citizens of the former British India were
segregated geographically, along roughly religious lines, into
modern India and Pakistan. The uprooting of so many people,
most of them farmers, for resettlement in one state or the other
over a short time period brought untold suffering, outbreaks of
violence, widespread rape of women and famine. At the end of
the process between 2.3 million and 3.2 million people were
'missing'[42], most of whom probably died of hunger. Another
reason for including the Indian partition is that its victims were
for the most part attempting to migrate to one state or the
other – and it is an early example of large-scale conflict and
starvation arising out of the mass movement of people. As such
it is likely to find fresh resonances in the twentyfirst century.

Categories of Food Conflict

We have explored the nature of the nexus between food and
conflict through the examples in these first two chapters. As
Santayana might remind us, many of the factors which drove
these wars and famines are still active in the world of the early
twentyfirst century and will continue to dictate events in the
mainstream of human history up to 2100 and beyond. Food
scarcity, in other words, is one of the chief propellants of armed
conflict, domestic and international, along with mass refugee-
ism – and also one of the most likely consequences of such
conflicts. While these conflicts can potentially arise almost anywhere, the global 'hot spots' most at risk of such events are
examined in Chapter 5.

Historical 'food wars' fall broadly into five categories:

- mass starvation as a result of the depredation of armies on
  the civilian population (The Thirty Years' War, Napoleonic
  Wars, Sino-Japanese War);
- mass starvation as a causative factor in civil war and regime
  change (France, Russia, Weimar Germany, Syria);
- mass starvation as a result of the destruction and
  displacement of farming populations, usually for ideological

or religious reasons (Soviet war on the Kulaks, Indian partition, Cambodian genocide, Chinese Cultural Revolution);

• mass starvation as a result of the denial of food sources to civilians by military action (World War I naval blockade and U-boat campaign, World War II German Hunger Plan and U-boat campaign); and

• deliberate weaponisation of food as a bludgeon of military strategy (World War I and World War II).

These may be more neatly packaged into three main issues that bind food and conflict almost inseparably in the contemporary world:

• famine/food insecurity, from any combination of natural or man-made causes (including deliberate and unintentional acts), leading to conflict;

• food deprivation as an overt weapon of politics or conflict; and

• food insecurity/famine resulting from conflict but potentially spawning further confrontations.[43]

Recent history displays a disturbing escalation from civilian hunger deaths being a collateral product of military action, to hunger becoming an accepted and acceptable weapon of war – albeit a largely ineffective one, viewed from a purely military standpoint. This has been accompanied by an almost total abandonment, by so-called 'civilised' nations, of the moral principle of sparing civilian suffering, to a state where ordinary citizens and their food supply are now a tacitly acknowledged target of warfare and much propaganda on all sides relies upon media coverage of civilian suffering and death. The Fourth Geneva Convention (1949) specifically bans the deployment of starvation as a weapon against civilian populations[44] – but in the twenty-first century it is a rule increasingly honoured in the breach.

Food insecurity is one the ten great existential threats facing humanity in the twentyfirst century (Chapter 6).[45] It is both a likely consequence of some threats (such as climate change, resource scarcity or ecological collapse) and a probable cause of others (such as nuclear wars, global toxicity, eco-collapse and disease pandemics). It is no exaggeration to say that the fate of human civilisation in this century may turn on the pivotal question of whether or not we can sustain the food that nourishes us through the peak in human numbers. Failure to do so, without a doubt, spells war.

3 THE STRATEGIC IMPORTANCE OF FOOD, LAND AND WATER

Dry Times – Land Losses – Climate Change:
Threat Multiplier

'*Anyone who believes in indefinite growth on a finite planet is either mad, or an economist.*'

David Attenborough

Food is a primary trigger for war in the twentyfirst century. Emerging scarcities of fresh water, topsoil and fertiliser, combined with the burgeoning impacts of climate change on resource availability and regional food production together pose the greatest threat to our food supply, worldwide, in all of history. *There has never been a situation faced by the entire human population at one time to compare with today's.*

Though supermarkets and their warehouses bulge with food in developed regions and complacent governments and their overfed citizenry are largely indifferent, the surplus could vanish almost overnight in the event of a food system failure in any of the world's major food growing regions. There are numerous documented events showing that packed supermarket shelves quickly empty, often in 24 hours or less, when a link in the modern food production and delivery chain breaks.[1] This high-lights the emerging strategic significance of food, land and water to human survival, health and wellbeing – as well as their role as drivers of conflict and mass migration to 2050 and beyond.

With the global population likely to hit 10 billion in the 2060s, along with continued economic growth, soil and water will become increasingly critical elements in global, regional and national security and must be factored into defence, security and sustainability planning at all levels. This is a potential worldwide catastrophe which can be anticipated – and which is largely avoidable, should we wish to do so.

Furthermore, the role of food, land and water security in keeping the peace and preventing mass refugee events involving tens or even hundreds of millions, needs to be more widely understood and acted on.

Dry Times

'Water... is linked to almost everything in the world. Water is a precondition for human existence and for the sustainability of the planet', observes the United Nations Water Programme[2], continuing:

> *Water is at the core of sustainable development and is critical for socio-economic development, healthy ecosystems and for human survival itself. It is vital for reducing the global burden of disease and improving the health, welfare and productivity of populations.*

> *Water is also at the heart of adaptation to climate change, serving as the crucial link between the climate system, human society and the environment. Without proper water governance, there is likely to be increased competition for water between sectors and an escalation of water crises of various kinds, triggering emergencies in a range of water-dependent sectors.*

Yet the UN's wise words pass largely unheeded by the bulk of humanity and the majority of governments. Sound, sustainable and honest water governance exists hardly anywhere in the world. Water systems generally are severely overexploited, contaminated, fragmented, disputed, subject to leakage, evaporation, decaying infrastructure and corruption, in almost every country on Earth. Most countries do not even know how much fresh water they have, exactly, and thus cannot manage, regulate or replenish it – even if they wished to do so. As a result, water crises are now arising in all continents, often with little warning.

Freshwater scarcity is emerging as a critical systemic risk worldwide – a potential cause of wars. Of all the emerging global resource scarcities (soil, strategic minerals, oil and gas, timber, fish, wildlife, clean air, etc.) it is the one arriving most rapidly and universally – and the one already causing the most actual death and suffering.[3] Freshwater availability is absolutely essential to the global food supply: 70 per cent of humanity's total usage of fresh water extracted from rivers, lakes and aquifers – 2500 out of 3800 cubic kilometres[4] – is used to grow the 40 per cent of the world food supply furnished by irrigation agriculture.[5]

The UN Food and Agriculture Organisation (2016) estimated that to feed the human population in the 2050s will require a 60 per cent increase in food production – and supplying that will entail an expansion of 20 per cent in global water use.[6] On the face of it, this would raise the share of world freshwater required by farming to 79 per cent.

This is never going to happen – because city and industrial demand for water is also exploding at the same time, with urban populations on track to double by the mid century. At current rates of growth, urban water demand could expand from 1050 cubic kilometres to 2100 cubic kilometres, or 60 per cent of total global fresh water availability (3800 cubic kilometres). A quarter of the world's city people already do not have access to clean drinking water or sanitation – so meeting their water needs in future will inevitably clash with the need to feed them. The water can either be used to grow food or supply cities: the way it is presently being managed, it cannot do both. If city and industrial water use were to double in line with urban population growth, as is presently happening, then the amount of fresh water available to grow food would drop from 70 per cent of global availability to 40 per cent. This in turn would reduce world food production by as much as one third by the 2050s – when there will be over nine billion mouths to feed – instead of increasing it by 60 per cent to meet their demand, as projected by the UN. Thus, water scarcity could reduce actual global food output to a level smaller than today's harvest – to feed a much larger, hungrier population. And this equation does not include the impact of climate change.

This looming clash between the water needs of cities and their industries, and the water needs of the farmers who feed the world, is one of the greatest and least carefully considered consequences of the explosion in human numbers and our resource demands on a finite planet. It is a collision that will affect the life history of every person in the world from the 2020s onwards. It is an issue that most governments do not even want to think about – and have consequently done little to solve.

Today's typical citizen of planet Earth uses around 1385 tonnes of fresh water a year, directly and indirectly.[7] This ranges from 2800 tonnes for the average American to 1000 tonnes for the typical Chinese or Indian. This 'water footprint' consists of all the water we use to produce our food, consumer goods, and to provide the services on which we rely: our indirect use of water is many times larger than our personal, direct use (Figure 3.1). While the global population has tripled over the past century, our use of water has grown sixfold.

Two thirds of the human population – more than four billion people – already face acute water stress at least one month a year. About half of these live in India and China.[8] By 2050 the number of people facing acute water scarcity will have risen to five billion, UNESCO has warned.[9]

Total water footprint [mm/y]
- 0 - 10
- 10 - 50
- 50 - 100
- 100 - 200
- 200 - 500
- 500 - 1,000
- > 1,000

Figure 3.1. World water footprint. Credit: Hoekstra and Mekonnen, 2012.

The combination of growing populations, rising economic demand for food, megacity and industrial water consumption and climate change mean that 'The ultimate consequence is that, by 2030, demand for water could be 40% greater than supply available', according to a study made by the UN University.[10]

This means that, among the various strategic threats to the global food supply, water scarcity is the hazard arriving most rapidly, and with the least effective global effort to address it. It is also a primary risk factor for conflict. And it is not simply a case of better allocating a finite amount of water among competing human uses – the actual volumes of water now available are also under growing threat.

'Rivers are the veins of the planet... they are the lifeblood of civilization', says National Geographic.[11] Yet the world's major river systems are in a dire state, especially in semi-arid regions where many have now run dry.

The world's rivers are in crisis, and the drivers of river degradation are numerous. While pollution in its many forms impairs the quality of our rivers' waters, dams impact both water quality and the very functionality of rivers, of planetary life cycle processes. Roughly two-thirds of the world's rivers have suffered harm from the 50,000 large dams that have been built over the past century

says International Rivers, a global scientific body that monitors their condition worldwide.[12]

Construction of new dams on rivers that flow across national borders – such as the Mekong, the Nile or the Tigris–Euphrates – is raising tensions between neighbouring countries, which many observers fear could lead to war. In a vivid example of where all this might lead, a particular source of contention between India and Pakistan is the Indus River. Of this, Pakistani Supreme Court advocate Dr Waseem Querishi writes 'India is eager to take control of all Pakistani water supplies by developing projects over the western rivers of the Indus Basin. Pakistan objects to these projects, fearing its water supplies are gradually diminishing. As a result, water conflicts between India and Pakistan are escalating. The global community fears these conflicts will escalate into full-scale water-wars, in a situation where both nations are nuclear powers'. The Pakistani view is that India is stealing their water – the Indian reply is that climate change is causing its loss. The risk is that the Indus Waters Treaty, which has kept the peace between them for years, may be abandoned.[13]

A similar picture is emerging of the plight of the world's lakes and inland seas, especially in heavily populated and intensively farmed regions and where their shorelines are shared by several countries. Many are drying up from the damming of their feeder rivers, over-extraction of their water and climate change, suffering from industrial and agricultural pollution, overfishing, deforestation, feral pests and acidification due to air pollution. Some may soon be gone forever.[14] In the tropics, flooding is more likely as a warming climate brings heavier dumps of rain for which twentieth-century drainage and flood-control systems are insufficient.

The Aral Sea in Kazakhstan is a notorious example of a major water body almost emptied by uncontrolled extraction of its inflowing water for cotton irrigation.[15] An even grimmer case is Lake Chad, once Africa's third largest lake and now nine tenths empty thanks to over-extraction and climate change, threatening its seven million surrounding inhabitants with starvation and war.[16] In China, Hubei, once known as the 'Province of 1000 Lakes' has lost 900 of them to development, rampant industrialisation and local maladministration.[17] In a study of the world's disappearing lakes, National Geographic also nominated Lake Poopo (Bolivia), Lake Urmia (Iran), the Salton Sea (USA), Lake Tanganyika (Tanzania), Lake Tai (China) and the Great Salt Lake (USA) as major waterbodies at risk of disappearing altogether under the combined human onslaught of climate change and overexploitation.[18] UNESCO adds 'Since the year 1900, an estimated 64–71% of the natural wetland area worldwide has been lost due to human activity'.[19]

The global scientific body, LakeNet, says: 'Experts predict that global climate change will affect lake water levels, water temperatures, precipitation and evaporation rates, chemical budgets, water quality, and biodiversity. Lake levels are likely to fall in some regions, as rising air temperatures produce rising water temperatures and increased evaporation. In other watersheds, lake levels may rise dramatically due to large increases in precipitation'.[20]

River, lake and wetland water is not only becoming unavailable for food production because of competing uses and climate change: it is also increasingly damaged by industrial chemicals, pesticides, urban runoff, fertiliser from farming, eroded soil and blooms of toxic algae. These are turning the world's once clear-running streams into turbid, brown flows unsuitable for any form of human use (unless cleansed) and unable to support their natural life of fish, insects, frogs and birds.

Though few people seem aware of it, the greatest resource of fresh water on the planet – 95 per cent of it, in fact – is beneath our very feet. Groundwater not only represents a vast store of the Earth's most precious resource, it also supplies much of the flow in our rivers, the content of our lakes and wetlands, up to a quarter of the food on our tables and half of the world's drinking water. Humanity is estimated to consume over 1000 cubic kilometres of groundwater every year[21]– so much, indeed, that when discharged as wastewater, it contributes to sea-level rise[22].

Being 'out of sight, out of mind' groundwater suffers from the endlessly repeated error that people extract it until the well runs dry – and then wonder why. Almost nowhere on the planet are groundwater resources systematically measured before exploitation begins. As a result, satellite studies by US space agency NASA have revealed that one third of the world's major groundwater basins are now rated 'in distress'.[23] Eight were classified as 'overstressed', with almost no natural replenishment to offset usage. A further five were rated 'extremely' or 'highly' stressed, depending upon the level of replenishment in each. Those aquifers were still being depleted but had some water flowing back into them, the agency said. The American Geophysical Union's grim assessment is that by 2050, 1.8 billion people will be living in regions whose groundwater has run out.[24] This will probably force most of them to move.

The UN Water Agency says about around a quarter of the world's food is supplied by irrigation areas that rely on groundwater to grow it, and there has been a tenfold increase in rates of extraction for agriculture in the past 50 years.[25] 'Freshwater is rapidly disappearing in many of the world's irrigated agricultural regions', scientists warned after using satellites to measure 34 different indicators of water availability.[26] Key regions affected by groundwater depletion include the Indo-Gangetic basin aquifers, which feed much of northern India and Pakistan, the Northern Saharan aquifer system in Africa, the Arabian system in the Middle East, which supports 60 million, the North China Plain, which provides food for around 400 million Chinese, and the High Plains Aquifers in the US midwest, a third of which are expected to run dry within 30 years. In this case, some of the Ogallala water now being mined for agriculture is up to 13,000 years old, which shows how long it may take such resources to recharge naturally, once they have been drained. In most cases, local authorities have little idea of the volumes of water left, or how soon they will be used up. Climate change, energy development, urban growth and food needs are ramping up demand, intensifying the problem of scarcity and leading to growing conflicts over whether water should be used for cities and industry – or reserved to grow food. The rising scarcity of groundwater has already sparked clashes between farming communities and gas or oil drillers ('frackers') and other miners in countries around the world over access to, and contamination of, these vital resources.

There is global alarm at the rate of melting of glacial ice in high mountain chains due to global warming. This ice, melting slowly, supplies the year-round flow of mighty rivers such as the Indus, Ganges, Brahmaputra, Jumna, Syr Darya, Amu Darya, Colorado and many smaller streams such as those of the South American Andes, all of which supply both farming and cities with year-round water. When the glacial 'water tower' is gone, the rivers will be dry for part of the year, food production will decline or cease and cities will go thirsty. 'The evidence is overwhelming: Earth is losing its ice', says Colorado University glaciologist Dr Twila Moon.[27] In America's Glacier National Park the number of glaciers has declined from 150 to just 30 in a century. The pattern is being repeated in Patagonia, the Andes, the Rockies, the Himalaya and Karakorum, Kilimanjaro and the European Alps. Switzerland is expected to lose half its glaciers within 20 years, while Western Canada will lose 70 per cent and Asia 30 per cent of their frozen water by 2100. In total, the US space agency NASA warns, the world's glaciers have shed around 400 billion tonnes of ice a year since the mid 1990s.[28] This is the equivalent of losing ten Three Gorges Dams – the world's largest water impoundment – every year for quarter of a century. Such losses are expected to reduce dramatically the volumes of water available to grow agricultural crops or pastures as well as supply cities in the world's most populous regions in coming decades.

The loss of the world's ice has another insidious effect on food production: it is causing the flooding and salinisation of low-lying farmlands by sea-level rise. The rapid melting of the Green-land and West Antarctic ice sheets is driving up sea levels at an accelerating rate, which has increased by 50 per cent from 2.2 millimetres to 3.3 millimetres a year. Between them, these two vast sheets hold enough ice to raise sea levels by 12 metres when it all melts – enough to drown many of the world's coastal cities, as well as key food-growing regions like the Indus, Ganges, Irrawaddy, Mekong, Mississippi and Nile deltas, and displace 150 million people. 'Multiple studies indicate that this irrevers-ible West Antarctic collapse is under way', Dr Twila Moon warns, adding that 'Much of the (ice) loss is irreversible and the result of human-caused climate change'.

The water crisis confronting world food production is being exacerbated by the increasing frequency and severity of droughts and disruption to normal rainfall patterns. Severe droughts were reported in all continents during the first quarter of the twentyfirst century. California and Australia experienced their worst droughts in over 1000 years. Cities such as Cape Town and São Paulo faced the threat of depopulation as water supplies ran close to exhaustion. India's capital, New Delhi, was warned by the Indian Supreme Court that it could run out of groundwater by the early 2020s.[29] Drought persisted across the African Sahel, struck eight provinces in China, hit central India, threatened water and food supplies in the Andean countries of South America and even affected countries with benign, wet climates such as the United Kingdom and New Zealand. The flip-side to climate-induced drought is climate flooding, which can have equally devastating effects on food production by flooding farmers' fields, destroying crops and stripping topsoil: the steady warming of the Earth's atmosphere leads inevitably to higher rates of evaporation, which in turn suspends more water in the atmosphere, resulting in heavier dumps of rain. In some cases, these manifest as more powerful and destructive typhoons, hurricanes and cyclones, in others as rainfall events that exceed the ability of drainage and storage systems designed for the twentieth century to cope with the water movements of the twentyfirst century. Consequently, both cities and farms are at increased risk of flooding. Furthermore, the surplus water is often contaminated and usually runs quickly to waste – and so cannot contribute to food production or recharge groundwater.

The risk of conflict over water scarcity has been flagged by many eminent figures, including successive UN chiefs including Boutros Boutros-Ghali and Ban Ki-Moon, who said: '(water scarcities) create tensions in conflict-prone regions. Too often, where we need water we find guns'. In 2018, Secretary General Antonio Guterres declared 'water is a matter of life and death', warning that one in four people live in a country where the lack of fresh water will be chronic or recurrent.[30]

Peter Gleick of the Pacific Institute has documented the gradual rise in both frequency and intensity of water conflicts over the past 5000 years, noting a particular increase in the early twentyfirst century[31] and adding that water can be both a trigger for conflict and also a weapon or casualty of conflict.[32] Other strategic analysts are ambivalent over the extent to which water will drive war in the twentyfirst century, but most acknowledge it has the potential to spark local conflicts which may build into regional wars:

Water stress is best understood as a precursor to conflict. While the environmental security community generally agrees that water disputes rarely lead to interstate violence, the same cannot be said of intrastate conflict. At the subnational level, water disputes and instability can trigger violent conflict, particularly in situations of existing social, political, or economic fragility. Water stress acts as an accelerant, increasing the likelihood of conflict. Moreover, water scarcity-fueled instability can have dangerous security implications for wider geographic regions.[33]

Even the world's great 'water powers' (i.e. those with the most available water) – Brazil, Russia, Canada, China and the USA – have regions where water availability is becoming critical: the city of São Paulo in Brazil, the North China Plain and the south-western United States are instances. The main regions afflicted by serious water scarcity in the early twentyfirst century are: North Africa, the Sahel, the Horn of Africa and the Middle East; India, Pakistan and south Asia; Central Asia. Many of these regions contain countries that are already conflict-prone.

Water crises and associated climate and food disasters have consistently ranked close to the top of the World Economic Forum's list of greatest global risks in recent years, in terms of impact.[34] One of the WEF's 'most likely' risks was 'largescale involuntary migration' triggered by 'conflict, extreme weather events (climate failure) and natural disasters'. The UN Food and Agriculture Organisation has also warned that worsening water shortages could soon force millions of people to leave their communities. Worst affected are those regions dependent on water for food production, added FAO chief José Graziano da Silva: 'Some among them, especially the poorest, may see no alternative to migrate in search of better livelihoods'.[35]

'Nigeria. Syria. Somalia. And now Iran', The New York Times reported, continuing:

In each country, in different ways, a water crisis has triggered some combination of civil unrest, mass migration, insurgency or even full-scale war. A water shortage can spark street protests: Access to water has been a common source of unrest in India. It can be exploited by terrorist groups: The Shabab has sought to take advantage of the most vulnerable drought-stricken communities in Somalia. Water shortages can prompt an exodus from the countryside to crowded cities: Across the arid Sahel, young men unable to live off the land are on the move. And it can feed into insurgencies: Boko Haram stepped into this breach in Nigeria, Chad and Niger. Iran is the latest example of a country where a water crisis, long in the making, has fed popular discontent.[36]

In the mid twentyfirst century water is a plainly emerging worldwide crisis for which few lasting solutions have yet been devised or implemented at global, national or even local level. It is both an ignition point and an accelerant for hunger and for future conflict. Potential solutions to this are discussed in later chapters.

Land Losses

More than 95 per cent of humanity's present food supply comes from the soil. However, it is already clear that this will not remain the case in future – or for long. In short, the food so many of us take for granted can no longer be guaranteed, if the soil, water, climate and nutrients needed to produce it are no longer sufficient to do so (Figure 3.2).

In the International Year of Soils, 2015, the first-ever comprehensive assessment of the world's soils concluded 'the majority of the world's soil resources are in only fair, poor or very poor condition... and that conditions are getting worse in far more cases than they are improving'. It continued: 'Further loss of productive soils will severely damage food production and food security, amplify food price volatility, and potentially plunge millions of people into hunger and poverty'.[37]

By 2018, *National Geographic* magazine was headlining '75% of Earth's Land Areas Are Degraded' and the livelihoods and well-being of 3.2 billion humans were at risk. 'If this trend continues, 95 per cent of the Earth's land areas could become degraded by

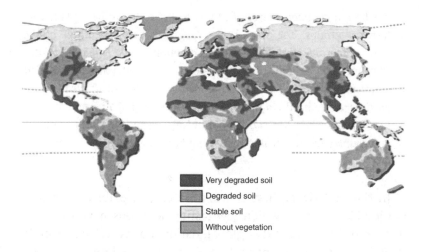

Very degraded soil
Degraded soil
Stable soil
Without vegetation

Figure 3.2. Map of global soil degradation. Credit: Philippe Rekacewicz, UNEP/GRID-Arendal, 2005

2050. That would potentially force hundreds of millions of people to migrate, as food production collapses in many places', reported Canadian science journalist Stephen Leahy.[38] The UN-backed IBPRES study underscored the urgent need for consumers, companies and governments to rein in excessive consumption – particularly of beef – and for farmers to draw back from conversion of forests and wetlands to farming land.[39]

A third of the planet's land is severely degraded and fertile soil is being lost at the rate of 24–40 billion tonnes a year, according to the UN Convention to Combat Desertification (UNCCD).[40] Using different methodology, the US Geological Survey calculated global soil loss as high as 75 billion tonnes a year.[41] The University of Sheffield estimated that nearly one third of the world's arable land was lost to erosion or pollution between 1975 and 2015.[42] If such rates persist, then the world will shed the equivalent of 1.5 million square kilometres of useful farmland by 2050 – an area the size of the entire grain-growing regions of India, which presently feed over a billion people.

The problem with such big numbers is that not many people can get their minds around their true significance. But here is one that everyone can understand: for *every* meal you eat, between 5 and 10 kilograms of soil are lost, plus 800 litres of fresh water. And that applies to every person on the planet, every meal, every day. The human jawbone is the most destructive implement ever to appear. It is presently devouring the Earth – and that is not a wise strategy for our long-term survival.

'A rough calculation of current rates of soil degradation suggests we have about 60 years of topsoil left', Professor John Crawford told *TIME* magazine. 'Some 40% of soil used for agriculture around the world is classed as either degraded or seriously degraded – the latter means that 70% of the topsoil, the layer allowing plants to grow, is gone. Because of various farming methods that strip the soil of carbon and make it less robust as well as weaker in nutrients, soil is being lost at between 10 and 40 times the rate at which it can be naturally replenished', he said.[43]

In the drylands, which account for 44 per cent of the world's food production system 'arable land loss (is) estimated at 30 to 35 times the historical rate', according to the UNCCD (United Nations Convention to Combat Desertification). On average 12 million additional hectares are being lost to desert each year. Paralleling this is a net loss in world forest cover of 6.6 million hectares/year, itself a major cause of lost topsoil.

Land degradation takes many forms:

- erosion by wind and floodwater of soils that have been cleared for farming, over-cultivated by machinery and over-grazed by livestock;
- destruction and over-clearing of forests, woodlands and savannahs;
- accelerated erosion due to drought and climate change;
- nutrient depletion from years of over-cropping and poor fertiliser practices, leading to a less nourishing food supply and more diseases caused by micronutrient depletion;
- the spread of acid soils from years of over-cropping and over-fertilisation, and acid rains from industrial fallout;
- loss of soil structure caused by heavy machinery (compaction) and loss of the ability of soils to take up and retain moisture and carbon;

- loss of carbon caused by land clearing, annual cropping practices and drought;
- poor irrigation practices leading to collapse in soil structure and salinisation;
- contamination by agricultural and industrial chemicals and plastics;
- contamination by chemicals such as nitrogen, mercury and ozone from air pollution;
- poorly designed urban development, waterways, drains and site construction;
- clearing of land for new cities, towns and suburbs;
- pressures from tourism, off-road vehicles and other land-damaging forms of recreation;
- infestations of weeds and insects introduced from other parts of the world which destroy local vegetation;
- changes in soil biota caused by pesticide use, tillage or the introduction of alien plants; and
- local extinctions of animals and plants, leading to a breakdown in the biotic systems that support life on Earth, including human life.

From this list it can be seen that global soil degradation is a multi-faceted problem, with many causes and a complex inter-relationship with other pressures in society, such as industrial development, economics, urban planning, climate or the innocent desire of citizens to spend time in nature. It is now occurring on such a scale that it cannot be addressed through agricultural policies alone, but only in a way that is integrated across all the various threats, pressures and stresses and particularly through the dietary choices of consumers.

Despite the shrinking availability of arable land, the UN Food and Agriculture Organisation has projected 'that for the world as a whole, net-land under crops may have to increase by some 70 million ha by 2050' in order to meet predicted global food needs.[44] However, statistics collected by the FAO and World Bank suggest that, far from growing, the world area of farm land is in fact already shrinking – from a peak of 49.4 million square kilometres in the year 2000, to 48.6 million square kilometres in 2015.[45] This suggests that humanity has already passed 'peak land'. The decline in land use at a time of rising food demand is probably due to a combination of factors including the spreading of cities and deserts, degradation of topsoil and consequent abandonment of farms, sea-level rise and other climatic factors, the very poor price incentives received by farmers from a profit-driven global supermarket and 'agribusiness' sector, and the urban drift of rural populations.

The central fact is unmistakable: *humanity now depends on a shrinking resource to create an expanding food supply*. Without radical change to the present global food production and consumption system, crisis is unavoidable.

Soil is not just soil. It is also land, territory, an economic possession, a sovereign realm, a national emblem, a political rallying cry. The United Nations Interagency Framework Team for Preventive Action in its report on land and conflict argues that 'land issues readily lend themselves to conflict. Land is an important economic asset and source of livelihoods; it is also closely linked to community identity, history and culture. Communities, therefore, can readily mobilize around land issues, making land a central object of conflict'.[46]

Traditionally, scholars have tended to view famine as a consequence, rather than a driver, of warfare. However, the Oslo Peace Research Institute (PRIO) has challenged this perception in a paper arguing the risks of conflict in recent decades were much higher in regions suffering insecurity of food, land and water – and very much lower in places (such as Europe, North America or Australasia) where those resources were secure.[47] This view turns the old model on its head and begs the question: if we can secure and sustain our sources of food, can we at the same time reduce the drivers of war? This question is explored in Chapter 7.

Finally, it should be noted that the world currently wastes up to 40 per cent of its food in the production/market chain – enough to feed three billion people. This means that 20–35 billion tonnes of the world's soil are being lost annually *in order to grow food that is never eaten*. In a profit-driven global food industry, no-one has yet been able to devise an affordable system for redistributing food from surplus regions to deficit regions (which cannot afford to pay for it on the scale required to overcome hunger). The proven solution lies in protecting and enhancing local food self-sufficiency in the deficit regions through care of land, water and the adoption of novel production systems that use little or no soil and water (Chapters 8 and 9).

Climate Change: Threat Multiplier

During the twentyfirst century our changing climate will dominate geopolitical security and the risk of conflict, primarily through its impacts on the food chain and water scarcity.

This impact is likely to be felt in harvest and pasture losses caused by more frequent and intense droughts, heavier flood events and hotter heatwaves stressing both crops and livestock, loss of water for irrigation, sea-level rise inundating or salinising low-lying farmlands, loss of food nutritional quality and more damaging outbreaks of crop diseases and insect pests. These will increase the uncertainty affecting world grain supplies and trade, a study by Britain's Chatham House cautioned.[48] For example, when Russia suffered a poor harvest in 2010, it immediately suspended grain exports in order to feed people at home; an unforeseen consequence of this was the bread crisis in Egypt and Tunisia, which led to the overthrow of their governments.

How severe future crop losses will prove depends on many, as yet unknown, factors – such as the extent to which science can overcome them by breeding more-resilient food crops and the rate of global warming, which in turn depends on how quickly or slowly we cease to use fossil fuels. However, for today's crop varieties, modelling projects that by 2100 under continued high greenhouse emissions, corn yields would decline by 20–40 per cent, wheat yields by 5–50 per cent, rice yields between 20–30 per cent, and soybean crops by 30–60 per cent.[49] On the face of it, such an outcome would be catastrophic for humanity, reducing world grain production by about one third *at the very time we are trying to double it* to meet both population and economic demands. The result would be worldwide famine – with 10 billion people trying to get by on food sufficient to feed only four billion. This would drop the caloric intake per person from a recommended 2000–2500 calories a day to 800–1000 calories, which is well below the level advisable for a healthy person, and into the realm of starvation for the average human.

Even as little as half a degree (0.5 °C) of global warming may make a profound difference. A scientific study of the difference between a 2 °C carbon emission target (the one set in the Paris Agreement) and a more stringent 1.5 °C target found, for example, that food security would improve in three quarters of developing countries under the lower target. In terms of local weather, this meant that 2 °C of warming would see the Ganges flood twice as often as under 1.5 °C, and the Amazon flow decrease by up to 25 per cent, along with more heatwaves and extreme rainfall events hammering food supplies across Asia, South America and Africa.[50]

A recent Chinese study based on data from 39 separate climate models, found that the Earth will warm by 4 °C, possibly as early as 2065 but probably before 2084.[51] This would be catastrophic for agriculture-based food production systems. With 3–5 °C of global warming – the likely result of failure by humanity to control its carbon emissions – hunger will soar worldwide and even people in less-affected regions will face food prices many times their present levels as scarcity causes global grain prices to skyrocket. Echoing events such as the 1930s US 'dustbowl', hundreds of millions of farmers worldwide will also be driven from the land by drought and economic hardship, impairing global capacity to restore food output for decades and destabilizing many urban societies and their governments.

Another study, by Chinese and Japanese researchers, found that one of the unpredicted consequences of climate change is a decline in the quality of foods such as rice, when produced under hotter conditions in an atmosphere richer in CO_2. They found that rice, which is a staple food for more than two billion people, lost protein, essential minerals like zinc and iron, and vitamin content when grown under these conditions, producing a diet less nourishing especially for poorer people in rice-dependent cultures.[52] In other words, more food will be needed to compensate as staple foods become less nutritious under the effects of climate change.

Clearly, such problems can be contained – and possibly overcome – by reducing or eliminating present levels of food wastage, which amount to 40 per cent of the world food supply, and by introducing new global diets and food production systems that do not depend on soil, water or a stable climate. These will be discussed in Chapter 9. Without such measures, it is doubtful if the world can avoid periods of extreme hunger from the mid century on, as a changing climate moves agriculture everywhere out of the Holocene 'sweet spot' in which it arose over the past 6000 years and into the Anthropocene world of sudden climate shocks, food shortages, contamination and collapsing agro-ecosystems.

Several of the world's leading militaries have already warned that climate change multiplies the risks generated through existing insecurity of the primary resources of food, land and water. Former US Secretary of State John Kerry observed in February 2014: 'In a sense, climate change can now be considered another weapon of mass destruction, perhaps the world's most fearsome weapon of mass destruction'. In 2015, a Pentagon study found climate change is a security risk, 'because it degrades living conditions, human security and the ability of governments to meet the basic needs of their populations'. Similarly, the UK's Climate Envoy, Rear Admiral Neil Morisetti, cautioned that the climate posed as grave a threat to Britain's security and economic resilience as terrorism and cyber-attacks. 'The areas of greatest global stress and greatest impacts of climate change are broadly coincidental... The increased threat posed by climate change arises because droughts, storms and floods are exacerbating water, food, population and security tensions in conflict-prone regions.'[53]

'The pressures caused by climate change will influence resource competition while placing additional burdens on economies, societies, and governance institutions around the world.

These effects are threat multipliers that will aggravate stressors abroad such as poverty, environmental degradation, political instability, and social tensions – conditions that can enable terrorist activity and other forms of violence', the US Department of Defense stated in its 2014 review of the defence landscape.[54] These threats were spelled out in greater detail in a subsequent defence report to the Congress.[55] A NATO report in 2017 used the same language, describing climate change as a threat multiplier and highlighting the Middle East as one region where climate, food and water issues posed a growing risk of violence. A year later, however, America had quietly swept the issue under the rug again as the Trump Administration sought to appease its fossil fuels lobby by expunging all references to climate change in US government reports.[56] Consequently, in 2018 the Pentagon scrubbed all reference to 'climate' from its National Defense Strategy update, thereby obeying the orders of its Commander-in-Chief, Trump, but deceiving itself, the US defence forces, the American people and the world in general as to its true thoughts.[57]

Not all US agencies were quite so compliant. 'The impacts of the long-term trends toward a warming climate, more air pollution, biodiversity loss, and water scarcity are likely to fuel economic and social discontent – and possibly upheaval', the US Director of National Intelligence, Daniel Coats, warned the American Congress in his 2018 annual briefing on threats.[58] 'Extreme weather events in a warmer world have the potential for greater impacts and can compound with other drivers to raise the risk of humanitarian disasters, conflict, water and food shortages, population migration, labor shortfalls, price shocks, and power outages.'

'Research has not identified indicators of tipping points in climate-linked Earth systems, suggesting a possibility of abrupt climate change', Coats cautioned. 'Accelerating biodiversity and species loss – driven by pollution, warming, unsustainable fishing, and acidifying oceans – will jeopardize vital ecosystems that support critical human systems. Water scarcity, compounded by gaps in cooperative management agreements for nearly half of the world's international river basins, and new unilateral dam development are likely to heighten tension between countries.'

In a commentary on the emerging crisis in water, soils and food, a former director of Australian Defence Intelligence, Major General John Hartley, commented: 'Years of variable food yield and volatile commodity prices, together with the certainty that food demand will increase substantially by the middle of the century, suggest increasing global instability and human suffering, with the possibility of widespread conflict. Political turmoil, social unrest, civil war and terrorism are all likely'. He continued: 'We need to inform food consumers and impress relevant decision makers that land and water systems, underpinning many of our key food-producing systems worldwide, are being stressed by unprecedented levels of demand and that climate change is expected to exacerbate these stresses'.[59]

The 2018 IPCC report[60] warned:

- at current rates, global warming is likely to reach 1.5 °C between 2030 and 2052 (high confidence);
- warming will last for hundreds to thousands of years and will cause further long-term impacts such as sea-level rise (high confidence);
- climate-related risks for nature and humans are higher for global warming of +1.5 °C than at present (+1 °C), but lower than at 2 °C (high confidence);
- impacts include hotter average temperatures in most regions, heavier rainfall events, greater likelihood of drought in some regions;
- damage, including extinctions and impact on food, land, freshwater and oceans will be lower at 1.5 °C than at 2 °C;
- risks to health, livelihoods, food security, water supply, human security and economic growth are projected to increase with global warming of 1.5 °C and increase further with 2 °C;
- a wide range of adaptation options can reduce the risks of climate change at lower temperatures (high confidence);
- human carbon emissions must drop by 45 per cent by 2030 and 100 per cent by 2075 to keep the global temperatures below +1.5 °C;

- this demands rapid and far-reaching transitions in energy, land, urban and infrastructure (including transport and buildings), and industrial systems (high confidence);
- a hotter climate will worsen poverty and inequality and undermine global sustainable development;
- at +2 °C, climate impacts on food and water will be much worse in the Middle East, Sub-Saharan Africa, Southeast Asia and Central and South America.

Instances of climate crises are accumulating internationally, say the Brookings Institution and others: over just three years from 2015 to 2017 severe floods hit Colombia, Sri Lanka, Canada, the USA, Thailand, Western and Central Europe, India, Bangladesh, Myanmar, Peru, Chile, Brazil and Niger.[61] Stronger hurricanes and typhoons made 2017 the most expensive year on record for storm damage, costing $320 billion, according to the World Meteorological Office.[62] All of these events had negative consequences for local agriculture and food production (Figure 3.3).

Global food crises are poised to worsen in key regions of the world as conflict and climate change intersect to damage agriculture, the Global Report on Food Crises 2018, co-authored by the UN FAO (the Food and Agriculture Organisation of the United Nations), the World Food Programme and the European Community, declared.[63] The report detailed how a combination of war and climate shocks had thrust 124 million people in

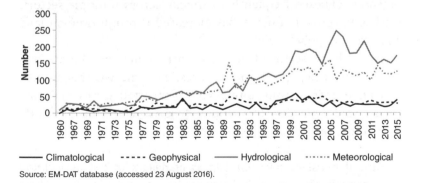

Source: EM-DAT database (accessed 23 August 2016).

Figure 3.3. Increasing frequency of floods and storms 1960–2015. Source: Emergency Events Database, 2016.

51 countries into a state of acute hunger and malnutrition. 'We must recognize that food crises are likely to become more acute, persistent and complex given current trends and their root causes – with devastating effects on the lives of millions of people', the EU Commissioner for International Cooperation & Development, Neven Mimica, said.

'Natural disasters' – from droughts to floods, storms to heat-waves, fires to disease outbreaks – are striking world food production hard. Together they wrecked crops conservatively worth $96 billion in the decade from 2005 to 2015, a UN FAO study found.[64] 'Protracted crises are the new norm, with 40 percent more ongoing food crises considered to be protracted than in 1990', it added. Many of these disasters are 'silent' meaning that they are local in impact and so escape attention by global media – but are serious nonetheless for the people and farms they affect. Climatic disasters affect not only agriculture, but also fishing and forestry. While farmers are the first and usually worst-hit by these disasters, their impacts cascade all along the food chain, affecting the livelihoods of millions and ultimately the prices paid in the shops by consumers.

That climate shocks to agriculture and fisheries are on the rise worldwide is documented in a study published in *Nature Sustainability* in 2019: 'Sudden losses to food production (that is, shocks) and their consequences across land and sea pose cumulative threats to global sustainability... some regions are shock hotspots, exposed frequently to shocks across multiple sectors. Critically, shock frequency has increased through time on land and sea at a global scale'.[65]

'Agriculture sectors face many risks, such as climate and market volatility, pests and diseases, extreme weather events, and an ever-increasing number of protracted crises and conflicts', said FAO director general José Graziano da Silva. He concluded:

> *Natural disasters have cost billions of dollars in lost agricultural production. The human food chain is under continuous threat from an alarming increase in the number of outbreaks of transboundary animal and plant pests and diseases. Conflict and protracted crises*

are forcing more and more people into conditions of poverty, food insecurity and displacement. This has become the "new normal," and the impact of climate change will further exacerbate these threats and challenges.

In this FAO report, buried under its habitual monotonic prose, it is possible to discern the emergence of an epochal new cycle – one in which climate changes and wars spawn food crises, which in turn spawn more wars and further climatic deterioration. Whereas in the past conflict may have sparked individual famines, and famines sparked individual conflicts, we are now in an age in which each can lead to the other continuously, giving rise to a fearsome, self-propagating cycle. One in which soil, water, climate, the food system and conflict interact and combine to multiply the threats facing our global civilisation.

One in which the agricultural food system which has stood by humanity for thousands of years, and which we respect, love and trust, can no longer be sustained, at least in its present form.

4 IS 'AGRICULTURE' SUSTAINABLE?

**Agriculture and Climate – Food and Poison –
Agriculture and Extinction – The Great Meat Debate –
Why Farmers Need a Payrise – Novel Farming Systems**

'If agriculture fails, everything else will fail.'
M. S. Swaminathan, father of India's Green Revolution

The basics of the global food system, which today feeds seven to eight billion people, were developed by the ancient Romans. Their model of mono-crop, broadacre export agriculture has been taken up worldwide, with science and machinery substituting for the slave labour and manual methods of the ancient world, to boost its yields of food in the modern era. It has been phenomenally successful – being the chief driver – coupled with vaccines, antibiotics and public health – in a tripling of the human population since the mid twentieth century.

Today's food is thus the product of an Iron Age system, super-charged and propped up by the addition of recent high-intensity technologies, chiefly chemistry, fossil fuels and biotechnology. There is good reason to question whether this is the most suitable, sustainable and stable form of food production for the hot, overcrowded world of the mid twentyfirst century, in which all resources and biological systems face acute stress.

Agriculture has been humanity's crowning achievement and one of the central dynamics in the ascent of civilisation: none of the technological wonders of the modern world would have been developed without it. Those early experiments in domesticating plants and animals in the Tigris–Euphrates, Indus and Yangtse valleys supplied the essential bedrock for today's cities, industries, professions, arts, religions, sciences and commerce. However, to assume that, because it was successful in the past, agriculture is the only way to produce food in the future is, at best, sentimental nonsense – and at worst, perilously unrealistic on an over-heated, over-populated, over-exploited planet.

What has changed is the sheer vastness of the human impact on the Earth. Had our population, society and its food and energy demands remained at the levels of the 1950s, then agriculture would be fine as the mainstay of food production in a stable world populated by 2.5 billion people with modest demands. In a world of seven to ten billion, each using five to ten times the amount of resources used by their grandparents, however, this ancient method of food production is looking increasingly shaky, imperilled by planetary changes now afoot – erratic climate, loss of soils, scarcity of water, global chemical pollution and ecosystem decline.

Back in the nineteenth century, when there were around one billion humans, we thought coal was sustainable forever too – though we understood it was dirty and caused disease. In the modern world, its massive over-use inflicts catastrophic damage on the Earth's atmosphere, climatic systems and human health in general with every day that passes. Coal and oil are implicated in the deaths of up to nine million people a year[1] – one in six – and are the primary drivers of global climate change: coal alone supplies 42 per cent of humanity's total carbon emissions.[2] The world at large has grasped this – barring a handful of corporate executives and their pet politicians, who do not care what becomes of their grandchildren – and is making the essential transition to clean, renewable energy and transport systems. Though maybe not nearly fast enough for traditional farming to have a future.

The footprint of agriculture has grown in proportion to the growth in human numbers and demands. Today it occupies around 37 per cent of the Earth's terrestrial land surface. This may not sound much – until one considers that only 71 per cent of that land is habitable. Thus, it can be seen that food production uses 52 per cent of the available world land area to feed humanity now – and could potentially occupy close to 70 per cent by the mid century.

This is not to suggest there is no future for agriculture – far from it, in fact. But it is to suggest that old-style industrial agriculture can no longer be the only source, or even the main source, of humanity's food supply when innumerable other options with less impact, lower vulnerability and greater bene-fits exist. And also, that the way we do agriculture in future will be very different from the way we do it today.

A warning that the present food system is on the way out was clearly articulated by a conference of food scientists from 17 countries held in Sydney in 2016. It concluded:

Access to diverse nutritious food and potable water is a right for all life. Our current food systems supporting humans, domestic animals and plants are neither sustainable nor ecologically sound. An inte-grated and holistic approach involving the whole of society is needed to reverse unsustainable trends within current food systems.[3]

A highly authoritative warning was sounded by the EAT-Lancet Commission in early 2019. In a report entitled *Food in the Anthropocene*, the Commission concluded: 'Food systems have the potential to nurture human health and support environmen-tal sustainability; however, they are currently threatening both', adding that 'Unhealthy and unsustainably produced food poses a global risk to people and the planet'. Boldly they then set out to describe a healthy, sustainable global diet, which included little or no meat. This diet met with a storm of criticism from both food and livestock fans, yet the critics did not undermine the Commission's essential point – that the modern food system is broken, and needs fixing.[4]

'As we race towards a population of nine billion, business as usual for farming is no longer a viable option. We must take a more ecological approach', argued two agricultural experts, Nina Moeller and Michel Pimbert, in an article in Britain's *The Independent* newspaper. They continued:

The failings of dominant food systems are becoming impossible to deny. Current production methods are severely polluting. They are the cause of malnutrition. They are also inequitable, and unjustifiably wasteful. And they are concentrated in the hands of few corporations. Entangled in the multiple crises humanity is facing, establishing global food security is considered a key challenge of our time.[5]

'The greatest barrier to hope on the hunger front is socio-political. Above all, it arises from a combination of ignorance, politics and the stresses on the world order from human over-population', add environmental scientists Paul Ehrlich and John Harte. 'The multiple harms that global warming is causing, especially to human access to adequate food supplies, will only increase if the science deniers continue to provide politicians with excuses to do nothing about the problem, while the media remains nearly silent.'[6]

That the existing industrial model of the food production system is unsustainable we have already seen in its impact on soil loss and water scarcity and its vulnerability to climatic extremes – with the added danger that this susceptibility may lead to war. This chapter considers other factors that make conventional industrial farming unsuited to feed the world in the future.

Agriculture and Climate

Agriculture is the offspring of the mild, temperate climate that arose when the last Ice Age ended, some 9000 years ago, the epoch known as the Holocene. Recent archaeological discoveries indicate that people were gathering and grinding wild grains in Australia possibly as far back as 65,000 years ago[7] – in the warmer period between the last two Ice Ages. Though there is vestigial evidence of cropping from Israel during the Ice Age 23,000 years ago[8], humanity in general does not seem to have progressed to the systematic planting and harvesting of crops or herding of animals until around 9000–10,000 years ago, as the grip of the ice sheets on the world's climatically favoured food-bowl regions finally began to ease.[9] Then, agriculture seems to have sprung into existence independently and more or less sim-ultaneously around the planet, in regions as widely separated as

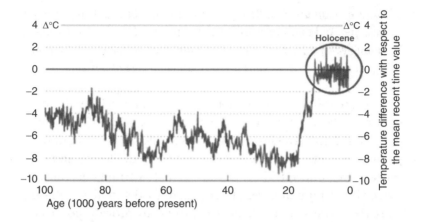

Figure 4.1. Climate fluctuated wildly during the Ice Ages, then settled into a temperate, stable state in which agriculture arose (right). Now it is becoming unstable again. Source: Steffen W. and Vostok Ice Core.

the Middle East, China's Yangtse Valley, Mexico, Egypt, India and Papua New Guinea.

If agriculture is the driving force for the ascent of human civilisation and its recent population overgrowth, then agriculture itself was driven by climate – a climate which, for several thousand years, was sufficiently stable, warm and moist to favour the growth, especially, of the grasses that became our cereal grains and pastures. Note the remarkable evenness depicted in the right-hand end of the graph in Figure 4.1: this was the Holocene, a mild, stable period uniquely suited to outdoor agriculture, which is now extinct. Farming's explosive expansion, to the point where it now dominates more than half of the habitable regions of the Earth, has wrought a geological change – from an era in which climate governed agriculture, to one where agriculture now influences climate and vice versa. This era is now known as the Anthropocene, a new geological age in which human activity has become a dominant influence in shaping the world climate, biosphere and oceans.

'At least one fifth of total greenhouse gas emission can be attributed to the agriculture sectors', UN Food and Agriculture Organisation director general Graziano da Silva noted, with that organisation's usual cautious underestimates, in his speech to the Paris climate conference, COP 13.[10] However, as others note 'Most studies estimate that between 20–35 percent of anthropogenic greenhouse gases are associated with the food and agriculture sector, while some have it as high as 50 percent'.[11]

First, a little chemistry: agriculture is a source for three major greenhouse gases: carbon dioxide (CO_2), nitrous oxide (N_2O) and methane (CH_4) – and a sink for atmospheric carbon dioxide (CO_2). The emitted CO_2 comes chiefly from land clearing, tillage and forest fires, the burning of fossil fuels by machinery, transport and the use of chemicals and fertilisers derived from fossil fuels. The nitrous oxide comes primarily from losses into the air and environment of nitrogen from fertilisers and legume crops. The methane is emitted mainly by bacteria in the stomachs of ruminant livestock (cattle, sheep, goats) digesting their feed and by bacterial action in the mud of rice paddies and dams. Agriculture's ability to soak up atmospheric CO_2 is mainly through plants absorbing it and transferring some carbon back into the soil via their root systems. If the carbon is stable and undisturbed within the soil, it is said to be 'sequestered' from the air and makes no contribution to global warming. If it is soon released again by tillage, drought or land use changes, then it escapes, trapping more heat within the Earth's atmosphere. The issue is one of balance: to what degree does agriculture's ability to lock up carbon offset its ability to release it? On present estimates, the world food sector is releasing a net 10–28 billion tonnes – depending on whose analysis you accept – of new carbon into the atmosphere every year (Figure 4.2).

Business-as-usual emissions, including from agriculture, are sufficient to drive the planet's temperature up by +4–5 °C by 2100 – a level at which most scientists agree, arable crops will fail and livestock will die globally.[12] The paradox of human history is that our modern food production system is so successful that it has become a major force for the very climate change which will destroy it – and possibly ourselves and our civilisation as well, unless we change our ways. Every time a farmer starts a tractor, uses a chemical spray or increases the size of

Million

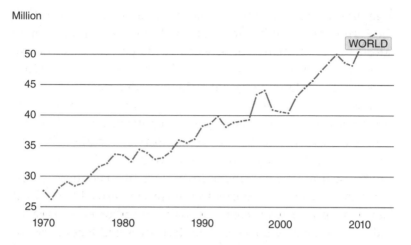

Figure 4.2. World annual greenhouse emissions, in million tonnes of CO_2 equivalents. Source: World Bank.

their herd, they help to create a climate less conducive to farming: the CO_2 he emits lingers in the atmosphere for a few years before cycling into the oceans, and then being re-released into the air. The net effect of this continual cycling is that our personal carbon emissions – including those of agriculture – continue to warm the planet for a period of between 500 and 1000 years. An agriculture that emits carbon thus contains the seeds of its own destruction and will affect up to 40 human generations to come.

In the long run, either agriculture must cease emitting carbon – i.e. replace fossil fuels and chemicals with clean energy and biological protectants – and cease land clearing, or else the bulk of the world's food must be produced by other, non-agricultural means. Or both.

Much more needs to be done to reduce these emissions and to simultaneously improve yields and build resilience, the FAO's da Silva says. This means adopting approaches such as agroecology and sustainable, climate-smart intensification, among others. 'Reducing deforestation; restoring degraded lands and forests; eliminating food loss and waste; enhancing soil carbon seques-tration; low-carbon livestock - these are only a few known solutions to address hunger, poverty and sustainability at the same time', he added. 'We cannot expect that smallholders, family farmers and pastoralists ... can tackle these challenges on their own. They will need national and international support.'[13]

The dilemma that farmers the world over face is that they now have little or no real power to determine what happens on their own farms. Their farming choices are largely dictated by the intense economic pressures imposed by a handful of giant corporations which recently came to dominate the global food supply and dictate the price of farm commodities, and a handful of giant corporations which dictate the cost of farming inputs like machinery, chemicals and fuel. Over these, farmers have no control at all. The decision to farm unsustainably and to destroy the agricultural environment is therefore taken, not on farms by farmers, but in boardrooms – and by people in suits with little technical insight or care for what it all means to humanity, but whose chief motive is money. This issue is further discussed below.

Food and Poison

'Someday we shall look back on this dark era of agriculture and shake our heads. How could we have ever believed that it was a good idea to grow our food with poisons?', renowned anthropologist Dr Jane Goodall asked rhetorically in her 2005 book *Harvest of Hope.*[14]

Goodall's is a point worth pondering: when is a poison, however specialised, ever consistent with a healthy, sustainable diet? And do we truly know what's poisonous and what isn't among the 6500 different man-made chemicals purposefully used in the production, formulation, preservation and packaging of the modern food supply? Or what their combined effect might be on our health and that of the planet?

Chemistry has become a mainstay of both agriculture and food processing, and hence of human population growth. The chemical industry likes to argue that, without it, millions would starve – but the antithesis is also true: without chemicals, millions would not exist *to* starve. Besides the 2000 and 4000 different chemicals and pesticides used on the farm,

> *More than 2,500 chemical substances are intentionally added to foods to modify flavor, color, stability, texture, or cost. In addition, an estimated 12,000 substances are used in such a way that they may unintentionally enter the food supply. These substances include components of food-packaging materials, processing aids, pesticide residues, and drugs given to animals. An unknown number of naturally occurring chemical contaminants also find their way into food*

the US National Institutes for Health cautioned, in a report written as long ago as 1983.[15] 'There has been no requirement to perform tests to determine carcinogenicity for most substances added to food', it added.

Many of the chemicals used in modern food production were approved in 1958, in the US Food, Drug, and Cosmetic Act. Though never stringently tested for human safety these chemicals were presumed safe merely because few cases of death or serious harm had been noticed *by 1958*. This presumed safety of food additives and agricultural chemicals was then grandfathered into worldwide chemical regulation – in Europe, Australasia, Japan and other countries whose food safety practitioners took their lead from the USA (where policy often conforms more to the needs of chemical corporations than it does to the needs of consumers) without bothering to test the chemicals they were using for safety. Since then, many cases of harm have emerged, and authorities have been backpedalling ever since to compensate for this bizarre oversight, introducing maximum residue limits, some retrospective testing and stricter approval rules for new chemicals. However, no test has yet been devised to assess the total 'cocktail effect' of thousands of different chemicals being deliberately or unintentionally administered to citizens the world over in their daily diet, and how this affects the health of billions, children especially. Humanity is still the involuntary guinea pig in a vast, worldwide chemistry experiment which, like the case of tobacco, assumes that everything is safe – until people become sick and start dying.

Rachel Carson blew the whistle on this global poisoning in her 1962 book *Silent Spring*, which focussed on one particular chemical, DDT, leading to a worldwide ban in 1972. Since she wrote her book, worldwide production and use of pesticides in agriculture has more than quadrupled, exceeding 5 million tonnes in 2017. China alone uses 1.8 million tonnes, and India is rapidly catching up. These volumes are on track to redouble again by the mid century, with industry predictions of pesticide sales soaring by half from $216 billion in 2016 to $308 billion by 2025.[16] In recent years, a growing flood of scientific papers has reported more and graver health impacts as a result of the chemicalisation of our food supply; for example, in 2018, Irva Herz-Picciotto and colleagues reported brain damage to unborn children and adult deaths resulting from exposure to organophosphate pesticides, which are widely used in agriculture all over the world. They called for the use of these chemicals in the food supply to be phased out and an immediate global education programme implemented.[17]

What consumers often fail to understand is that many of these toxic chemicals used in food production do not just vanish after they have been used. They, or their daughter compounds, may continue to cycle through the natural world, lingering in the soil and concentrating up the food chain to result in doses often many times stronger by the time they reach humans. The US Department of Health conducts an annual national survey in which it finds, unsurprisingly, that most Americans are contaminated by hundreds of toxic industrial chemicals linked to cancers or other diseases. Many of these are sourced to foods produced by the modern industrial food system.[18]

Together, humans emit more than 250 billion tonnes of chemicals every year[19] – four times the scale of our climate emissions – and while the bulk of these are a byproduct of mining, mineral extraction and energy production, a very large part of them are nevertheless a product of modern industrial agriculture, the soil its dislodges, the gases and nutrients it releases and the biocidal chemicals it distributes throughout the environment.

In *Poisoned Planet* I presented the mounting scientific and medical evidence that this colossal chemical release is implicated in a global pandemic of cancers, brain damage, sexual dysfunction, allergies, hormonal and developmental disorders, the like of which has never before been seen in human history. Rates of these diseases are certainly far higher today than they were one or two generations ago, in most societies. As Harvard professors Philippe Grandjean and Philip Landrigan put it:

> *Neurodevelopmental disabilities, including autism, attention-deficit hyperactivity disorder, dyslexia, and other cognitive impairments, affect millions of children worldwide, and some diagnoses seem to be increasing in frequency. Industrial chemicals that injure the developing brain are among the known causes for this rise in prevalence.*[20]

To take just one example, the conditions known as autism spectrum disorder (ASD):

- in the 1950s it is estimated that 1 in 25,000 children was diagnosed with autism;
- in the 1970s and 1980s, about one in 2500 children was diagnosed with ASD;
- in 2000, the US Centers for Disease Control (CDC) reported that ASD affected 1 in 150 American children;
- in 2004 this figure had reached 1 in 125 children;
- in 2006 the figure was one in 110 children,
- in 2008 this figure reached 1 in 88, based on the CDC's ADDM network of 14 monitoring areas across the USA;
- in March 2013, the US National Health Statistics Report indicated that 1 in 50 children across the USA were diagnosed with ASD. In heavily populated US cities this recently reached 1 in 27 children.[21] Surveys of parents indicated the rate may be as high as one child in nine.

A thousandfold increase, from 1-in-25,000 to 1-in-27 children, cannot be explained by the development of better diagnosis alone. At the same time, numerous foods, food additives and chemical dyes (made from oil and coal but often included as ingredients in food) were implicated by science in child behavioural disorders. Some were banned by the European Union, though not by the USA – as those who have eaten food-chain hamburgers on both sides of the Atlantic would be aware, from the striking colour difference in the cheese.

This is not to argue that all autism originates with the diet, or any single source. Some is undoubtedly genetic, and other cases probably relate to the chemical environment in which the child was raised: for example, a famous study among US nurses by Harvard School of Public Health found that autism rates in their children were double for those who lived close to freeways and industrial areas with heavy air pollution.[22] The parsimonious explanation for the rise in autism, ADHD, reduced IQ and other emergent childhood mental disorders is the intense sensitivity of the developing human brain to poisons in the child's environment – in air, water, food and living conditions. Because they consume far more of these things per kilogram of bodyweight, infants are also far more susceptible than adults to brain damage.

Exposure to toxic chemicals begins in the womb, as a famous study by the US-based Environmental Working Group (EWG) demonstrated, when it identified 287 different industrial chemicals – 217 of which were known to cause cancer – in the blood of new-born babies.[23] After birth, the poisoning continues: in 2017, the World Health Organisation reported banned, highly toxic industrial contaminants and agricultural pesticides in mothers' milk in 68 different countries.[24]

The effects are not confined to babies and young children: a study revealed that male sperm counts (fertility) in North America, Europe, Australia and New Zealand have crashed by 50–60 per cent since 1981[25]; while the reason is unknown, the researchers note that 'sperm count has been plausibly associated with multiple environmental and lifestyle influences, both prenatally and in adult life. In particular, endocrine disruption from chemical exposures or maternal smoking during critical windows of male reproductive development may play a role in prenatal life, while lifestyle changes and exposure to pesticides may play a role in adult life'. More disturbing still is mounting evidence that pesticides in the food supply can cause inherited genetic disorders several generations into the future.[26]

Modern food is also implicated in another condition, previously uncommon, but now galloping through the human population: depression. The WHO notes that the number of people living with depression worldwide increased by 18.4 per cent between 2005 and 2015 to 322 million. Depression is now the world's leading single cause of ill health and disability, and responsible for nearly a million deaths a year.[27] The drivers of this global upsurge in brain damage are still unclear but scientists note that 'Modern populations are increasingly overfed, malnourished, sedentary, sunlight-deficient, sleep-deprived, and socially-isolated'.[28] In other words, the modern diet, with all its chemical additives and poor nutritional design, may be an important causative factor.

Similarly, the modern industrial diet is implicated in the pandemic of obesity and diabetes. 'The modern diet is the main reason why people all over the world are fatter and sicker than ever before. Everywhere modern processed foods go, chronic diseases like obesity, type 2 diabetes and heart disease soon follow', states the US-based consumer health website *Healthline*.[29] The statement is founded on two decades of intensive medical and dietetic research. In 2016, said the World Health Organisation, 1.9 billion adults and a third of a billion children – almost a third of the human population – were overweight or obese: this was two and a half times the number suffering hunger (0.81 billion).[30] Paralleling this, the number of diabetics quadrupled from 108 million in 1980 to 422 million in 2014 and the disease was killing around 3 million a year. This self-acquired disease was on track to become the world's seventh largest killer by 2030. While the large intake volumes, high sugar, fat and salt content and poor nutritional quality of the modern industrial diet are the primary reason for the increase in premature deaths among its consumers, there are subtler strands to the story: scientists are now convinced that hormone-disrupting chemicals in the food supply are partly to blame: 'A substantial body of evidence suggests that a subclass of endocrine-disrupting chemicals (EDCs), which interfere with endocrine signalling, can disrupt hormonally regulated metabolic processes, especially if exposure occurs during early development. These chemicals, so-called "obesogens" might predispose some individuals to gain weight despite their efforts to limit caloric intake and increase levels of physical activity'.[31] These chemicals derive partly from trace amounts of certain pesticides and preservatives, partly from cooking of meat, partly from soy and its products, but chiefly from the plastic film, packaging, drink bottles, cups and utensils in widespread use by supermarkets and fast food chains especially.[32] Their effects include changing the way the body regulates its energy use and storage, causing obesity, changing both male and female hormonal systems (including gender identity and sexual preference), sensory disruption, mental problems causing social difficulties and impaired immunity to other diseases.

While not solely responsible, the modern industrial food system is, nonetheless, a major contributor to a universal web of toxicity that will entrap and poison the human species, our descendants and the environment they live in for centuries to come. This is a web of toxicity that hardly existed three generations ago and, previously, did not exist at all for the entirety of human history – until the age of fossil fuels and industrial chemistry unleashed it.

A growing mountain of worldwide research testifies to the havoc being wrought by agricultural pesticides in soils, rivers, among farm workers, among bees, birds, frogs, fish and small mammals and even in the oceans and their food chains. As many as 200,000 people die each year directly from agricultural pesticides and many millions are poisoned.[33] Farm chemicals, which may have been relatively safe when used in small quantities and over limited areas a generation or two ago, are now deployed in such vast quantities and so universally they have become a significant threat to life on the planet. The Earth is now subject to a universal chemical bombardment, a macro-scale version of the destruction of the forests and rice paddies of Vietnam in the US 'Agent Orange' campaign of the 1970s. The job of most farm chemicals is to kill something – whether it is an insect or a plant – and their dispersal through the global environment ensures that many non-target species, including people, birds, frogs, honeybees and soil micro-organisms, are killed, injured or have their reproductive, neurological and developmental systems damaged. 'The mechanism for toxic action is not restricted to target pests, and toxicity is exerted also on nontarget similar organisms causing damage to biodiversity and ecosystems health.'[34]

As the UN Human Rights Council put it, 'Evolving technology in pesticide manufacture, among other agricultural innovations, has certainly helped to keep agricultural production apace of unprecedented jumps in food demand. However, this has come at the expense of human health and the environment'.[35]

> *Sick, unbalanced soils have problems that are symptoms of the management that disrupts soil food webs. Symptoms include compaction, soil crusting, acidity, salinity and soil borne diseases. They are the result of gross oversimplification of fertilisation and plant protection practices that use harsh synthetics and ignore the delicate balance of microbiota, trace minerals, nutrients and carbon in the soil. There is increasing awareness, however, that the synthetics used compromise the environment, food quality and human health*

explains biological farming scientist Dr Martin Stapper.[36] He says unhealthy foods originate from current farming practices because of the following.

- Foods from plants grown on 'sick soils', where microbial activity is low, have much lower nutrient (e.g. minerals, vitamins, proteins) and phytonutrient (e.g. antioxidant) content because there are not enough microbes to release them.
- Plants bred for high yield, without factoring in their mineral content, have a large production of plant material but their food value remains low. High yields are thus said to dilute

food quality. The essential minerals are in the soil but are not taken up by the force-fed plant due to low soil microbial activity.

- Fresh foods produced under high-input systems have a much higher water content, driven by the use of nitrogen fertiliser, which also dilutes their nutritional value.
- As soils become 'sicker', increasingly large doses of fertiliser and chemical protectants are needed to grow crops, with consequences for human health.

An alarming dimension of planet-wide chemical release by the food industry is what scientists now refer to as 'the global nitrogen crisis'. 'In the past half-century, humans have increased the amount of nitrogen in the environment more than any other major element', says science writer Fred Pearce. 'Sewage, livestock waste, fossil-fuel burning, and especially our use of synthetic fertilizer have all contributed to a doubling of nitrogen flows. Half the world's crops today are grown with the aid of fertilizer made by capturing inert nitrogen from the air.'[37]

The world uses more than 120 million tonnes of nitrogen fertiliser to feed crops every year and the volumes are soaring as developing countries resort to fertilisers to boost domestic crop yields. This is on top of the nitrogen released by organic sources such as animal manures, crop wastes and legumes. The result is calamity for the world's waterways – from China and the USA to India, Africa, South America and Europe rivers and lakes are choking under an assault from toxic blue-green algae and excessive nutrient runoff. Four hundred 'dead zones' have materialised in the world's oceans near the mouths of great rivers and bays. Whole seas, like the Baltic, are at risk, their fisheries being decimated. A dead zone at the mouth of the Mississippi in the Gulf of Mexico reached 23,000 square kilometres in 2017. Off the southern coast of the Arabian Peninsula, a vast dead zone – more than 80,000 square kilometres in extent – has been growing since the 1990s, scientists report. 'The Arabian Sea is the largest and thickest dead zone in the world. But until now, no-one really knew how bad the situation was because piracy and conflicts in the area have made it too dangerous to collect data. Our research shows that the situation is actually worse than feared – and that the area of dead zone is vast and growing. The ocean is suffocating', said Dr Bastien Queste of the University of East Anglia.[38] Thus, agriculture plays a direct role in the destruction of the world's fisheries, even as they are being overfished.

Human nitrogen pollution of the hydrosphere is in striking parallel with the impact of humanity's carbon release on the atmosphere – but far less is being done to understand, quantify and remedy it. Indeed, the type of crops being grown worldwide and modern industrial farming systems will tend to increase nutrient pollution, not reduce it. Scientists working on the issue of 'safe global boundaries' calculate humanity as a whole releases a surplus of 150 million tonnes of nitrogen and 36 million tonnes of phosphorus into the environment every year, quantities which are far beyond the natural capacity of the planet to safely reabsorb and cycle. Along with climate and species collapse, there is a critical 'safe boundary' for nutrients that humans have already breached.[39]

Agriculture and Extinction

Normally, when we think of world population, we tend to count the number of people on the planet – eight billion rising to ten billion in the 2060s. Not Vaclav Smil. In his efforts to work out how many of us the Earth can in fact support, the Canadian biologist decided to measure humans in terms of the millions of tonnes of organic carbon we consist of. He concluded that in 1900 there were 13 million tonnes of carbon in human form and, a century later in 2000, 55 million tonnes, as we grew fatter and more numerous.[40] But humans also rely on vast quantities of domestic animals – cattle, sheep, goats, pigs, poultry, horses, pets, etc. – and their combined tonnage is more than twice that of humanity. Smil then calculated the percentage shares of all vertebrates on the planet by weight and found almost two thirds were now livestock, just under a third were humans – and a

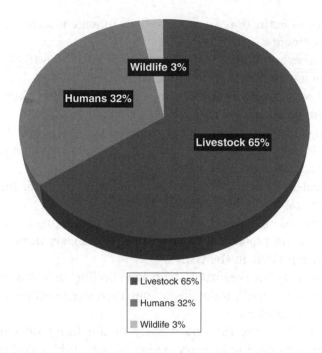

Figure 4.3. World land vertebrate biomass in the early twentyfirst century. Source: after Vaclav Smil.

microscopic 3 per cent was wildlife, from elephants and antelope to birds, frogs, lizards and crocodiles (Figure 4.3).

This explains, in terms anybody can understand, why, without radical change to the present food system, the world's wildlife will mostly be dead and gone, long before the end of this century. As humans seek to eat more, the space left for wild animals to exist will dwindle to practically nothing.

It is now widely acknowledged by science that the modern food system is the primary cause of the Sixth Extinction of life on Earth.[41] The main drivers are land clearing, which destroys the habitat of wild animals and plants, water extraction, which denies them adequate clean water, climate change driven by emissions from food production and distribution (along with emissions from industry, travel, etc.), and worldwide pollution by pesticides, nutrients and eroded soil.

Rates of extinction are now well-documented, across species and continents:

- present rates of extinction are estimated at 100–1000 times the normal rate before humans emerged[42];
- 60 per cent of the world's large wild animals have been eliminated since 1970[43];
- mass die-offs of wildlife are common and increasing[44];
- of 83,000 species assessed by science, 24,000 were found to be at risk of extinction[45];
- species richness has fallen below a critical point for human survival across two thirds of Earth's landmass[46];
- bees and other insects responsible for pollinating a third of the world's food crops face collapsing numbers worldwide[47] but especially in the USA;
- scientists have reported a 'shocking decline' in bird numbers across Europe[48], following an observed steep decline in insect numbers.

'Biodiversity – the essential variety of life forms on Earth – continues to decline in every region of the world, significantly reducing nature's capacity to contribute to people's wellbeing. This alarming trend endangers economies, livelihoods, food security and the quality of life of people everywhere', a report compiled by more than 550 scientists from over 100 countries said.[49] The study, which covered the entire planet except the poles and open oceans, sounded the clearest possible warning that loss of the Earth's wildlife will, in the end, come back to bite humans in a deadly way – and that current methods of food production are deeply implicated.

In a subsequent study by the same group, they found a million species are under threat of extinction. 'Nature is declining globally at rates unprecedented in human history – and the rate of species extinctions is accelerating, with grave impacts on people around the world now likely', Intergovernmental Science-Policy Platform on Biodiversity and Ecosystem Services (IPBES) chair Sir Robert Wilson said. 'The health of ecosystems on which we and all other species depend is deteriorating more rapidly than ever. We are eroding the very foundations of our economies, livelihoods, food security, health and quality of life worldwide'.[50]

Another way in which modern industrial food systems shoot themselves in the foot is through the erosion of genetic diversity. This occurs when agribusiness systems place too much emphasis on the profitability of a very narrow range of plants and animals at the expense of other important traits like disease resistance, climate tolerance, suitability to local conditions, balanced nutrition and so on. In contrast to the varied diets of times past, the modern diet consists chiefly of six plants and six animals, and a small number of strains of each. It consists chiefly of 200–300 plants, or just 1 per cent, of an available world total of 30,500 edible plants.[51]

This has led to the replacement of traditional varieties, indigenous species and landraces with genetically uniform, high-yielding, modern cultivars where the accent is on quantity, not farming sustainability or nutritional quality. 'Crop genetic resources are being wiped out at the rate of 1–2% every year. Since the beginning of this century, about 75% of the genetic diversity of agricultural crops has been lost', writes Hope Shand, research director for the Canada-based Rural Advancement Foundation International (RAFI).[52] Examples are the loss of more than 6000 US apple varieties since 1900 and the replacement of dozens of native rices with just two modern varieties over 98 per cent of the rice-growing area of the Philippines. As industrial agriculture spreads through the developing world scientists estimate 50% of indigenous goat breeds, 20% of indigenous cattle breeds, and 30% of indigenous sheep breeds are in danger of disappearing.

The danger this wipe-out poses to world food security was underlined in a striking report by the FAO in 2019. It found that, while biodiversity is essential to agriculture, 'Many key components of biodiversity for food and agriculture at genetic, species and ecosystem levels are in decline'.[53] The advent of genetically modified crops and livestock has raised further concerns. Though evidence of their toxicity to humans is, as yet, limited, GMO varieties nevertheless contribute to a trend of narrowing the human diet and making the industrial food system ever more reliant on chemicals and artificial inputs. Furthermore, there remain unanswered questions about their environmental and biological safety, should the engineered genes escape into wild relatives of food crops or produce unanticipated side-effects when interacting with any of the tens of thousands of other genes in the plant genome. However, the chief concern over GMOs is the dishonesty of the debate around them – on both sides.[54] While critics may be guilty of exaggerating their risks, their proponents are equally guilty of concealing them and of trying to force GMO food down the throats of consumers worldwide without telling them. Since most people feel they have a right to choose what they eat, this has provoked a global backlash against gene modification that is entirely the fault of the biotech companies themselves and their tame scientists, for arrogantly presuming to dictate to humanity what it should eat, simply because it is profitable to them. This has, to a significant degree, bred worldwide consumer distrust and retarded the adoption by farmers of what may otherwise be a valuable technology, especially for combatting pests, diseases and climatic changes. Failure to consult the public or be transparent about the risks (as well as the advantages) of GMOs, has made them a world case study in how *not* to introduce a powerful, disruptive new technology.

In brief, the narrowing of the genetic base of the modern food supply, solely to meet the profit-driven needs of industrial food companies, is escalating the risk of harvest failures and livestock plagues, especially in unsettled climatic times. It is also furnishing a poorer and less nutritious food supply for the world community, which is compounding global obesity, diabetes and other diet-related pandemics.

This has brought about a situation in which two thirds of humans now 'die by their own hand' – the hand holding the fork or chopsticks. For humanity at large, the main causes of death are now diet related – heart and circulatory diseases, cancers, diabetes, kidney and liver ailments, obesity, malnutrition and fatal mental conditions. In developed societies as many as four people in five now die from a diet-related or other non-communicable disease.[55] A food system that helps kill from two thirds to three quarters of its customers cannot last; it will be forced by public anger, concern and informed consumer choices, to change.

Modern industrial agriculture and food processing is thus sowing the seeds of its own demise – not only that of the wider world around it. Besides the direct damage it inflicts on soils, water and climate it is reducing the fertility of soils by killing off their microbial and plant life with pesticides, wiping out the very pollinators that fertilise many crops and fruit trees, destroying many beneficial insects and birds that protect crops, undermining the genetic diversity of farm animals and crops, and harming the health of its consumers. Such a system will not survive in the long run. Trying to prop it up by force-feeding it with ever more machinery, fossil energy, chemistry and biotechnology – a process known as 'agricultural intensification' – has the same quality of logic to it as Josef Stalin shooting more farmers in his attempts to increase food production.

These ugly features of the modern food supply foreshadow escalating global food vulnerability, instability and insecurity – and those, as we have seen, raise the national and international tensions which lead to revolution and war. This view is receiving increasing acceptance among international agencies. The UN's Global Environment Foundation (GEF), for example, says:

> Humans depend on Earth's ecosystems and the services they provide. These include provisioning services such as food and clean water, regulating services such as disease and climate regulation, cultural services such as spiritual fulfillment and aesthetic enjoyment, and supporting services such as primary production and soil formation. The degradation of these services often causes significant harm to human well-being which ... explicitly includes human security.[56]

The Great Meat Debate

One of the most emotive debates of recent times is whether or not humans should continue to eat meat. This has been highlighted in many recent books, notably Michael Pollan's *The Omnivore's Dilemma*, which explores the food chains and their wider impacts for various types of industrial and 'whole' foods,[57] and Vaclav Smil's *Should We Eat Meat?*.[58]

That humans are omnivores is apparent from a glance in your mirror. Those are not the teeth of a sheep, nor yet those of a wolf. You have spent the last four million years carefully evolving a specialised dentition to cope with a variety of foods. The face that we so worship and photograph is in fact a product of our eating habits. You have teeth that can chop or tear meat, and teeth that can grind up raw plant matter or crunch insects. The inclusion of meat protein in the diet saved early humans at least two million 'chews' a year – which is a lot of spare energy for other things. Your gut and its resident bacteria are now adapted to a mix of foods. Moreover, a high protein meat diet, especially with cooking, helped supply the energy for a rapidly expanding human brain. *Homo sapiens* is, as Smil puts it, 'a perfect example of an omnivorous species'. People are by descent mixed feeders, and it is therefore quite difficult – though not impossible – to separate them from this genetic heritage.

That said, a large part of humanity – even a majority – has subsisted quite happily and successfully as vegetarians or near-vegetarians – the majority of the Indian population being one example, and that of China prior to the introduction of modern industrial agriculture, another.

What has changed in the long human history of mixed feeding is the massive worldwide growth in meat consumption and production that has taken place since the mid twentieth century – matching and far exceeding even the growth in human population. The amount of meat eaten per head of humanity grew from 24 kilograms in 1965 to 42 kilograms in 2015 and is forecast to reach 45 kilograms per person by 2030.[59] This all happened as human numbers swelled from 3.3 billion to 8 billion.

Consequently, global meat consumption nearly quadrupled in just half a century, from 79 million tonnes in the mid 1960s to 310 million tonnes in the mid 2010s: much of this expansion was due to the rise in affluence of Chinese consumers and their demand for pork and poultry and to the industrialisation of livestock production led by America. Based on these trends, the FAO anticipates global meat consumption will continue to grow, by about 73 per cent by 2050, bringing it to a world total of around 540 million tonnes (Figure 4.4).[60]

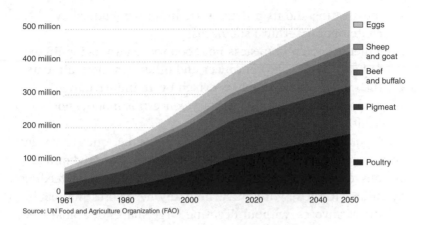

Figure 4.4. Global meat consumption to 2050. Source: FAO, 2013.

Whether such growth can, in fact, eventuate is open to question, as feeding so many animals will require the global production of an additional 2.5 billion tonnes of feedgrains or fodder crops, on a planet in which crop and pasture yields are under growing climatic stress in the form of heat, storm, disease and drought. It also means, in effect, we will need to discover the equivalent of two or three more 'North Americas' to grow enough grain to feed all those extra animals. On Google Earth, undiscovered continents appear in short supply. Furthermore vegetarian and vegan groups advocate, with growing stridency, an end to livestock as food on the grounds that it constitutes your single biggest impact on Earth.[61]

Its proponents argue the case against meat eating, basically, on six grounds:

- its huge cost to the global environment: the numbers of livestock and the vast areas of grain needed to feed them impose massive environmental damage on soil, pollute water and cause the extinction of other species;
- its impact on the climate: ruminant livestock are major contributors to climate change, while even pigs, poultry and fish contribute via their feed requirements;
- meat animals, especially pigs and poultry, are a primary source of pandemic diseases that affect humans;

- meat eating and its processes are inhumane judged by contemporary ethical standards;
- a diet over-rich in meat is not good for health, being linked to heart disease, bowel cancer and other common ailments;
- the modern meat supply is driven by an industrialised corporate sector whose primary concern is money, not healthy or sustainable food.

On the other hand, proponents of meat in the diet, such as Vaclav Smil, argue 'We could produce globally several hundred millions of tons of meat without ever-larger confined animal feeding operations (CAFOs), without turning any herbivores into cannibalistic carnivores, without devoting large shares of arable land to monocropping that produces animal feed and without subjecting many grasslands to damaging overgrazing'.[62] Sustainable grazing advocate Alan Savory is another who argues that, stocked at conservative densities and moved frequently (as wild game herds move), grazing animals can be used to manage and restore the world's rangelands and combat climate change.[63]

Furthermore there may be life-threatening risks in reducing world meat, dairy and egg consumption, especially for people in poorer countries on low-protein diets. 'Global efforts to limit or reduce the consumption of meat, milk and eggs over environmental concerns should exclude pregnant and breastfeeding women and babies under the age of two, especially in low-income settings', argue Delia Grace and colleagues. 'Consuming livestock-derived foods – meat, milk and eggs – in the first 1,000 days of life can improve a child's prospects of growth, cognition and development.'[64]

Thus, supporters of continued meat consumption argue as follows.

- Cattle and sheep, especially if grazed at sustainable stocking rates, can enrich soils, manage weeds and help to lock up carbon.
- Controlled grazing offers a way to restore and manage the world's rangelands sustainably. This may help to bring back threatened wild grazing animals.

- Meat is a human right and a tradition in most cultures.
- Meat is part of a balanced human diet, providing protein, iron and other essential nutrients, especially for mothers and infants.
- There is no necessity to produce meat in ways that are cruel to either animals or people. Indeed, pasture-fed animals are likely to be happier and produce healthier meat.

An important trend in world carnivory is that, outside the newly-affluent classes, meat consumption per head is in fact falling, notably in traditional big meat-eating cultures like the USA, Britain, Germany and Australia. Even China has announced a plan to cut meat consumption by half.[65] The trend away from meat is thought to reflect a widening range of alternative food choices, along with rising consumer concerns about health, ethics, corporate control of food and climate change. It suggests that, after the rapid increase in meat consumption that accompanies the rise in their incomes, people's meat intake tends to level off and then slowly fall as they become more concerned for their own health and for the planet's. Ardent vegetarians nevertheless argue that eating meat must go, if humanity is to avoid the worst of climate change[66], on the grounds that a meat- and dairy-rich diet produces eight times more greenhouse gas than a mainly vegetable diet.[67] However, insightful critics, like British organic farmer Isabella Tree, respond 'We should, at the very least, question the ethics of driving up demand for crops that require high inputs of fertiliser, fungicides, pesticides and herbicides, while demonising sustainable forms of livestock farming that can restore soils and biodiversity, and sequester carbon'.[68]

However, convincing billions of consumers to abandon meat, not to mention several hundred million livestock producers, is unlikely. In the end the argument over whether humans should, or should not, eat meat, may prove academic. There are scientific developments in the wind which could change our meat, dairy and egg consumption patterns for all time. These are explored in Chapter 9.

Why Farmers Need a Payrise

The world's farmers need a payrise – or, come the mid century, the other eight billion of us may well find we do not have enough to eat. The simple reason is that, globally and in the developed world, food has become far too cheap. This is having a range of unfortunate – and potentially dangerous – effects, which include:

- negative economic signals to farmers everywhere, discouraging them from growing more food;
- increasing degradation of the world's soil and water;
- a downturn in the global rate of harvest yield gains;
- a lack of capital, which hinders farmers from investing in eco-agriculture and other more sustainable systems;
- a deterrent to external investment because agriculture is less profitable than alternatives;
- the decline and obliteration of many local food-producing industries as big global supermarket chains shop around the world for the cheapest commodities;
- discouragement of young people to find work in agriculture or agricultural science;
- loss of agricultural skills, rural community dislocation and increased poverty as farmers are forced off the land and into cities;
- reduced national and international investment in agricultural research and extension;
- the waste of over a third of the world's food (for no good reason);
- a pandemic of obesity and degenerative disease that sickens and kills most consumers of the 'modern diet', resulting in
- budget blowouts in healthcare costs in all countries;
- the failure of many developing countries to lay the foundation for stable governance and economic development – a secure food and agriculture base – imposing direct and indirect costs on the rest of the world through poverty, war and mass refugee movements.

From this list it can be seen that low farm incomes have far wider consequences for humanity in general than most people imagine. Indeed, in a world where food security is increasingly at risk, it may be argued that low farm incomes can lead to wars – and thus, they endanger every one of us.

Reasons for the low farm incomes are not hard to find: farmers are weak sellers, trapped between muscular global food firms who drive down the prices they get for their produce, and muscular industrial firms who drive up the costs of farming. This pincer movement has become far worse in recent decades, with world food power concentrating in fewer and fewer hands: around two dozen corporate titans now dominate the world trade in food[69], compared with the thousands of traders who did in the 1980s and 1990s. To offer their customers the cheapest possible food and compete with one another, these giants prowl the world looking for farmers who can sell them produce or grain a bit cheaper. When they find them, they ditch their previous suppliers and move offshore. Thus, they move from country to country, abandoning and collapsing entire farming industries and communities in their wake. The average producer now competes against some struggling farmer in a far-away country, rich or poor, who is also simply trying to survive by selling at the lowest price.

Farmers have no real power, even collective, to resist this constant downward price pressure. Some become independent suppliers – but the cost and complexity of the modern food supply chain usually overwhelms them. Some farmers have resorted to the early twentieth-century solution of sellers' co-operatives, but even these have next to no power against the corporate giants, who can undercut them all along the chain.

The power of the global farm input suppliers – of fuel, machinery, fertiliser, chemicals, seeds and other farm requirements, has also grown as they concentrate and globalise.[70] This makes it far easier for them to raise the prices of products that are essential to agriculture than it is for farmers to obtain more for their wheat, rice, livestock or vegetables or to withstand input cost hikes.

As a consequence of this double market failure, millions of the world's farmers are being forced from their farms and industries – as they were in the USA, Japan, Europe and Australia in the 1930s and again in the latter part of the twentieth century. In some cases their farms are bought up by larger farmers who uphold the corporate model of agriculture – in others by corporations themselves. This corporatist trend has lately been exacerbated by what is known as the 'financialisation' of agriculture – the progressive shift of private equity, hedge, pension and superannuation funds, financial institutions and merchant banks into farming investments, food and commodity markets. 'The crucial question the world is facing is "Will an increasingly financialised food system feed the world, and do so in an equitable manner?"' ask authors Lawrence, Sippel and Burch.[71]

> Global entities like the World Bank, IMF and WTO, grain traders and free-trade inspired governments answer with a resounding "yes". Critics point to the significant dislocations that have occurred, and are occurring, throughout the agri-food industries, along with the destructive outcomes for rural livelihoods and the environment and answer "No". Social protest movements, despite their increasing presence, remain vocal but seem powerless...Yet if food prices increase and basic foods become unavailable to urban populations, we are likely to see the reappearance of food riots

they caution.

The core issue of financialisation is whether it is a good idea to repose the future of the human food supply, and hence world peace and stability, in the hands of virtually the same set of idiots as those who brought you the Global Financial Crisis of 2008. That idle gamblers and speculators should play with the world's currencies, money markets and pension funds is bad enough. That they should control our food supply, using it as one more gambling chip in their unending, selfish game, is a calamity.

While some still argue that corporatisation and financialisation make for greater 'economic efficiency', the logical outcome of unrestrained global market power will eventually evict a billion smallholder farmers, especially in Asia and Africa, with devastating consequences for the landscapes they manage, for the stability of the societies they belong to and ultimately, for the security of food production and for world peace. In a world in which classical economics still treats all the real costs of agriculture, human as well as geophysical and ecological, as if they belonged to some other planet, it is one more symptom of a system disconnected from reality and approaching crisis.

It is an article of contemporary agribusiness doctrine that all 'modern' food must be produced by an intensive combination of chemicals and machines. Having travelled the world for almost half a century, speaking to farmers in over 50 countries, I have found very few indeed who think this is a good or a sustainable way to grow food. Were it not for the brutal economic pressures they face, most farmers would naturally choose to farm at lower intensity, preserving more elements of the farm landscape including its wildlife, using far fewer chemical sprays, less fertiliser and fewer big machines, and pursuing grazing systems kinder to both human and beast. Once farmers are owned by banks, supermarkets and speculators, however, their freedom to choose how they farm is drastically curtailed. They find themselves on an economic treadmill, forced to mine their soils, water and landscapes to 'compete' (i.e. to stay afloat while receiving a dwindling income from their produce).

It can thus be seen that the main driver of our unsustainable world food system is money. Paying farmers too little for their produce, in order to offer consumers food at way below its true cost of production, is degrading soil on a global scale, extinguishing wildlife, poisoning rivers and oceans, exploiting, evicting and even killing farmers (many of whom commit suicide, at rates far higher than city people), releasing far too much carbon for the safety of humanity and ruining consumers' health with toxins and an utterly deficient diet of industrially processed foods with added chemicals. Money is, of course, a figment of the human imagination and therefore infinite: soil, water, biodiversity, the atmosphere and oceans are all distinctly finite. If you use an

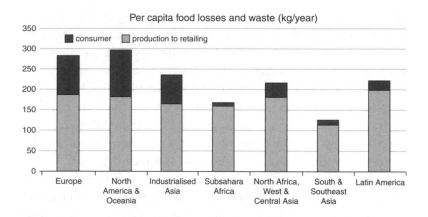

Figure 4.5. World food waste in kilograms per person, per year, by region. Source: FAO, 2018.

infinite amount of money to ruin a finite planet, you will run out of planet long before you run out of money.[72] The current monetary system will therefore crash world agriculture, even if climate change doesn't.

Please don't blame farmers for the modern food system – it isn't the one most would naturally have chosen, had they the freedom to decide. Instead, it was foisted on them a bit at a time by giant 'agribusiness' corporations and their tame research scientists and economists who decided that agriculture could be run on the same industrial principles as Henry Ford's car factories. This is a fantasy, since farming systems are biological and ecological, whereas cars are inorganic – and living plants, soils and animals are far more complicated than mere metal and plastic.

Another aspect of the modern food system which everyone talks about but which few do anything about is its colossal waste (Figure 4.5). Nearly half the effort of todays' farmers ends up in landfill. Worldwide, between 30 per cent and 50 per cent of all food produced is lost[73] – either in the field, in storage, in transport, processing, distribution, cooking, consumption and its component nutrients in urban sewage and landfills. That's enough to feed 2–3 billion people, in a world where 800 million still go hungry.

So, not only is the present system producing far too much food and harming the biosphere, it is also failing to overcome critical problems like hunger and inequity of access to nutrition. This waste is chiefly driven by five factors:

- post-harvest losses due to poor infrastructure and handling in developing countries;
- high rates of discarded food in the developed world so supermarkets can sell produce with high visual appeal and quick turnover to make fat profits;
- consumers, for whom food is now so cheap they have lost all respect for it, and think nothing of throwing it away;
- badly planned urban garbage and sewage disposal systems that are designed to waste everything, especially nutrients and water; and
- badly planned food regulations which encourage consumers to throw away edible food.

Waste varies across food sectors, being about 30 per cent for cereals, 40–50 per cent for root crops, fruits and vegetables, and 20 per cent for oilseeds, meat and dairy. And, in a world where catches of wild fish have been in decline since 1995, 35 per cent of all fish caught are wasted.

Another way to look at this issue is that food production systems of the eighteenth and nineteenth centuries were mainly sustainable, because they were local, involved farming at smaller scales and much lower intensities, and recycled their nutrients in the form of composts and manures. The modern food system isn't, because it is in reality a mining industry, not a farming industry. It mines and then squanders nutrients, soil, water, wildlife, food and people. It is a well-known fact that all mines eventually run out. Such a system cannot last more than a few decades at such colossal rates of extraction, waste and destruction. It will be forced to change – and the concluding chapters of this book explain how.

Today's food is too cheap. Too cheap for the survival of agriculture and farmers, for the health of the planet or for the health and safety of consumers. A hundred years ago, the average family spent a third of its income on food. Today, in the affluent world, the figure is 10 per cent or less. However, this is not an insoluble problem. There are ways to overcome it, including the following.

1. Price: through an educated community consensus that results in willingness on the part of consumers, supermarkets and food processors to pay the real cost of food, so as to protect the resource base and enable farmers to invest in cleaner, more sustainable systems or transition to new ones.

2. Subsidy: by the payment of a social wage to farmers by governments for their stewardship on behalf of society of soil, water, atmosphere and biodiversity, separate from their commercial food production.

3. Regulation: limiting by law those practices or technologies which degrade the food resource base and endanger consumer health; encouraging those which protect them.

4. Taxation: by levying a resource tax on all food (like a carbon tax) which reflects its true cost to the environment to produce, and by reinvesting the proceeds directly into more sustainable farming systems, R&D, rural adjustment, agroforestry and landscape regeneration (including carbon farming and rewilding).

5. Market solutions: establish markets for key farm resources (e.g. carbon or water) that reward farmers for wise and sustainable production.

6. Widespread public education about how to eat more sustainably and healthily; industry education about sustainability standards and techniques.

7. A combination of these measures.

Novel Farming Systems

Debate over the future of food production systems has begun in earnest around the world. However, it is confused by the many different terms and schools of thought on the matter – and by a grave lack of scientific support, until recently, for low-intensity, sustainable farming systems. For almost half a century, most of the high-powered science has gone into systems and crop varieties that support global agribusiness and favour the increased use of chemicals, fertilisers and machines – despite mounting evidence of the harm they cause. Agricultural science internationally has thus been conscripted – some would say corrupted – into pursuing a single, failing, model of food production.

Around the world, however, thousands of enthusiastic groups of farmers who are fully aware the present system cannot last, are hard at work designing new ones, many with a strong accent on natural principles. Among the best-known examples are the following.

- From the USA, Wes Jackson's The Land Institute explained in 2017 *Why farming is broken (and always has been)*. 'Led by a team of plant breeders and ecologists working in global partnerships, we are developing new perennial crops to be grown in ecologically functional mixtures known as polycultures. Our goal is to create an agriculture that mimics many aspects of natural ecosystems in order to produce ample food and reduce the negative impacts of industrial agriculture', they explain.[74]

- From Australia, the worldwide Permaculture Movement has spent half a century developing a similar philosophy of 'Consciously designed landscapes which mimic the patterns and relationships found in nature, while yielding an abundance of food, fibre and energy for provision of local needs. People, their buildings and the ways in which they organise themselves are central to permaculture. Thus, the permaculture vision of permanent or sustainable agriculture has evolved to one of permanent or sustainable culture'.[75]

- Joel Salatin of Polyface Farms, Virginia, USA, propounds a global mission 'To develop environmentally, economically, and emotionally enhancing agricultural prototypes and facilitate their duplication throughout the world', with an accent on greatly improved nutrition.[76]

- South African Alan Savoury leads a crusade to restore the world's grasslands and rangelands through a philosophy of holistic management of landscapes, plants and livestock, again based on close observation of natural systems.[77]

- Centres like Britain's Rothamsted Research and America's Rodale Institute have been trying for around a century to apply scientific principles to organic farming systems – and having considerable success.

The 'new agriculture' or 'eco-agriculture' movement now sweeping the planet has one thing in common – a desire to get away from industrial farming systems and back to more natural modes of food production harmonious with their environment and the nutritional needs of people. Beyond that, it bears a disturbing resemblance to the early days of monotheistic faith, with various cults, schisms and congregations disputing vigorously over who is right, accompanied by a general lack of hard, testable evidence.

The following are among the main 'alternative' approaches.

Eco-farming: not identical to organic farming, but borrowing from its thinking, eco-farming involves maximising ground cover to prevent soil loss and improve water infiltration and carbon uptake while minimising mechanical, chemical and other disruption of the ecological systems and services that support food production. Techniques include no-till, multispecies cover crops, polycropping (growing several symbiotic crop species together), strip cropping, terrace cultivation, shelter belts, pasture cropping and agroforestry. In the USA, eco-farming tends to be synonymous with no-till chemical farming, whereas in Europe it tends to be an alternative name for organic agriculture, eschewing chemicals, and is regulated as such. Its stricter adherents define it as ensuring 'healthy farming and healthy food for today and tomorrow, by protecting soil, water and climate, (which) promotes biodiversity, and does not contaminate the environment with chemical inputs or genetic engineering'.[78]

Climate-Smart Agriculture (CSA): CSA 'is an approach that helps to guide actions needed to transform and reorient agricultural systems to effectively support development and ensure food security in a changing climate', according to the FAO.[79] It has three main aims: to sustainably increase agricultural productivity and incomes; to adapt and build resilience to climate change; and to reduce and/or remove greenhouse gas emissions, where possible. Its over-arching goal is to secure world food supplies in a climate increasingly hostile to agriculture. Another buzz-phrase (like 'sustainable intensification', below), its critics have argued the term is being used as a Trojan horse by agribusiness corporations to increase sales of fertilisers, chemicals and genetically modified crops and so impair the sustainability of the global farming system.[80]

Organic Farming: Organic agriculture is an integrated farming system that aims for sustainability by enhancing soil fertility and biological diversity while in most cases avoiding the use of synthetic pesticides, antibiotics, synthetic fertilisers, genetically modified organisms and growth hormones.[81] Founded on long-standing, pre-industrial farming principles, it applies to about 1 per cent of global farmland area, and yields $60–70 billion's worth of produce a year to meet a rising consumer demand for clean, safe food. It is extensively regulated and guided, especially in Europe. It remains controversial whether this system can feed all humanity – or might cause mass starvation, as its critics aver. To this its supporters retort that organic farming already feeds half the world's population, chiefly on small farms and in developing countries. Recent analysis suggests that organic agriculture can deliver greater benefits to ecosystems and consumers than industrial farming – but may have to be used along with other more intensive systems to feed the world.[82]

Biodynamic Farming: a school or subset of organic farming, it derives from the thinking of German philosopher Rudolf Steiner. It treats soil fertility, plant growth and livestock care as ecologically interrelated tasks, but also accentuates spiritual and mystical perspectives.[83]

Permaculture: a food and social system modelled on the systems used by nature itself for cycling energy, nutrients and water. Its founder, Australian Bill Mollison, said 'Permaculture is a philosophy of working with, rather than against nature; of protracted and thoughtful observation rather than protracted and thoughtless labour; and of looking at plants and animals in all their functions, rather than treating any area as a single product system'.[84] Besides offering an alternative way to farm in a rural setting, permacultural design promises to be a vital ingredient in the design of the megacities of the future, without which they may struggle to survive. See Chapter 8.

Sustainable Intensification: is a recent buzz-phrase for the next evolution in current agricultural systems. It has been defined as increasing food production from existing farmland while minimising pressure on the environment.[85] 'However, it remains unclear what sustainable intensification entails and what it means to those working on this grand challenge', say two scientific experts.[86] What it does involve, it is now fairly clear, is increased use of energy, chemistry, machinery, robotics and IT in order to force more food from existing farming systems, hopefully without ruining the planet and its ecosystems that support life in the process. It is certainly intensified – whether it is truly sustainable, or the name is just 'greenwash', is open to doubt.

Owing to a lack of definition, or agreement, about what some of these terms mean, reinforced by a dearth of reliable global scientific data for comparing their actual performances, agriculture has become more like a religious marketplace than a laboratory for practical food solutions, in that many of these competing ideologies and philosophies rely more on the convictions of their adherents than they do on trustworthy, testable evidence. This has not been helped by the secretiveness of some producers in refusing to share the details of their operations with others or the conscription of the global agricultural science effort by a handful of giant, profit-driven, agrichemical companies. It is all very confusing for consumers who are trying to eat sensibly, safely and sustainably and find out just how their food is grown.

Attempts to remedy this situation are being made around the world, an example being the Australian project *Soils for Life*, which is documenting, scientifically analysing and disseminating the best practices of hundreds of farm managers in a range of environments so as to help others to regenerate their soils, conserve water and preserve the natural environment.[87] The rise of the global internet and social media means that practical advice such as this – whether gleaned in Australia, the Americas, Asia or Africa – can now be shared among farmers worldwide at, literally, the speed of light. Whichever farming systems evolve in future, the effective planet-wide sharing of knowledge will be a key determinant – not only among farmers, but also among the consumers who drive the demand that drives the corporations that drive the farming economy that drives farmers' individual choices.

This raises the obvious point that urban consumers are today more cut-off from the sources of their food by sprawling, opaque food-chains, than they have ever been in all of history. They are more ignorant of its origins and the means by which it is produced – and more blithely unaware of the consequences for themselves of a system that may break down. If consumers demand cheap food produced by unsustainable methods, and use their dollar purchasing power to reinforce this signal, then the world food system will collapse – because that is what the money is instructing it to do. It is no good telling farmers they 'have to change', if consumers refuse to do so. It is no good telling agribusiness executives they 'have to change', as they are obliged by corporate practice to look to the dollar, not the planet.

It turns out that the central actor in reshaping the global food supply for the twentyfirst century is you. The consumer. Our own personal knowledge or ignorance about how food is produced will determine the risk of conflict and the fate of human civilisation, within today's lifetimes.

5 HOTSPOTS FOR FOOD CONFLICT IN THE TWENTYFIRST CENTURY

Recent Food Conflicts – Future Food Wars – The Human Tide

'In preparing for battle I have always found that plans are useless, but planning is indispensable.'

Dwight D. Eisenhower

Where and how the next major food war or planet-wide conflict will break out is anybody's guess, because human behaviour and our collective responses to crises such as famine, political mass murder and water scarcity are unpredictable. That food wars will happen is *totally* predictable – on the strength of what has occurred regularly during the past 20,000 years, and what is happening right now in terms of rising food demand from a shrinking resource base.

This chapter reviews several existing conflicts and the role of food in them, and goes on to assess various regions around the world where the balance between human needs and food, land and water is so precarious as to constitute an elevated risk of major conflict by the mid twentyfirst century.

Recent Food Conflicts

Syria

The Syrian civil war, which began in 2011, grew out of the 'Arab Spring' – a people's movement discontented with the authoritarian rule of many Arab states and especially, in this case, that of the Syrian dictator, Bashar Al-Assad. It was inflamed by the religious, political and ethnic divisions in Syria and the external intervention of Hezbollah, Sunni groups, the Iraqi Kurds, the self-proclaimed Islamic State of Iraq and the Levant (ISIL), Russia and America. The conflict progressed rapidly from public protest to armed revolt, in the course of which several cities were almost totally destroyed, chemical weapons were used and, up to 2019, half a million Syrians had perished and 12 million had fled their homes, around half of whom sought haven in other countries. So runs the commonly known narrative – but that is only half the story.

Deeper analysis of the conflict's drivers by several scholars reveals that food played a potent role in fomenting popular discontent with the Assad regime. Inhabited for tens of thousands of years, Syria stands astride a belt of country once known as the Fertile Crescent, which connected the Tigris–Euphrates basin in the east with the Mediterranean coast in the west. Once consisting of well-watered fertile river flats, well-vegetated rangelands and dense forests, this region has been progressively clear-felled, grazed to desert and farmed to exhaustion over the past 3000 years – but especially in recent times as local population pressures soared.

The world's earliest poem, the Akkadian *Epic of Gilgamesh*, composed more than 4000 years ago and recorded on clay tablets, recounts the adventures of its hero, Gilgamesh, King of Uruk. One of these takes place in a deep, dark forest that is thought once to have cloaked the lands where the almost treeless modern states of Lebanon, Syria and southern Turkey now stand.[1] If it truly existed, this forest has since been utterly lost, probably due to a combination of man-made drought and to the felling of its timber to build the Egyptian, Phoenician, Roman and Levantine merchant and naval fleets. This episode in the *Epic of Gilgamesh* may thus represent the lingering memory of a world that humans have since devastated by clearing all its trees and releasing its topsoil.

Likewise, the Biblical account of Abraham, a thousand or so years later, has him born in Chaldea (now Iraq) and travelling from the ancient city of Ur (near modern Baghdad) across the Fertile Crescent with his flocks and herds, to reach Canaan (Israel/Palestine) around 1400 BC. The land's verdance so delighted him that he and his family decided to settle there. Not long after this, in 1272 BC, the army of the Egyptian Pharaoh Ramses II met with the Hittites advancing from the north (Turkey) in a tremendous clash known as the Battle of Kadesh (Qadesh, near Homs in modern Syria) involving around 5000–6000 chariots on both sides, at which the Egyptians were soundly defeated. Such a massive display of horsepower – probably more than 15,000 animals in all – is eloquent testimony to the well-vegetated character of the countryside through which the armies moved and foraged at the time, in stark contrast to its depauperate, desert-like state today.

The prevailing fertility of the region in ancient times was a key factor in the military ascendancy of the Assyrian Empire between 2500 BC and 610 BC, extending over northern Iraq and northeastern Syria, a reliable food and forage supply enabling it to maintain larger professional armies than its neighbours. But the age when

The Assyrian came down like the wolf on the fold,
and his cohorts were gleaming in purple and gold;
And the sheen of their spears was like stars on the sea,

as Byron put it, could not endure the harsher pressures of land and water degradation and climate change that followed.

Today it is well understood that the loss of vegetation changes local rainfall patterns. This is due to disruption of the 'small water cycle', the local transpiration and re-condensation of water which contributes a half or more of local rainfall, as described by Mikal Kravik in his important work *Water for the Recovery of the Climate – A New Water Paradigm*.[2] Essentially, if you clear a landscape, the trees and shrubs which pump water from rainfall back into local atmospheric moisture that falls again as dew or rain, are no longer there to perform this vital recycling – the land becomes much drier and a desert may result. In the case of the Fertile Crescent, a combination of logging (for fuel and ship-building), over-grazing of rangelands and over-farming of river flats for centuries has formed the barren, denuded landscapes that characterise Syria, Jordan, Lebanon, Israel, Turkey and Iraq today – in contrast with the verdant landscapes and forests of antiquity. Conversely, argues Kravik, if you regreen a region, you can expect it to become wetter, more fertile and lock up more carbon.

In one sense, the deep origins of the Syrian crisis may lie in the bronze axes, flocks and ploughs which stripped the Fertile Crescent in antiquity and in more recent times into an arid, bare, eroded landscape, prone to drought and at increased risk under climate change. Climate scientists have concluded that drought and water scarcity linked to climate change in this harsh landscape played a driving role in the twentyfirst-century Syrian crisis: 'extreme dryness, combined with other factors, including misguided agricultural and water-use policies of the Syrian government, caused crop failures that led to the migration of as many as 1.5 million people from rural to urban areas. This in turn added to social stresses that eventually resulted in the uprising…'.[3] According to the news network *Al Jazeera*, 'Severe drought plagued Syria from 2007–10… exacerbating poverty and social unrest'.[4] Food prices soared as the Syrian government was forced to increase food imports tenfold, adding to the discontent. Following the outbreak of fighting, food was then weaponised by the Assad regime in an attempt to starve insurgent cities into submission.[5]

'There is evidence that the 2007–2010 drought contributed to the conflict in Syria. It was the worst drought in the instrumental record, causing widespread crop failure and a mass migration of farming families to urban centers', wrote Colin Kelley and colleagues in a scientific assessment of the causes of the conflict. They continued:

Century-long observed trends in precipitation, temperature, and sea-level pressure, supported by climate model results, strongly suggest that anthropogenic forcing has increased the probability of severe and persistent droughts in this region, and made the occurrence of a 3-year drought as severe as that of 2007–2010 2 to 3 times more likely than by natural variability alone. We conclude that human influences on the climate system are implicated in the current Syrian conflict.[6]

The Syrian dominoes began to tumble elsewhere. Refugees fleeing from the war and famine flooded into neighbouring countries and then across Europe, unleashing local food, water and energy crises, anger against refugees and political turmoil. ISIL-led terrorism gathered support internationally. The delicate Middle Eastern power balance tilted towards Iran. European countries were targeted by terrorists and shaken by the sheer numbers of refugees.[7] Syria stands as a clear warning of the resounding impact even a relatively localised food crisis and conflict can have on the wider world.

Monique Barbut, the executive secretary of the UN Convention to Combat Desertification (UNCCD) drew a parallel between events in Syria and contemporary conflicts in the Sahel, Mali and Darfur: 'When land degradation reaches a level where it seriously threatens people's livelihoods, it can turn into a security issue. Data ... shows that 80% of major armed conflicts affecting society occurred in vulnerable dry ecosystems'.[8]

In a separate paper Barbut argued

The livelihoods of over 2 billion people worldwide depend on 500 million small-scale farmers for their food security; however, one-third of all agricultural land is now considered either highly or moderately degraded. The impacts of land degradation not only pose a serious challenge to sustainable development but also amplify the underlying social and political weaknesses at the local and national level, which in turn can contribute to global threats of illegal migration, cross-border conflict, and other forms of violence that feed human insecurity.[9]

Land degradation drives instability in three main ways, she explained, as summarised here.

- When more land is needed to feed a growing population, less land is available for other uses. This increases competition for scarce resources and tensions between competing groups. Since 1960, between 40 per cent and 60 per cent of armed conflicts have been linked to natural resource scarcity.

- Fifty million African farmers occupy less than two hectares each. When the land is too small to support the whole family, young people leave and drift to underdeveloped cities where unemployment is high. This increases the likelihood of them becoming radicalised. Extremist groups prey on their sense of hopelessness and take advantage of their cross-border mobility to recruit them as child soldiers, militias and terrorists.

- Massive outmigration from rural areas leads to land abandonment. These abandoned lands and their natural resources become, in some cases, a base and a source of funding for insurgents, radicals and extremists. This is seen in at least 14 fragile African states.[10]

Water scarcity couples with land degradation as a conflict multiplier, leading to a world in which geopolitics and international relationships are increasingly riven by resource and related food issues, argued analysts Peter Engelke and Russell Sticklor:

> (There is) a growing list of countries suffering through a perfect storm of rapid population growth, resource depletion, poor governance, economic stagnation, and unsettling climate change impacts, all within the context of chronic aridity. The most water-fragile among them are concentrated in a strategically significant belt stretching from North Africa across the Middle East and Horn of Africa into Central, South, and East Asia. It is in these naturally arid or semi-arid countries where water scarcity has the greatest potential to inflict serious harm.[11]

While seldom leading to interstate wars, within countries water disputes often trigger violent conflict, particularly where social, political or economic systems are fragile. Water stress acts as an accelerant, increasing the likelihood of conflict. Moreover, water scarcity-fuelled instability has grave security implications for the wider geographic region.

All this makes Syria a model for many likely conflicts in the twentyfirst century, where food insecurity, land degradation and water scarcity combine with repressive governance, religion and/or politics and mischief by the superpowers to spark a chain reaction of events and consequences whose culmination is a war that embroils nations and societies around the planet. Importantly, while the actual outbreak of wars is never easy to forecast, the pattern of these preconditions is easily seen and makes the likelihood of this type of conflict far easier to predict: declining food, land and water security are flashing warning lights on the road to war.

Yemen

Yemen is one of the most ancient civilizations of the Middle East, its premier seaport, Aden, associated in some mythology with the Biblical Garden of Eden, and the kingdom with the legendary Queen of Sheba. Settled from around 5000 BC it was home in succession to the Sabaean, Qataban, Minaean and Himyaritic civilisations. The classical historian and geographer Ptolemy, writing in the first century AD, characterised it as Arabia Eudaimon, or 'fortunate Arabia', a hint at a forgotten prosperity founded on a wetter climate and more fertile soils – in what has in recent history become the poorest country on the Arabian Peninsula.

Known to many as the home of *Arabica* coffee, Yemen has a long farming history reaching back over 7000 years and consisting of dryland grain production, irrigated fields fed from small dams built across *wadis* (natural water channels) and one of the world's largest systems of terrace farming of steep mountain valleys. Its crops ranged from staples such as barley, millet, sorghum, wheat, olives and vegetables to luxuries like coffee, myrrh and frankincense. These were evidently bounteous enough to support the rise of small cities and towns, from about 5000 years ago – and their ancient fortifications as well as obsidian and bronze weapons testify to a long warrior culture of fighting over them.[12] The key to Yemen's subsequent prosperity was not agriculture alone – it was also due to the country's fortunate location astride the main sea routes from Egypt and western Arabia to the Horn of Africa, the Persian Gulf and India, a location that also made it all the more attractive to invaders.

This proved the case with the British, who seized Aden in 1839 at a time when a new Suez Canal (to replace the old Pharaonic ones) was being mooted by French engineers, and for much the same reasons they had already acquired Gibraltar and Cape Town: it was a strategic choke point astride a major world sea route. The opening of the canal in 1869 made Aden a way-station and coaling port on the route between Europe and India, a fortress controlling the mouth of the Red Sea and a prosperous *entrepôt*. The hinterland continued to be governed by its Yemeni rulers, under a British protectorate, until a growing insurgency in the 1960s – armed and funded by Nasser's Egypt and the USSR – finally overthrew them, forcing the British to pull out in 1967. A long period of sporadic fighting between North and South Yemen ensued, until the country was unified in 1990 under strongman Ali Abdullah Saleh, who in turn fell victim to the Arab Spring in 2012, which launched Yemen into a fresh civil war. Saleh himself was ambushed and shot by a sniper in 2017. The subsequent Yemeni conflict was between the Houthis (the pro-Saleh faction) and supporters of his opponent and successor, Abdrabbuh Mansur Hadi. Saudi Arabia and other Arab states then intervened in support of the Hadi regime, with the backing of the USA and UK. Terrorist factions like Al Qaeda exploited the ongoing chaos.

In these wars, farming became a primary military target. The area of Yemeni land under terrace farms halved and many dryland farms were abandoned, as a combined result of economic pressures, physical destruction and loss of manpower. By 2012, the World Food Programme reported 'ten million Yemenis, nearly half of the population, were food insecure'. Five years later the figure had swollen to 17 million, and two years after that to 22 million. The country's economic, transport and health systems were in collapse.

With the men drafted into the fighting, much of the farm work had to be done by women. From being a country largely self-sufficient in food at the time of the British protectorate, Yemen had ended up importing three quarters of its grain needs including, by the mid 2010s, 96 per cent of the wheat required to make its daily bread. Successive regimes talked big about agricultural development and 'fighting poverty' but achieved little or nothing. Hunger thus became a critical driver of the civil unrest and sporadic warfare that erupted following the Arab Spring – and an equally important weapon of war between the competing factions and their foreign backers.[13]

Much of this 'war on food' escaped world attention. Emerita Professor Martha Mundy, of the London School of Economics, explained: 'Simply put, (rural Yemen) represents the bulk of the country: 65% of Yemen's population still lives in dispersed villages, and over half of the population relies in part or in whole on agriculture and animal husbandry. Villages, sites of food production, are inevitably less "visible" in media than the urban centres'.[14] With foreign embassies closed, journalists and international institutions alike for a long time overlooked this aspect of the conflict, chiefly because of the difficulty in safely reaching the rugged interior of Yemen, and partly because of a long-established media myopia that rates politics of more interest than food, and cities more interesting than farms.

Mundy traces a gradual evolution in the war from its early days when military installations were the primary targets, to its latter phases when cultural, economic and civilian targets – including the food supply in particular – were deliberately selected. Around half of Yemen's farmers and farm workers were forced by these actions to flee their land, she said. Between 2015 and 2016, agriculture was by far the most heavily targeted sector in air strikes by the US-backed Saudi-led coalition, she said (Figure 5.1).

'Don't be fooled by pictures showing hungry people in arid landscapes: the weather had nothing to do with the famine. More than seven million people in Yemen are hungry; far more

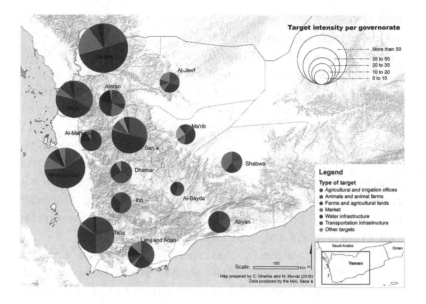

Figure 5.1. Air strikes against agricultural targets in the Yemen war. Credit: Cynthia Gharios and Martha Mundy based on data from Yemeni Ministry of Agriculture and Irrigation, Sana'a, 2015–16.

are likely to die of starvation and disease than in battles and air raids', wrote Alex de Waal, executive director of the World Peace Foundation. Military intervention led by Saudi Arabia and the United Arab Emirates had strangled the country's economy: Saudi aircraft bombed ports, roads, bridges and markets, while the opposing Houthi forces blockaded several cities.[15] Ports and land routes were blockaded by the coalition, severing food imports and hastening starvation and disease.

'Food is the biggest weapon, and lack of food the biggest killer, in the Yemen war', de Waal stated. Asked in late 2016 whether the Yemeni Ministry of Agriculture was keeping a record of damage to farming infrastructure, an official replied 'No. All has already been bombed'.[16]

The same programme of air strikes that wrecked Yemeni agriculture also targeted water supplies and medical facilities, leading to one of the worst outbreaks of cholera in recent history. Deprived of both food and clean water, more than a million

Yemenis were laid low by the twin horsemen, Famine and Pestilence. Aid programmes, aimed at cities, were powerless to assist the bulk of the population which lived in rural, often remote and mountainous, areas.

The case of Yemen evinces many of the horrors of the Nazi Hunger Plan and Stalin's war on the kulaks (*Holodomor*) but in a twentyfirst-century context – and with the tacit support of supposedly civilized nations such as the USA and UK and even the UN Security Council.

The deliberate targeting of farmers, the wrecking of water supplies, transport facilities and even farmers' fields may evoke the mediaeval villainies of the Thirty Years' War, but they represent a very clear warning that the destruction of civilian and farming populations through hunger is an accepted, even approved, contemporary means of waging war. They signal, beyond a doubt, that this is how wars will be fought in future – and that there is no country, no matter how food secure it may deem itself, that is immune from this type of conflict once politics, climate, environmental collapse and military power compound their lethal brew. Though it is a small country, remote from the mainstream of world politics, Yemen must be remembered and understood as the harbinger of future food conflicts in the twentyfirst century.

Rwanda and the Horn of Africa
Whenever people hear or read of the little African state of Rwanda, the chilling term 'genocide' rises first in the mind, and then connects it with a long-simmering power struggle between two major tribes, the Tutsi and Hutu, which is how the story has usually been told in world media and even in many scholarly works. But in truth the deep origins of this tragedy lie, as they so often do nowadays, with a dwindling supply of food.

The mass killing took place over barely 100 days in 1994, from early April to mid July when between 500,000 and a million people were slain – mostly with machetes – 300,000 women were systematically raped and a further two million people became refugees. This outbreak of extreme violence was planned by the Hutu-led government as part of a wider civil conflict with Tutsi-backed rebels that had been simmering since 1990. Of the actual victims of the genocide, 70 per cent were Tutsis and 30 per cent from the pygmy Batwa tribe.

A study by the FAO explains: 'Prior to the colonial period, Tutsi and Hutu, as the dominant ethnic groups of Rwanda, had a working relationship which balanced nutrient flows within the farming system. This was accomplished by the Hutu herding Tutsi cattle in return for receiving excess male offspring, manure and milk. As a result, the Hutu farmland maintained or increased its soil fertility'.[17] The FAO study continues:

> This led, by the 1940s, to increases in both human and animal populations – and land previously used for grazing was converted to cropping... Farm size became smaller and livestock forage was reduced. Livestock ownership from 1967 to 1993 decreased from 1 in 2 households owning cattle to 1 in 4. These changes resulted in a reduction in nutritional quality and access to food since fewer animal products, pulses or cereals were being produced and people were relying more on tubers.

> This led to continuous cultivation and increased vulnerability to soil erosion; reduced pastures resulted in fewer animals and less manure; and farmers were forced to try buying manure. Over 40% of survey respondents cited lack of manure as a major reason for declining soil fertility.

> This combination of poverty, population pressure and resource degradation led to the eruption of one of the worst civil wars in modern times. Livestock provided an important and stabilizing component of the farming system by maintaining soil nutrients. Their increasing absence contributed to the destabilization of a previously balanced system.

It may appear incredible to many of today's urban citizens, living what they fondly imagine to be a food-secure existence, that an event as horrifying as the Rwandan genocide could spring out of something as innocuous as a shift in the ratio of

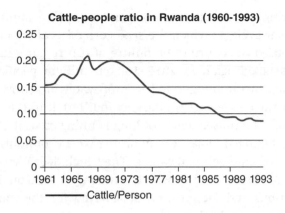

Figure 5.2. Ratio of cattle to people, Rwanda, 1960–93. Source: FAO, 1997.

cattle to people (Figure 5.2), or a lack of manure to fertilise the fields. Yet, in a sense, the origins of the Rwandan tragedy differ little from the drivers in so many other conflicts in the history of civilisation – the modest success of agriculture leading to an overgrowth in human numbers too great for the local environment and traditional agricultural methods to sustain, leading to degradation in land and water, leading to increased tensions between various groups according to ethnic, religious or political divisions, leading to fear, hatred, extreme violence and the mass flight of refugees.

Similar factors were also at work on the Horn of Africa, where man-made drought (caused by over-grazing and over-cropping as regional populations grew, urbanised and their food demands rose) played a key role in touching off decades of fighting in Somalia, and between Ethiopia and Eritrea. In the first case, 'Outside urban centres, different clans contest(ed) over resources such as water, livestock and grazing land', says Professor Afyare Elmi of Qatar University[18]. In the second, disputes over border lands played their part in stoking a war 'over rival hegemonic claims in the Horn of Africa and over "national pride" and "territorial integrity"'.[19] In both cases clan identity, which is often tied to land, was a primary factor.

These conflicts in turn collapsed much of what was left of the agricultural system in a previously fertile region of Africa, engendering an almost insoluble and unending famine–war–famine–war cycle, in which the seed corn of local crop varieties was devoured, so assuring the failure of future harvests. When the rains failed again in 2015–16, ten million people in the region faced acute hunger and lack of water in a world which had, over the decades, grown largely indifferent to their plight.

However, the consequences of long-running crisis in the Horn of Africa impinged more heavily on the world community than did those of landlocked Rwanda. They included a spectacular upsurge in maritime piracy which randomly preyed on the ships of all nations and the creation of a haven for the training of terrorists who could then show up anywhere on the planet to pursue their violent aims, floods of refugees and an unceasing demand for food, medicines, infrastructure, peacekeepers and other forms of aid.

In such cases it is reasonable to theorise that early and comparatively inexpensive intervention to secure the food supply and limit population growth might have forestalled the long slide into hunger, violence and cyclical war.

South Sudan

The conflict in Darfur/South Sudan, which raged on-and-off between 1980 and 2010, was characterised in western media reports as an insurgency by various factions including the Sudan Liberation Movement, Jinjaweed and the Sudanese government, stoked by long-standing religious tensions between Christian and Moslem factions and rivalry between various tribal groups. As with a great many conflicts, political, ethnic and religious factionalism is but part of the story.

The war in Darfur was dubbed 'the world's worst humanitarian crisis' by the UN at the time of its peak, between 2003 and 2010. In total the conflict is thought to have claimed more than 300,000 lives, mainly from starvation, and displaced four million people – half the population – as refugees, mostly across borders. For a time it was labelled a genocide – of 'Africans' by 'Arabs' – though in reality the region had long been a racial melting pot and people of all origins fought on all sides. (In fact, use of the term was partly a ploy, intended to conjure up the spectre of another Rwanda and so induce the international community to intervene.) The creation of the new, but struggling, state of South Sudan in 2011 brought no end to the crisis, with acute food scarcity affecting nearly six million in 2018. In the worst-affected areas, food was used as a weapon of war, with trade blockades and security threats leaving people marooned in swamps with no access to food or health care, the FAO said.

'The... Darfur conflict is a product of an explosive combination of environmental, political, and economic factors', wrote scholar Ahmad Sikainga.[20] Darfur was part of Sudan, which, at the time of the outbreak of conflict, was the largest country in Africa. Four in every five of the six million inhabitants of its southernmost province of Darfur were rural villagers, farmers and herders, comprising dozens of small ethnic groups, many speaking different languages. As Sikainga explains, in Sudan the term 'Arab' is more a description of a person's occupation than their racial origin – the 'Arabs' were graziers and herders and the 'Africans' were small farmers. The southern part of the country is lush, receiving regular tropical rainfall and is heavily farmed, whereas the north is semi-desert and arid rangeland. Darfur's lack of a seaboard and poor road links to its neighbours made it critically reliant on its own home-grown food supplies – and thus, highly vulnerable to a shortfall.

During the 1980s and 1990s the combination of a growing population, a fierce drought, landscape degradation and shifting patterns of land ownership fuelled the underlying tensions and lesser conflicts that were to erupt into a general civil war in 2003. For centuries, camel-owning nomads of the north had relied on customary access rights granted by settled farmers, to feed their herds as they moved between northern and southern pastures following the flush of feed provided by the changing seasons. Dry times, spreading desert and the growth of settled pastoralism and farming led to 'range war'-style clashes between the nomads and the settled farmers, which the declining native system of mediation failed to resolve.

'Environmental degradation and competition over resources can be understood as principal causes of communal conflict in Darfur', wrote Sikainga, 'but the ongoing carnage is also a product of a long history of ethnic marginalization and manipulation by Sudan's ruling elites'. Landscape decline along with disputes over grazing rights, and access to both land and water thus furnished the tinder which ignited into rebellion and war.

Others pointed to the probable role of the Earth's steadily warming climate in worsening the bleak environmental conditions that led to war:[21] 'In the decades leading up to the 2003 outbreak of war, the Sahel region of northern Sudan had witnessed the Sahara Desert advance southward by almost a mile each year and a decrease in annual median rainfall of 15 to 30 percent'. The rapid spreading of the desert combined with drought eroded the capacity of Darfur's natural resources to support its people's traditional livelihoods. Longstanding pasture and grazing corridors shrank at a rate that traditional systems of land tenure could not handle. Chaos and violence ensued.

In 2007, UN Secretary General Ban Ki-Moon observed: 'Almost invariably, we discuss Darfur in a convenient military and political shorthand – an ethnic conflict pitting Arab militias against black rebels and farmers. Look to its roots, though, and you discover a more complex dynamic. Amid the diverse social and political causes, the Darfur conflict began as an ecological crisis, arising at least in part from climate change'.[22]

'Two decades ago, the rains in southern Sudan began to fail', he continued. 'Scientists at first considered this to be an unfortunate quirk of nature. But subsequent investigation found that it coincided with a rise in temperatures of the Indian Ocean, disrupting seasonal monsoons. This suggests that the drying of Sub-Saharan Africa derives, to some degree, from man-made global warming. It is no accident that the violence in Darfur erupted during the drought. Until then, Arab nomadic herders had lived amicably with settled farmers.'

Such conflicts may be far from over – and far from confined to the region of South Sudan, Ban warned. 'The stakes go well

beyond Darfur. Jeffrey Sachs, the Columbia University economist and one of my senior advisers, notes that the violence in
Somalia grows from a similarly volatile mix of food and water
insecurity. So do the troubles in Ivory Coast and Burkina Faso.'

The war in Darfur which, in essence, was ignited by competition over food, land and water, is a red light for similar future
conflicts in Africa, South and Central Asia, the Middle East and
Central America especially.

Future Food Wars

The mounting threat to world peace posed by a food, climate and
ecosystem increasingly compromised and unstable was empha-
sised by the US Director of National Intelligence, Dan Coats, in a
briefing to the US Senate in early 2019. 'Global environmental
and ecological degradation, as well as climate change, are likely
to fuel competition for resources, economic distress, and social
discontent through 2019 and beyond', he said. 'Climate hazards
such as extreme weather, higher temperatures, droughts, floods,
wildfires, storms, sea level rise, soil degradation, and acidifying
oceans are intensifying, threatening infrastructure, health, and
water and food security. Irreversible damage to ecosystems and
habitats will undermine the economic benefits they provide,
worsened by air, soil, water, and marine pollution.' Boldly, Coats
delivered his warning at a time when the US President, Trump,
was attempting to expunge all reference to climate from government documents.[23]

Based upon these recent cases of food conflicts, and upon the
lessons gleaned from the longer history of the interaction
between food and war, several regions of the planet face a
greatly heightened risk of conflict towards the mid twentyfirst
century.

Food wars often start out small, as mere quarrels over grazing
rights, access to wells or as one faction trying to control food
supplies and markets. However, if not resolved quickly these
disputes can quickly escalate into violence, then into civil con-
flagrations which, if not quelled, can in turn explode into crises

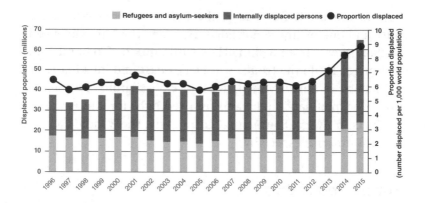

Figure 5.3. Number and proportion of refugees 1997–2016. Source: UNHCR.

that reverberate around the planet in the form of soaring prices, floods of refugees and the involvement of major powers – which in turn carries the risk of transnational war. The danger is magnified by swollen populations, the effects of climate change, depletion of key resources such as water, topsoil and nutrients, the collapse of ecosystem services that support agriculture and fisheries, universal pollution, a widening gap between rich and poor, and the rise of vast megacities unable to feed themselves (Figure 5.3).

Each of the world's food 'powderkeg regions' is described below, in ascending order of risk.

United States

In one sense, food wars have already broken out in the United States, the most overfed country on Earth. Here the issue is chiefly the growing depletion of the nation's mighty groundwater resources, especially in states using it for food production, and the contest over what remains between competing users – farmers, ranchers and Native Americans on the one hand and the oil, gas and mining industry on the other. Concern about the future of US water supplies was aggravated by a series of savage droughts in the early twentyfirst century in the west, south and midwest linked to global climate change and declining snowpack in the Rocky Mountains, both of which affect not only agriculture but also the rate at which the nation's groundwater reserves recharge.

'Groundwater depletion has been a concern in the Southwest and High Plains for many years, but increased demands on our groundwater resources have overstressed aquifers in many areas of the Nation, not just in arid regions', notes the US Geological Survey.[24]

Nine US states depend on groundwater for between 50 per cent and 80 per cent of their total freshwater supplies, and five states account for nearly half of the nation's groundwater use. Major US water resources, such as the High Plains aquifers and the Pacific Northwest aquifers have sunk by 30–50 metres (100–150 feet) since exploitation began, imperilling the agricultural industries that rely on them. In the arid southwest, aquifer declines of 100–150 metres have been recorded (Figure 5.4).

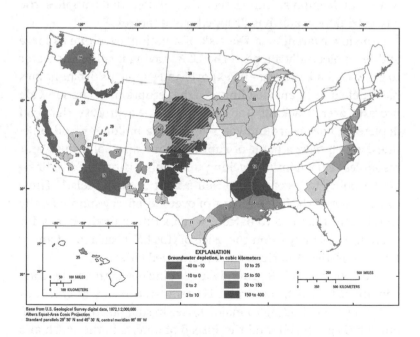

Figure 5.4. US cumulative groundwater depletion. Source: US Geological Survey, 2016.

To take but one case, the famed Ogallala Aquifer in the High Plains region supports cropping industries worth more than US $20 billion a year and was in such a depleted state it would take more than 6000 years to replace by natural infiltration the water drawn from it by farmers in the past 150 years. As it dwindles, some farmers have tried to kick their dependence on groundwater – other users, including the growing cities and towns of the region, proceeded to mine it as if there was no tomorrow.[25] A study by Kansas State University concluded that so far, 30 per cent of the local groundwater had been extracted and another 39 per cent would be depleted by the mid century on existing trends in withdrawal and recharge.[26]

Over half the US population relies on groundwater for drinking; both rural and urban America are at risk. Cities such as New Orleans, Houston and Miami face not only rising sea levels – but also sinking land, due to the extraction of underlying groundwater. In Memphis, Tennessee, the aquifer that supplies the city's drinking water has dropped by 20 metres.

Growing awareness of the risk of a nation, even one as large and technologically adept as the USA, having insufficient water to grow its food, generate its exports and supply its urban homes has fuelled tensions leading to the eruption of nationwide protests over 'fracking' for oil and gas – a process that can deplete or poison groundwater – and the building of oil pipelines, which have a habit of rupturing and also polluting water resources. The boom in fracking and piping is part of a deliberate US policy to become more self-reliant in fossil fuels.[27] Thus, in its anxiety to be independent of overseas energy suppliers, the USA in effect decided to barter away its future food security for current oil security – and the price of this has been a lot of angry farmers, Native Americans and concerned citizens.

The depletion of US groundwater coincides with accelerating climate risk, which may raise US temperatures by as much as 4–5 °C by 2100, leading to major losses in soil moisture throughout the US grain belt, and the spread of deserts in the south and west. Food production will also be affected by fiercer storms, bigger floods, more heatwaves, an increase in drought frequency and greater impacts from crop and livestock diseases. In such a context, it is no time to be wasting stored water.

The case of the USA is included in the list of world 'hot spots' for future food conflict, not because there is danger of a serious shooting war erupting over water in America in the foreseeable future, but to illustrate that even in technologically advanced countries unforeseen social tensions and crises are on the rise over basic resources like food, land and water and their depletion. This doesn't just happen in Africa or the Middle East. It's a global phenomenon.

Furthermore, the USA is the world's largest food exporter and any retreat on its part will have a disproportionate effect on world food price and supply. There is still plenty of time to replan America's food systems and water usage – but, as in the case of fossil fuels and climate, rear-guard action mounted by corporate vested interests and their hired politicians may well paralyse the national will to do it. That is when the US food system could find itself at serious risk, losing access to water in a time of growing climatic disruption, caused by exactly the same forces as those depleting the groundwater: the fossil fuels sector and its political stooges. The probable effect of this will, in the first instance, be a decline in US meat and dairy production accompanied by rising prices and a fall in its feedgrain exports, with domino effects on livestock industries worldwide.

The flip-side to this issue is that America's old rival, Russia, is likely to gain in both farmland and water availability as the planet warms through the twentyfirst century – and likewise Canada. Both these countries stand to prosper from a US withdrawal from world food markets, and together they may negate the effects of any US food export shortfalls.

Central and South America

South America is one of the world's most bountiful continents in terms of food production – but, after decades of improvement, malnutrition is once more on the rise, reaching a new peak of 42.5 million people affected in 2016.[28] 'Latin America and the Caribbean used to be a worldwide example in the fight against hunger. We are now following the worrisome global trend', said regional FAO representative Julio Berdegué.[29]

Paradoxically, obesity is increasing among Latin American adults, while malnutrition is rising among children. 'Although Latin America and the Caribbean produce enough food to meet the needs of their population, this does not ensure healthy and nutritious diets', the FAO explains. Worsening income inequality, poor access to food and persistent poverty are contributing to the rise in hunger and bad diets, it adds.[30]

'The impact of climate change in Latin America and the Caribbean will be considerable because of its economic dependence on agriculture, the low adaptive capacity of its population and the geographical location of some of its countries', an FAO report warned.[31]

Emerging food insecurity in Central and Latin America is being driven by a toxic mixture of failing water supplies, drying farmlands, poverty, maladministration, incompetence and corruption. These issues are exacerbated by climate change, which is making the water supply issue worse for farmers and city people alike in several countries and delivering more weather disasters to agriculture.

- Mexico has for centuries faced periodic food scarcity, with a tenth of its people today suffering under-nutrition. In 2008 this rose to 18 per cent, leading to outbreaks of political violence.[32] In 2013, 52 million Mexicans were suffering poverty and seven million more faced extreme hunger, despite the attempts of successive governments to remedy the situation. By 2100 northern Mexico is expected to warm by 4–5 °C and southern Mexico by 1.5–2.5 °C. Large parts of the country, including Mexico City, face critical water scarcity. Mexico's cropped area could fall by 40–70 per cent by the 2030s and disappear completely by the end of the century, making it one of the world's countries most at risk from catastrophic climate change and a major potential source of climate refugees.[33]
- The vanishing lakes and glaciers of the high Andes confront montane nations – Bolivia, Peru and Chile especially – with

the spectre of growing water scarcity and declining food security. The volume of many glaciers, which provide meltwater to the region's rivers, which in turn irrigate farmland, has halved since 1975.[34] Bolivia's second largest water body, the 2000 square kilometres Lake Poopo, dried out completely.[35] The loss of water is attributed partly to El Niño droughts, partly to global warming and partly to over-extraction by the mining industries of the region. Chile, with 24,000 glaciers (80 per cent of all those in Latin America) is feeling the effects of their retreat and shrinkage especially, both in large cities such as the capital Santiago, and in irrigation agriculture and energy supply. Chile is rated by the World Resources Institute among the countries most likely to experience extreme water stress by 2040.[36]

- Climate change is producing growing water and food insecurity in the 'dry corridor' of Central America, in countries such as El Salvador, Guatemala and Honduras. Here a combination of drought, major floods and soil erosion is undermining efforts to raise food production and stabilise nutrition.

- Food production in Venezuela began falling in the 1990s, and by the late 2010s two thirds of the population were malnourished; there was a growing flood of refugees into Colombia and other neighbouring countries. The food crisis has been variously blamed on the Venezuelan government's 'Great Leap Forward' (modelled on that of China – which also caused widespread starvation), a halving in Venezuela's oil export earnings, economic sanctions by the USA, and corruption. However, local scientists such as Nobel Laureate Professor Juan Carlos Sánchez warn that climate impacts are already striking the densely populated coastal regions with increased torrential rains, flooding and mudslides, droughts and hurricanes, while inland areas are drying out and desertifying, leading to crop failures, water scarcity and a tide of climate refugees.[37] These factors will tend to deepen food insecurity towards the mid century. Venezuela's climate refugees are already making life more difficult for neighbouring countries such as Colombia.

- Deforestation in the Brazilian Amazon has, in recent decades, removed around 20 per cent of its total tree cover, replacing it with dry savannah and farmland. At 40 per cent clearance and with continued global warming, scientists anticipate profound changes in the local climate, towards a drying trend, which will hammer the agriculture that has replaced the forest.[38] Brazil has already wiped out the once-vast Mata Atlantica forest along its eastern coastline, and this region is now drying, with resultant water stress for both farming and major cities like São Paulo. Brazil's outlook for 2100 is for further drying – tied to forest loss as well as global climate change – increased frequency of drought and heatwaves, major fires and acute water scarcity in some regions. Moreover, as the Amazon basin dries out, it will release vast quantities of CO_2 from its peat swamps and rainforest soils. These are thought to contain in excess of three billion tonnes of carbon and could cause a significant acceleration in global warming, affecting everyone on Earth.[39]

Latin America is the world capital of private armies, with as many as 50 *major* guerrilla groups, paramilitaries, terrorist, indigenous and criminal insurgencies over the past half century – exemplified in familiar names like the Sandanistas (Nicaragua), FARC (Colombia) and Shining Path (Peru).[40] Many of these drew their initial inspiration from the international communist movement of the mid twentieth century, while others are right-wing groups set up in opposition to them or else represent land rights movements of disadvantaged groups. However, all these movements rely for oxygen on simmering public discontent with ineffectual or corrupt governments and lack of fair access to food, land and water generally. In other words, the tendency of South and Central America towards internal armed conflict is supercharged significantly by failings in the food system which generate public anger, leading to sympathy and support for anyone seen to be challenging the incumbent regimes. This is not to suggest that feeding every person well would end all insurgencies – but it would certainly take the wind of popular support out of a lot of their sails. In that sense the revolutionary tendency of South America echoes the preconditions for revolution in France and Russia in the eighteenth and twentieth centuries.

Central Asia

The risk of wars breaking out over water, energy and food insecurity in Central Asia is high.[41] Here, the five main players – Kazakhstan, Uzbekistan, Turkmenistan, Tajikistan and Kyrgyzstan – face swelling populations, crumbling Soviet-era infrastructure, flagging resource cooperation, a degrading landscape, deteriorating food availability and a changing climate. At the heart of the issue and the region's increasingly volatile politics is water: 'Without water in the region's two great rivers – the Syr Darya and the Amu Darya – vital crops in the downstream agricultural powerhouses would die. Without power, life in the upstream countries would be unbearable in the freezing winters', wrote Rustam Qobil.[42]

Central Asia's water crisis first exploded onto the global consciousness with the drying of the Aral Sea – the world's fourth largest lake – from the mid 1960s[43], following the damming and draining of major rivers such as the Amu Darya, Syr Darya and Naryn. It was hastened by a major drought in 2008[44] exacerbated by climate change, which is melting the 'water tower' of glacial ice stored in the Tien Shan, Pamir and Hindu Kush mountain ranges that feed the region's rivers. The Tien Shan alone holds 10,000 glaciers, all of them in retreat, losing an estimated 223 million cubic metres a year. At such a rate of loss the region's rivers will run dry within a generation.[45] Lack of water has already delivered a body blow to Central Asia's efforts to modernise its agriculture, adding further tension to regional disputes over food, land and water.

'Water has always been a major cause of wars and border conflicts in the Central Asian region', policy analyst Fuad Shahbazov warned. This potential for conflict over water has been exacerbated by disputes over the Fergana valley, the region's greatest foodbowl, which underwent a 32 per cent surge in population in barely ten years – while more and more of it turned to desert.[46]

The Central Asian region is ranked by the World Resources Institute as one of the world's most perilously water-stressed regions to 2040 (Figure 5.6). With their economies hitting rock bottom, corrupt and autocratic governments that prefer to blame others for their problems and growing quarrels over food, land, energy and water, the 'Stans' face 'a perfect storm', Nate Shenkkan wrote in the journal *Foreign Policy*.[47] Increased meddling by Russia and China is augmenting the explosive mix: China regards Central Asia as a key component of its 'Belt and Road' initiative intended to expand its global influence, whereas Russia hopes to lure the region back into its own economic sphere. Their rival investments may help limit some of the problems faced by Central Asia – or they may unlock a fresh cycle of political feuding, turmoil and regime change.[48]

A 2017 FAO report found 14.3 million people – one in every five – in Central Asia did not have enough to eat and a million faced actual starvation, children especially. It noted that after years of steady improvement, the situation was deteriorating. This combination of intractable and deteriorating factors makes Central Asia a serious internal war risk towards the mid twentyfirst century, with involvement by superpowers raising the danger of international conflict and mass refugee flight.

The Middle East

The Middle East is the most water-stressed region on Earth (see Figure 5.5 above). It is 'particularly vulnerable to climate change. It is one of the world's most water-scarce and dry regions, with a high dependency on climate-sensitive agriculture and a large share of its population and economic activity in flood-prone urban coastal zones', according to the World Bank.[49]

The Middle East – consisting of the 22 countries of the Arab League, Turkey and Iran – has very low levels of natural rainfall

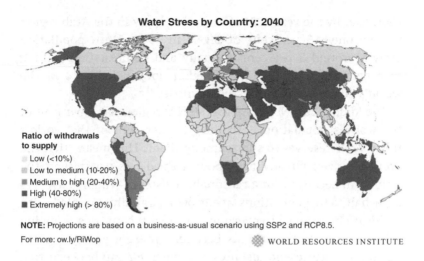

Water Stress by Country: 2040

Ratio of withdrawals
to supply

Low (<10%)
Low to medium (10-20%)
Medium to high (20-40%)
High (40-80%)
Extremely high (> 80%)

NOTE: Projections are based on a business-as-usual scenario using SSP2 and RCP8.5.
For more: ow.ly/RiWop   WORLD RESOURCES INSTITUTE

Figure 5.5. World's most water stressed countries in 2040. Source: World Resources Institute.

to begin with. Most of it has 600 millimetres or less per year and is classed as arid. 'The Middle East and North Africa [MENA] is a global hotspot of unsustainable water use, especially of groundwater. In some countries, more than half of current water withdrawals exceed what is naturally available', the Bank said in a separate report on water scarcity.[50]

'The climate is predicted to become even hotter and drier in most of the MENA region. Higher temperatures and reduced precipitation will increase the occurrence of droughts. It is further estimated that an additional 80–100 million people will be exposed by 2025 to water stress', the Bank added.

The region's population of 300 million in the late 2010s is forecast to double to 600 million by 2050. Average temperatures are expected to rise by 3–5 °C and rainfall will decrease by around 20 per cent. The result will be vastly increased water stress, accelerated desertification, growing food insecurity and a rise in sea levels displacing tens of millions from densely populated, low-lying areas like the Nile delta.[51] The region is deemed highly vulnerable to climate impacts, warns a report by the UN Development Programme. 'Current climate change projections show that by the year 2025, the water supply in the Arab region will be only 15 per cent of levels in 1960. With population growth around 3 per cent annually and deforestation spiking to 4 per cent annually... the region now includes 14 of the world's 20 most water-stressed countries.'[52]

The Middle East/North Africa (MENA) region has 6 per cent of the world's population with only 1.5 per cent of the world's fresh water reserves to share among them. This means that the average citizen already has about a third less water than the minimum necessary for a reasonable existence – many have less than half, and populations are growing rapidly. Coupled with political chaos and ill governance in many countries, growing religious and ethnic tensions between different groups – often based on centuries-old disputes – a widening gap between rich and poor and foreign meddling by the USA, Russia and China, shortages of food, land and water make the Middle East an evident cauldron for conflict in the twentyfirst century.

Growing awareness of their food risk has impelled some oil-rich Arab states into an international farm buying spree, purchasing farming, fishing and food processing companies in countries as assorted as South Sudan, Ethiopia, the Philippines, Ukraine, the USA, Poland, Argentina, Australia, Brazil and Morocco. In some food-stressed countries these acquisitions have already led to riots and killings.[53] The risk is high that, by exporting its own food–land–water problems worldwide, especially to regions already facing scarcity, the Middle East could propagate conflicts and government collapses around the globe. This is despite the fact that high-tech solar desalination, green energy, hydroponics, aquaponics and other intensive urban food production technologies make it possible for the region to produce far more of its own food locally, if not to be entirely self-sufficient.

Dimensions of the growing crisis in the Middle East include the following.

- Wars have already broken out in Syria and Yemen in which scarcity of food, land and water were prominent among the tensions that led to conflict between competing groups.

- Food, land and water issues feed into and exacerbate already volatile sentiment over religion, politics, corruption, mismanagement and foreign interference by the USA, China and Russia.
- The introduction of cheap solar-powered and diesel pumps has accelerated the unsustainable extraction of groundwater throughout the region, notably in countries like Libya, Egypt, Saudi Arabia and Morocco.[54]
- Turkish building of new dams to monopolise waters flowing across its borders is igniting scarcity and potential for conflict with downstream nations, including Iraq, Iran and Syria.[55]
- Egypt's lifeline, the Nile, is threatened by Ethiopian plans to dam the Blue Nile, with tensions that some observers consider could lead to a shooting war.[56]
- There are very low levels of water recycling throughout the region, while water use productivity is about half that of the world as a whole.
- There is a lack of a sense of citizen responsibility for water and food scarcity throughout the region.
- Land grabs around the world by oil-rich states are threatening to destabilise food, land and water in other countries and regions, causing conflict.
- A decline in oil prices and the displacement of oil by the global renewables revolution may leave the region with fewer economic options for solving its problems.
- There is a risk that acquisition of a nuclear weapon by Iran may set off a nuclear arms race in the region with countries such as Saudi Arabia, Syria and possibly Turkey following suit and Israel rearming to stay in the lead. This would translate potential food, land and water conflicts into the atomic realm.

Together these issues, and failure to address their root causes, make the Middle East a fizzing powder keg in the twentyfirst century. The question is when and where, not whether, it explodes – and whether the resulting conflict will involve the use of weapons of mass destruction, including nuclear, thus affecting the entire world.

China

China is the world's biggest producer, importer and consumer of food. Much of the landmass of the People's Republic of China (PRC) is too mountainous or too arid for farming, but the rich soils of its eastern and southern regions are highly productive provided sufficient water is available and climate impacts are mild. Those, however, are very big 'ifs'.

In 1995, American environmentalist Lester R. Brown both irked and aroused the PRC Communist Party bosses with a small, hard-hitting book entitled *Who Will Feed China? Wake-Up Call for a Small Planet.*[57] In it he posited that Chinese population growth was so far out of control that the then-agricultural system could not keep up, and China would be forced to import vast amounts of grain, to the detriment of food prices and availability worldwide. His fears, so far, have not been realised – not because they were unsoundly based, but because China managed – just – to stay abreast of rising food demand by stabilising and subsidising grain prices, restoring degraded lands, boosting agricultural science and technology, piping water from south to north, developing high-intensity urban farms, buying up foreign farmland worldwide and encouraging young Chinese to leave the country. What Brown didn't anticipate was the economic miracle that made China rich enough to afford all this. However, his essential thesis remains valid: China's food supply will remain on a knife-edge for the entire twentyfirst century, vulnerable especially to water scarcity and climate impacts. If the nation outruns its domestic resources yet still has to eat, it may well be at the expense of others globally.

Some western commentators were puzzled when China scrapped its 35-year 'One Child Policy' in 2015, but in fact the policy had done its job, shaving around 300 million people off the projected peak of Chinese population. It was also causing serious imbalances, such as China's huge unmarried male surplus. Furthermore, rising urbanisation and household incomes meant Chinese parents no longer wanted large families, as in the past. Policy or no policy, China's birthrate has continued to fall and by 2018 was 1.6 babies per woman – well below replacement, lower than the USA and nearly as low as Germany. Its population was 1.4 billion, but this was growing at barely 0.4 per cent a year, with the growth due at least in part to lengthening life expectancy.[58]

For China, female fertility is no longer the key issue. The critical issue is water. And the critical region is the north, where 41 per cent of the population reside. Here surface and ground-waters – which support not only the vast grain and vegetable farming industries of the North China Plain but also burgeoning megacities like Beijing, Tianjin and Shenyang – have been van-ishing at an alarming rate. 'In the past 25 years, 28,000 rivers have disappeared. Groundwater has fallen by up to 1–3 metres a year. One consequence: parts of Beijing are subsiding by 11 cm a year. The flow of the Yellow River, water supply to millions, is a tenth of what it was in the 1940s; it often fails to reach the sea. Pollution further curtails supply: in 2017 8.8 per cent of water was unfit even for agricultural or industrial use', the Financial Times reported.[59] On the North China Plain, annual consump-tion of water for all uses, including food production, is about 27 billion cubic metres a year – compared with an annual water availability of 22 billion cubic metres, a deficit that is made up by the short-term expedient of mining the region's groundwater.[60]

To stave off disaster, the PRC has built a prodigious network of canals and pipelines from the Yangtse River in the water-rich south, to Beijing in the water-starved north. Hailed as a 'lifeline', the South–North Water Transfer Project had two drawbacks: first, the fossil energy required to pump millions of tonnes of water over a thousand kilometres and, second, the fact that while the volume was sufficient to satisfy the burgeoning cities for a time, it could not supply and distribute enough clean water to meet the needs of irrigated farming over so vast a region in the long run, nor meet those of its planned industrial growth.[61] Oft-mouthed 'solutions' like desalination or the piping of water from Tibet or Russia face similar drawbacks: demand is too great for the potential supply and the costs, both financial and envir-onmental, prohibitive.

China is already among the world's most water-stressed nations. The typical Chinese citizen has a 'water footprint' of 1071 cubic metres a year – three quarters of the world average (1385 cubic metres), and scarcely a third that of the average American (2842 cubic metres).[62] Of this water, 62 per cent is used to grow food to feed the Chinese population – and 90 per cent is so polluted it is unfit to drink or use in food processing. Despite massive investment in water infrastructure and new technology, many experts doubt that China can keep pace with the growth in its demand for food, at least within its own borders, chiefly because of water scarcity.[63] Adding to the pressure is that China's national five-year plans for industrialisation demand massive amounts more water – demands that may confront China with a stark choice between food and economic growth. 'The Chinese government is moving too slowly towards the Camel Economy. It has plans, incentives for officials; it invests in recycling, irrigation, pollution, drought resistant crops; it leads the world in high voltage transmission (to get hydro, wind and solar energy from the west of China). None of this is sufficient or likely to be in time', the Financial Times opined.[64]

As the world's leading carbon emitter, China is more responsible for climate change than any other country. It is also, potentially, more at risk. The main reason, quite simply, is the impact of a warming world on China's water supply – in the form of disappearing rivers, lakes, groundwater and mountain glaciers along with rising sea levels. To this is coupled the threat to agriculture from increasing weather disasters and the loss of ecosystem services from a damaged landscape.[65]

China is thus impaled on the horns of a classic dilemma. Without more water it cannot grow its economy sufficiently to pay for the water-conserving and food-producing technologies and infrastructure it needs to feed its people. Having inadvertently unleashed a population explosion with its highly successful conversion to modern farming systems, the challenge for China now is to somehow sustain its food supply through the population peak of the mid twentyfirst century, followed by a managed decline to maybe half of today's numbers by the early twentysecond century. It is far from clear whether the present approach – improving market efficiency, continuing to modernise agricultural production systems, pumping water, trying to control soil and water losses and importing more food from overseas – will work.[66]

China has pinned its main hopes on technology to boost farm yields and improve water distribution and management. Unfortunately, it has selected the unsustainable American industrial farming model to do this – which involves the massive use of water, toxic chemicals, fertilisers, fossil fuels and machines. This in turn is having dreadful consequences for China's soils, waters, landscapes, food supply, air, climate and consumer health. Serious questions are now being asked whether such an approach is not digging the hole China is in, even deeper. Furthermore, some western analysts are sceptical whether the heavy hand of state control is up to the task of generating the levels of innovation required to feed China sustainably.[67]

Plan B, which is to purchase food from other countries, or import it from Chinese-owned farming and food ventures around the world, faces similar difficulties. Many of the countries where China is investing in food production themselves face a slow-burning crisis of land degradation, water scarcity, surging populations and swelling local food demand. By exporting its own problems, China is adding to their difficulties. While there may be some truth to the claim that China is helping to modernise food systems in Africa, for example, it is equally clear that the export of food at a time of local shortages could have dire consequences for Africans, leading to wars in Africa and elsewhere. How countries will react to Chinese pressure to export food in the face of their own domestic shortages is, as yet, unclear. If they permit exports, it could prove catastrophic for their own people and governments – but if they cut them off, it could be equally catastrophic for China. Such a situation cannot be regarded as anything other than a menace to world peace.

Around 1640, a series of intense droughts caused widespread crop failures in China, leading to unrest and uprisings which, in

1644, brought down the Ming Dynasty. A serious domestic Chinese food and water crisis today – driven by drought, degradation of land and water and climate change in northern China coupled with failure in food imports – could cause a re-run of history: 'The forthcoming water crisis may impact China's social, economic, and political stability to a great extent', a US Intelligence Assessment found. 'The adverse impacts of climate change will add extra pressure to existing social and resource stresses.'[68]

Such events have the potential to precipitate tens, even hundreds, of millions of emigrants and refugees into countries all over the world, with domino consequences for those countries that receive them. Strategic analysts have speculated that tens of millions of desperate Chinese flooding into eastern Russia, or even India, could lead to war, including the risk of international nuclear exchange.[69]

Against such a scenario are the plain facts that China is a technologically advanced society, with the foresight, wealth and capacity to plan and implement nationwide changes and the will, if necessary, to enforce them. Its leaders are clearly alert to the food and water challenge – and its resolution may well depend on the extent of water recycling they are able to achieve. As to whether the PRC can afford the cost of transitioning from an unsustainable to a sustainable food system, all countries have a choice between unproductive military spending and feeding their populace. A choice between food or war. It remains to be seen which investment China favours.

However, it is vital to understand that the problem of whether China can feed itself through the twentyfirst century is not purely a Chinese problem. It's a problem, both economic and physical, for the entire planet – and it is thus in everyone's best interest to help solve it. For this reason, China is rated number 3 on this list of potential food/war hotspots.

Africa

Food wars – that is, wars in which food, land and water play a significant contributing role – have been a constant in the story of Africa since the mid twentieth century, indeed, far longer. In a sense, the continent is already a microcosm of the world of the twentyfirst century as climate change and resource scarcity combine with rapid population growth to ratchet up the tensions that lead competing groups to fight, whether the superficial distinctions between them are ethnic, religious, social or political.

We have examined the particular cases of Rwanda, South Sudan and the Horn of Africa – but there are numerous other African conflicts, insurgencies and ongoing disturbances in which food, land and water are primary or secondary triggers and where famine is often the outcome: Nigeria, Congo, Egypt, Tunisia, Libya, Mali, Chad, the Central African Republic, the Maghreb region of the Sahara, Mozambique, Cote d'Ivoire and Zimbabwe have all experienced conflicts in which issues of access to food, land and water were important drivers and consequences.

The trajectory of Africa's population in the first two decades of the twentyfirst century implies that the number of its people could quadruple from 1.2 billion in 2017 to 4.5 billion by 2100 (Figure 5.6). If fulfilled, this would make Africans 41 per cent of the world population by the end of the century. The UN Population Division's nearer projections are for Africans to outnumber Chinese or Indians at 1.7 billion by 2030, and reach 2.5 billion in 2050, which represents a doubling in the continent's inhabitants in barely 30 years.[70] While African fertility rates (babies per woman) remain high by world standards – 4.5 compared with a global average of 2.4 – they have also fallen steeply, from a peak of 8.5 babies in the 1970s. Furthermore, the picture is uneven with birthrates in most Sub-Saharan countries remaining high (around five to six babies/woman), while those of eight, mainly southern, countries have dropped to replacement or below (i.e. under 2.1). As has been the case around the world, birth rates tend to drop rapidly with the spread of urbanisation, education and economic growth – whereas countries which slide back into poverty tend to experience rising birthrates. Food access is a vital ingredient in this dynamic: it has been widely observed that better-fed countries tend to have much lower rates of birth and population growth, possibly

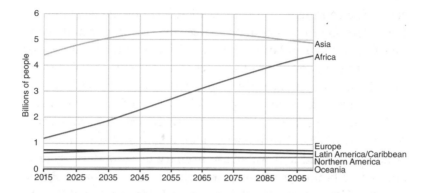

Figure 5.6. Africa: UN population projections to 2100. Source UNPD, 2017.

because people who are food secure lose fewer infants and children in early life and thus are more open to family planning. So, in a real sense, food sufficiency holds one of the keys to limiting the human population to a level sustainable both for Africa and the planet in general.

Forecasting the future of Africa is not easy, given the complexity of the interwoven climatic, social, technological and political issues – and many do not attempt it. However, the relentless optimism of the UN and its food agency, the FAO, is probably not justified by the facts as they are known to science – and may have more to do with not wishing to give offence to African governments or discourage donors than with attempting to accurately analyse what may occur. Even the FAO acknowledges however that food insecurity is rising across Sub-Saharan Africa as well as other parts.

In 2017, conflict and insecurity were the major drivers of acute food insecurity in 18 countries and territories where almost 74 million food-insecure people were in need of urgent assistance. Eleven of these countries were in Africa and accounted for 37 million acutely food insecure people; the largest numbers were in northern Nigeria, Democratic Republic of Congo, Somalia and South Sudan

the agency said in its Global Report on Food Crises 2018.[71]

The FAO also noted that almost one in four Africans was undernourished in 2016 – a total of nearly a quarter of a billion people. The rise in undernourishment and food insecurity was linked to the effects of climate change, natural disasters and conflict according to Bukar Tijani, the FAO's assistant director general for Africa.[72]

Even the comparatively prosperous nation of South Africa sits on a conflict knife-edge, according to a scientific study: 'Results indicate that the country exceeds its environmental boundaries for biodiversity loss, marine harvesting, freshwater use, and climate change, and that social deprivation was most severe in the areas of safety, income, and employment, which are significant factors in conflict risk', Megan Cole and colleagues found.[73]

In the Congo, home to the world's second largest tropical forest, 20 years of civil war had not only slain five million civilians but also decimated the forests and their ecological services on which the nation depended. Researchers found evidence that reducing conflict can also help to reduce environmental destruction: 'Peace-building can potentially be a win for nature as well, and... conservation organizations and governments should be ready to seize conservation opportunities'.[74]

As the African population doubles toward the mid century, as its water, soils, forests and economic wealth per capita dwindle, as foreign corporations plunder its riches, as a turbulent climate hammers its herders and farmers – both industrial and traditional – the prospect of Africa resolving existing conflicts and avoiding new ones is receding. The mistake most of the world is making is to imagine this only affects the Africans. The consequences will impact everyone on the planet.

A World Bank study has warned that 140 million people will have to leave just three regions of the world as climate refugees before 2050 – and the vast majority of these, some 86 million, would be displaced from their homes in Sub-Saharan Africa.[75] The second decade of the twentyfirst century has already witnessed a blow-out in the number of Sub-Saharan Africans fleeing north, across the desert into the already dangerously over-stressed region of North Africa. From there many have headed by boat for Europe, with shocking loss of life on the way – up to 5000 deaths due to drowning in a single year. The number of Africans fleeing across the Mediterranean has fluctuated, climbing as high as a third of a million people (in 2016) with most of them headed for Italy, followed by Greece, Cyprus and Spain. By this time Europe already had a population of five million Sub-Saharans.[76]

It is worth recalling, for a moment, that a food failure in the North African grainbowl in the third and fourth centuries was a primary factor in the collapse and demolition of the Roman Empire, from Britain to Asia Minor.

The risk of a tsunami of people attempting to escape Africa for Europe, and to a lesser degree the Middle East, in coming decades is building with ominous intensity. The stress in Sub-Saharan Africa is already forcing conditions in North African countries closer to crisis point. Were their food systems to fail in domino-succession, the scale of potential movement of desperate people into Europe can only be guessed – but is certainly in the range of tens to hundreds of millions. Large enough, in other words, to swamp the nations of Italy, Spain and Greece and eliminate their governments altogether, forcing many of their own people in turn to flee into northern Europe. Given the crisis caused by a million Syrians fleeing into Europe in 2013, the consequences for European stability and the world economy of an African eruption tens or hundreds of times the size can only be imagined.

The good news is that, in the view of the World Bank, up to 80 per cent of Africa's climate refugees could be prevented from leaving their homes in the first place by timely climate and development (i.e. food, land and water) action taken by the rest of the world. The bad news, however, is that most of the world's large oil and coal companies and their climate-denying puppet governments remain implacably opposed to the sort and scale of action necessary, preferring to pull the global house down on their own heads.

Canadian ecologist Paul Chefurka argued in a far-sighted paper that the outlook for Africa by 2040 was grim, even if the contin-ent were able to lock in a 1 per cent year-on-year increase in farm yields. Even then Africa might still be forced to spend half its wealth – an almost impossible proportion – on food imports by 2050, assuming sufficient affordable food was available globally to supply them. Chefurka argued the solutions were:

> First, the developed world must get its act together when it comes to foreign aid. Our lack of performance with regard to the Millennium Development Goals is beyond contemptible. A minuscule sliver of the GDP of the richest nations could help prevent a catastrophic outcome for hundreds of millions of people and scores of countries. That we have failed our African brothers and sisters so egregiously is a shame that should follow all of us into the afterlife.

> Second, and most importantly, we must develop an immediate crash program of education and contraception in all the regions at risk from this gathering storm. Africa may be the first, but the conditions are ripe for much of South Asia to follow in their footsteps. We must blanket Africa with schools and family planning clinics.[77]

There is substance to both points. Unfortunately expanding conventional farming with a view to feeding all the Africans in 2050 and 2100 is unlikely to succeed. It is a twentieth-century solution to a twentyfirst-century problem, even with more advanced farming technologies added. It would unleash cataclysmic soil and water loss, gross pollution, the spread of deserts and animal, plant and human diseases, accelerate climate change (through land clearing and the use of fossil fuels and fertilisers) and extinguish the last of Africa's wildlife. The combined outcome of this would be war, potentially on a continent-wide scale – and it is for this reason Africa ranks second on this list of world food and war hotspots.

Where the true solutions to Africa's and the world's food challenges may lie is dealt with in the concluding chapters of this book.

South Asia
The constellation of burgeoning food demand, water scarcity, degrading land, a turbulent climate, social, political and

religious feuding and rampant militarisation make the region of South Asia – India, Pakistan, Bangladesh and Sri Lanka – the most dangerous of all for civilisation during the twentyfirst century.

The population of the region has more than tripled since the 1960s. India alone is looking at a population of 1.73 billion by 2050, Pakistan at 306 million, Bangladesh 202 million and Sri Lanka at 23 million – a combined total approaching 2.3 billion.[78] The Indo-Gangetic Plain is the bread-basket of the three largest countries and currently feeds more than 900 million from both surface and groundwater.

'India is facing a perfect storm in managing water. Centuries of mismanagement, political and institutional incompetence, indifference at central, state and municipal levels, a steadily increasing population that will reach an estimated 1.7 billion by 2050, a rapidly mushrooming middle class demanding an increasingly protein-rich diet that requires significantly more water to produce – together, these are leading the country towards disaster', says Professor Asit Biswas of the National University of Singapore.[79] 'India is now facing a water situation that is significantly worse than any that previous generations have had to face. All Indian water bodies within and near popu-lation centres are now grossly polluted... Not a single Indian city can provide clean water that can be consumed from the tap on a 24×7 basis', he adds. This was underlined by a warning from the Indian Supreme Court in 2018 that the capital, New Delhi – population 25 million – was on track to run out of groundwater completely.[80] Facing similar water scarcity were 20 other Indian cities, including Bangalore and Hyderabad – heartbeat of the Indian high-tech boom – menacing the lives and jobs of 600 mil-lion Indians.[81]

Free electricity and cheap diesel pumps led to an explosion in the extraction of groundwater across the Indo-Gangetic plain. 'The best estimate is that at present India uses 230–250 cubic kilometres of groundwater each year. This accounts for about one-quarter of the global groundwater use. More than 60% of irrigated agriculture and 85% of domestic water use now depends on groundwater.' Over large areas, India's groundwater levels have been falling precipitously, in places at rates of a metre or more a year, since the start of the twentyfirst century and scientists fear its reserves will be largely exhausted by 2050.[82]

The World Resources Institute, which keeps a hawk-like gaze on global water issues, notes that more than half of India is already water stressed, affecting more than 600 million people – and the situation will become extremely grave towards 2040 (Figure 5.7).[83]

Climate change is only making matters worse for South Asia – the rising intensity of droughts, floods and heatwaves threatens to undermine the region's fragile ability to feed itself. Indeed, according to some projections, parts will be so hot as to become uninhabitable and unfarmable.[84] Recent climate modelling identified India as the world's second most vulnerable country for

Figure 5.7. India: facing high to extreme water stress. Source: World Resources Institute 2015.

climate-related hunger, and Bangladesh third, with the situation worsening towards 2 °C of global warming.[85] The Indian Ministry of Finance concurs, warning that climate could shrink agricultural incomes by as much as 25 per cent in unirrigated farmland and 18 per cent in irrigated areas by 2100.[86]

South Asia's main water reserve, the glacial ice of the Hindu Kush and Himalaya which supports two billion people, is in dire straits, according to a study by 210 scientists. A third of it will be gone by 2100, in a 'climate crisis you haven't heard of', said lead author Philippus Wester. Its loss due to global warming holds catastrophic consequences for rivers, groundwater, food production and the cities that rely on it.[87]

'Climate change is likely to have a detrimental effect on South Asia out to 2030 and beyond, mainly because of its ability to exacerbate one of South Asia's biggest challenges: an expanding population and the challenge of feeding, housing, clothing, watering and employing it', wrote analyst Benjamin Walsh.[88] Melting glaciers, increased evaporation and swelling cities are all intensifying existing food and water insecurity and, since climate change cannot be prevented in the short run, governments had better prepare for it, he said. In this sense, Walsh and Biswas tender similar advice: whether or not South Asia can ride out the 'perfect storm' will depend on the competence and determination of hitherto somewhat inept governments in taking the essential steps to conserve water and find new ways to produce food. The subcontinent's existing food and water model is broken and cannot survive the mid century.

On the positive side is the enthusiasm with which South Asia has embraced renewable energy and the IT revolution, expressed in the region's strong economic growth. These demonstrate that vast and rapid national and regional changes are possible. Water, land and food, however, present far more intractable problems – social, political and technical – on which age-old disputes over religion, ethnicity and caste lie like a pall.

Since India and Pakistan partitioned in 1947, there has been ongoing low-level conflict over the waters of the Indus and the territory of Kashmir. Pakistan considers India is stealing its water and trying to assert hegemony through dam-building, while India claims Pakistan is losing water due to climate change: the scarcer water becomes for either country, the more the tensions escalate. Both sides are heavily armed: India has 2.1 million soldiers under arms, and Pakistan 644,000. Both nations have 120+ nuclear warheads. Between them, they spend US$65 billion a year on their militaries.[89] How close they have been to open war is highlighted by legal expert Dr Waseem Quereshi: 'The tension over water conflicts between India and Pakistan has been soaring. India has threatened that it will scrap the IWT [Indus Waters Treaty] entirely. In response, Pakistan has stated that such a revocation of a bilaterally agreed treaty would be considered an act of war'.[90]

Large-scale food, land and water failures anywhere on the Indian subcontinent could spark immense refugee movements in the tens or hundreds of millions, capable of obliterating neighbour countries and igniting wars. They are liable to be on a scale that dwarfs the Syrian refugee problem into insignificance, with worldwide repercussions. For example, some 130 million people on the subcontinent inhabit low-lying coastal regions that will be under the sea by 2100[91], and that is but a single dimension of the climate–water crisis. The World Bank rates the Indian subcontinent the world's second most vulnerable region for enforced climate migration, with 40 million climate refugees alone in India by 2050.[92] These estimates take no account of the scale of migration that could result from major failures in food or water, or people fleeing resulting conflicts.

The scenario of major collapse in the South Asian food and water system is so appalling that no government or agency, as yet, seems prepared even to contemplate its possibility, or to risk the displeasure of South Asian governments and peoples by speaking openly about it. As a result, the world at large is doing little to forestall or prevent it. However, for whatever the *vox populi* is worth, when the website *Debate.org* asked readers to vote on the question "Will India Collapse?", 76 per cent of respondents (mostly Indians) were of the view that it would.[93] The Oslo

Peace Research Institute, in a rather more structured attempt to predict the likelihood of future conflicts based on past behaviour, rated Pakistan, India, Afghanistan and Sri Lanka among the countries more likely to face wars up to 2050.[94]

The great issue for humanity is South Asia's combined arsenal of 250+ nuclear weapons. Though many of these are thought to be 'battlefield' or tactical nukes (as opposed to city busters), there are enough of them to cause a worldwide famine affecting everybody and lasting several years. This insight arises out of the increasing sophistication of global climate models, which can now describe the impact of nuclear release on the global climate system with far greater precision than ever before. Meteorologist Alan Robock from Rutgers University and physicist Brian Toon from the University of Colorado have devoted 30 years to projecting the effects of nuclear war. They estimate that a *limited* nuclear exchange between India and Pakistan would throw up at least five million tonnes of dust and smoke from burning forests and incinerated cities, lofting it into the high atmosphere where it will linger for up to 20 years. In climatic terms, this would be the equivalent of an asteroid impact on Earth or a large volcanic eruption, they said – enough to unleash a worldwide 'nuclear winter'.[95]

'We put it into a NASA climate model and found it would be the largest climate change in recorded human history', Brian Toon told a journalist. 'The basic physics is very simple. If you block out the Sun, it gets cold and dark at the Earth's surface'.[96]

He continued: 'We hypothesized that if each country used half of their nuclear arsenal, that would be 50 weapons on each side. We assumed the simplest bomb, which is the size dropped on Hiroshima and Nagasaki – a 15 kiloton bomb. The answer is the global average temperature would go down by about 1.5 degrees Celsius. In the middle of continents, temperature drops would be larger and last for a decade or more'. The effects of this snap cooling on agriculture worldwide were then calculated. The answer was equally chilling: harvests would crash by 20–40 per cent for five years, and for the next five years, linger 10–20 per cent below the pre-war norm. This would result in

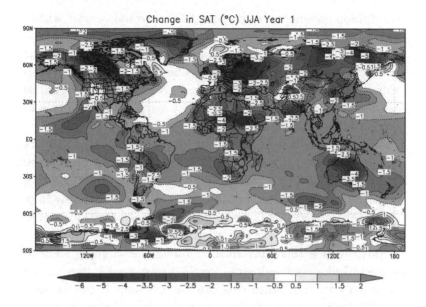

Figure 5.8. Global temperature falls following a small nuclear war. Credit: Robock, Oman and Stenchikov, 2007 (http://www.nucleardarkness.org/warconsequences/globaltemperaturesaftersmall/).

malnourishment, if not outright starvation, for most of the world's population (Figure 5.8).

Such an event would be more severe than the Little Ice Age of the eighteenth century – which was, it may be recalled, a likely contributing factor in the hunger that led to the French Revolution – or the cool period that brought down the Roman Empire in the fourth century. In today's overcrowded world it would unleash global hunger, reducing the average daily caloric intake from 2900 to 1900–2000 calories or fewer, which is borderline malnutrition. For people already hungry, such an outcome would be fatal.

Yet that is not the worst of it. A report by International Physicians for the Prevention of Nuclear War (IPPNW) concluded that China, lying immediately downwind of India/Pakistan, would be worst affected by the nuclear winter effects of even a limited atomic war in South Asia. Chinese winter wheat production would fall by up to half, and the rice crop by 21 per cent.

Two billion people in India and China would starve within months, government in both countries would probably disintegrate and, in an echo of their own and Roman histories, the remnants of society would doubtless be riven among local warlords. Most of the nations of Southeast, West, North and Central Asia on their borders would be swept away before the tide of people fleeing the catastrophe.[97]

How such events would play out for the rest of the world are not easy to predict – but, in all likelihood, the panic occasioned by rising global hunger, soaring global food prices and the loss of two of its largest traders would crash the world economy, toppling more governments and igniting further civil and international conflict, some of it potentially nuclear.

Thus, even a relatively limited nuclear exchange, such as between India and Pakistan, could bring civilisation as we know it to an end. From this brief assessment it can be seen that the Indian subcontinent, more than any region on Earth, holds the key to the future of world food security and hence, the fate of civilisation in this century. For this reason, the South Asian region is rated as the Number One Risk on this list, in terms of food, land and water insecurity and conflict risk, above all others.

The Human Tide

Since lack of food, or fear of it, is a primary motive for people to leave their homes, the number of refugees and displaced people worldwide offers stark testimony to the increasing pressures facing human civilisation and its food supply, as we bang up against the finite limits of the planet we inhabit.

The actual number of refugees and internally displaced people more than doubled in the first two decades of the twentyfirst century, from 32 million in the late 1990s to 68.5 million in 2018.[98] Furthermore, the proportion of the world population in flight rose nearly tenfold, from 0.1 per cent to almost 1 per cent, meaning – as the World Economic Forum pointed out – that around one person in every hundred has fled their home.[99] In

2018, the UN High Commissioner for Refugees noted these were 'the highest levels of displacement on record', that nearly half of all refugees were children under 18 and that, on average, 20 people were being displaced every minute.

On top of this the UN reported 258 million 'economic migrants' in 2017,[100] mostly from Asia and mainly educated people who had foreseen potential trouble in their homelands, including China and India, and had the resources to move themselves and their families out of harm's way and to other more secure parts of the globe. Together, then, almost a third of a billion human beings now roam the planet every year in search of new homes and opportunities, freedom from war or hunger. Such a vast number of people already on the road – equivalent to the entire population of the USA – gives some inkling of the colossal people movements which could eventuate from large scale conflicts over food, land and water as the century advances.

It is time to face the fact that movements of a billion humans or more are now entirely possible over a comparatively short time – even though many may die in the process.

In case anyone should consider such vast movements to be impossible, the World Bank notes that the number of global tourists alone already exceeds 1.25 billion a year – which simply goes to illustrate the capacity of modern transport systems.[101] Most of those tourists travel by air, road, rail or passenger vessel – however, it should be noted the world also has 52,000 merchant ships, 312,000 general aviation aircraft, 4.6 million fishing boats and tens of millions of larger recreational craft[102] capable of being commandeered by fleeing people, should their needs be fierce enough.

As mentioned before, the Bank anticipated that at least 140 million 'climate refugees' may be forced to quit just three highly vulnerable regions by the mid twentyfirst century: Sub-Saharan Africa, South Asia and Latin America.[103] In the Bank's analysis, the main drivers for these immigrants, it should be noted, are factors such as water scarcity, crop failure, sea-level rise and storm surges – not the wars these impacts may also ignite. They would make the exodus much larger. Furthermore, the Bank's analysis does not include other at-risk regions such as China, Central Asia and the Middle East/North Africa.

The FAO, in its report on the state of world food security,[104] commented as follows.

- 'The number of conflicts is... on the rise. Exacerbated by climate-related shocks, conflicts seriously affect food security and are a cause of much of the recent increase in food insecurity.'

- 'Conflict is a key driver of situations of severe food crisis and recently re-emerged famines, while hunger and undernutrition are significantly worse where conflicts are prolonged and institutional capacities weak.'

It is important to understand that such disasters are preventable, with sufficient forward recognition of the driving factors, early implementation of suitable preventative strategies and with the co-operation of the global community. At present this cooperation is fragmentary, and few countries feel responsible for preventing the kinds of events described in this chapter, especially those taking place in distant, overseas countries. Yet it is increasingly in their own interests to do so, in view of unavoidable consequences for themselves, both physical and economic.

In the twentyfirst century the risk of mass migration and conflict driven by insecurity of food, land and water is higher than in any previous age of human history. The World Economic Forum (WEF) rated enforced mass migration as the sixth most likely of its top 30 global risks in 2018 and the second worst in terms of its societal impact. It identified 'profound social instability' as the risk factor most highly connected to the prevailing range of global trends.[105] Furthermore, the ominous and destabilising rise of right-wing populism and renascent fascism in western countries, especially, is in part a direct response to rising fears of mass immigration.[106]

Eight out of the WEF's top ten risks of 2018 related to global food security. Furthermore, the World Food Programme (WFP), in its report *At the Root of Exodus: Food Security, Conflict and International Migration*, drew a direct line between food, war and mass migration: 'The WFP study found that countries with the highest level of food insecurity, coupled with armed conflict, have the highest outward migration of refugees. Additionally, when coupled with poverty, food insecurity increases the likelihood and intensity of armed conflicts; something that has clear implications for refugee outflows', it said.[107]

Food, land and water must therefore now be viewed as strategic components of defence and international security as elemental as naval fleets, air power, armies or weapons. There is no logic to arming ourselves against the possibility of global conflict if, by ignoring its causes, we inadvertently set in motion the very machinery that drives it. Neglecting the strategic importance of food, land and water will deliver increased risk of war and mass migration – while the opposite is also true: attending to them can yield a vital peace dividend by extinguishing or damping down an important *casus belli*. This issue is developed in Chapter 7.

6 FOOD AS AN EXISTENTIAL RISK

Extinction and Ecological Collapse – Resource Scarcity – Weapons of Mass Destruction – Climate Change – Poisoned Planet – Food Security – Pandemic Disease – Population and Megacity Failure – Uncontrolled Supertechnologies – Self-Delusion – Solving the Risks

'This is the first century in the world's history when the biggest threat is from humanity'
Emeritus Professor Martin Rees, UK Astronomer Royal

Around the world more and more people – scientists, concerned grandparents and thoughtful millennials especially – are daring to voice the questions: 'Are we in the endgame of human history? Is the twentyfirst century likely to be our last, as a civilisation – or maybe even as a species?'

The probable answers to these questions are contained in tens of thousands of scientific papers, articles and books, in which researchers have described their findings from countless tests, experiments, models and monitoring of global conditions that are the fallout from mass human behaviour and activity. The answers are entirely based on evidence that has been carefully measured and even more carefully checked by independent reviewers. They aren't based on belief, hunch, superstition or uninformed conviction – but on solid, accumulated fact. Fact that has been tested, and re-tested, independently. Mountains of fact. Indeed, so mountainous that it is impossible for any ordinary citizen to read even a small part, especially as much of it is published in specialist scientific journals, some of which are priced beyond the reach of the general public. To make this essential understanding of our world more widely available

was the aim of *Surviving the 21st Century* – a book in which
I documented the ten greatest threats to humanity that are
now building up around us, the main scientific evidence for
them and what we – both as a society and as wise and responsible individuals – can and should do about them.[1]

Humanity is facing its greatest test in the million-year ascent
of our kind. This isn't a single challenge. It's a constellation of
huge man-made threats, now coming together to overshadow our
civilisation's stability and even, maybe, its future survival. These
ten intersecting risks are: ecological collapse, resource depletion,
weapons of mass destruction, climate change, global poisoning,
food insecurity, population and urban failure, pandemic disease
and uncontrolled new technologies (like killer robots, artificial
intelligence and universal surveillance) – reinforced by a prodigious capacity for human self-delusion. But sticking our heads in
the sand and trying to ignore them will not remove the danger.

These threats are known as 'existential risks' because they
imperil our future existence, both as individuals, as a civilisation
and maybe even as a species.

Their most important feature is the fact that they are not
isolated from one another. They are deeply interwoven. They
play into and feed one another. They cannot be addressed separ-
ately or singly, because to do so creates a situation where
curbing one risk only makes other risks worse. Together they
constitute a single existential emergency facing all of humanity.

An example of why they cannot be addressed piecemeal is
trying to solve the global food problem by intensifying agriculture worldwide using fossil fuels, fertilisers and petrochemicals:
this will only destroy the very climate, resources and ecosystem
services on which agriculture, itself, depends – and is not, consequently, a viable or enduring solution. Other answers must be
sought. Another example is that trying to end the Sixth Extinction of wildlife on our planet by turning half of it back to forest
and grassland will not work on its own, because it would involve
the sacrifice of half the current human food supply: consequently, we need a solution that achieves both aims – sustainable food for all and a sufficient haven for the Earth's other

species. So, the problem of extinction needs to be solved, in part, by solving the problem of food – and that, in turn, entails solving the problems of climate, global poisoning, resource depletion and other mega-risks. It is absolutely clear from this that the solutions we adopt must be *cross-cutting*. They must comprehensively address *all* the perils we face, not just one or a handful of them.

Take these ten great risks together and what you have is the focal issue of our time – the greatest and most profound challenge ever to confront human civilisation. The risks are all self-inflicted, a direct result of the overgrowth in human numbers and our unbridled demands on the planet – for food, resources, space and a healthy environment. By solving them together, we ensure our future. By denying them or failing to solve them all in time, we knowingly create untold misery and suffering for most of humanity and generations to come through the centuries ahead. We are gambling with the very survival of our civilisation and species. The risks are described below, along with observations about how they play into the *Food or War* scenario. The detail, the scientific sources and the solutions, collective and individual, to each risk are described in more detail in *Surviving the 21st Century*.[2]

Extinction and Ecological Collapse

More than half of the large animals that once inhabited the Earth have been wiped from it by human action since 1970, according to the Worldwide Fund for Nature's Living Planet Index.[3] So, too, have half the fish in the sea on which humans rely for food.[4] Humans are, in the words of the great biologist E. O. Wilson, 'tearing down the biosphere', demolishing the very home that keeps us alive.[5]

Extinction, it should be noted, is a part of life: 99.9 per cent of all species ever to evolve on this planet have disappeared, and new ones like ourselves have arisen to replace them. But extinction rates like today's – a hundred to a thousand times faster than normal – are a freak occurrence that usually takes tens of millions of years, not mere decades. Animal, plant and marine species are presently vanishing so fast that scientists have dubbed our time "the Sixth Extinction" – the sixth such mega-death in the geological history of the Earth.[6] By the end of the present century, Wilson says, it is possible that up to half of the eight million species thought to exist here will be gone. Furthermore, in all previous extinctions, natural events like asteroid strikes and vast volcanic outbursts have been to blame. This will be the only time in the Earth's history when the wipe-out was caused by a single species. Us.[7]

The probability of humans becoming extinct during the twentyfirst century is not high – but there are scenarios, such as an all-out nuclear war, runaway climate change (+5–10 °C or more), or a compound collapse in the Earth's main life support systems, in which it must be regarded as a possibility – and the fact that it is unpleasant to contemplate is no excuse for doing nothing to stop it.

However, there are also a number of credible scenarios in which large-scale ecosystem collapse could endanger civilisation and cause very high mortality among the world's population. These revolve around the notion of 'environmental security' which is, in turn, very closely tied to human security – i.e. peace or war. An ecosystem is a biological community of mutually dependent species – and the removal of one species after another can undermine it and render it dysfunctional, in the same way that pulling one brick at a time out of your home will eventually cause it to fall down. Ecosystems support all life on the planet, and maintain the quality of air, water and soil on which it depends. For humans, they provide food and clean water (provisioning services), disease and climate regulation (regulatory services), spiritual and aesthetic fulfilment (cultural services), useful chemical energy (from plants) and soil formation (support services). As ecosystems decay, the decline and loss of these services often causes significant harm to human wellbeing and can inflame the tensions that lead to conflict.

The most destructive object on the planet, as we noted in Chapter 3, is the human jawbone. The need to keep it fed is responsible, every year, for the loss of up to 75 billion tonnes of topsoil, the wasting of six trillion tonnes of water, the release of five million tonnes of pesticides, and 30 per cent of the world's climate-wrecking carbon emissions. In addition, the contemporary food system is the chief driver of deforestation, desertification, wildlife extinctions and impaired ecosystems. Among the most striking examples of food's impact on the wild world are the 400+ 'dead zones' spreading through the world's oceans from the Arabian Sea, to the Baltic and the Mississippi delta. These are oxygenless layers in the sea, where fish cannot survive. They are caused by topsoil dislodged by land clearing, over-farming and over-grazing, the use of huge quantities of artificial fertilisers, toxic chemicals and human sewage. Along with overfishing they contribute to an ongoing collapse in world wild fisheries and are a clear example of how the activity of one part of the food system can impair another. Similarly, most inland rivers and lakes in populated regions are eutrophic and polluted – and no longer capable of producing as much food as in the past. The loss of wild fisheries increases tensions between nations and fishers over what remains and can lead to 'fish wars'.[8]

The existing global food production system is therefore a major contributor to the decline and failure of ecosystem services needed to support the human population. This in turn rebounds on the food system itself. Furthermore, the extinction of wild animals and plants deprives the food industry of many edible species that may be needed as part of a healthy, diverse global diet in future.

The solution to the extinction crisis is to cease farming and grazing on about half the currently farmed area of the planet (25 million square kilometres), transfer food production to the cities where it can take advantage of all the nutrients and water currently being wasted, and employ many of the world's farmers and indigenous people as Stewards of the Earth to manage the rewilding and regeneration of former farmlands. Food production can continue on the remaining 24 million square kilometres using eco-agriculture. This process is further described in *Surviving the 21st Century* and in Chapter 9 of this book.

How the existing food system plays into the risk of war can also be viewed through the lens of environmental security: war damages environments, making it harder for humans to sustain and feed themselves – and ruined environments themselves become cauldrons of war. This is plainly to be seen in the cases of Syria, South Sudan, Yemen and the Horn of Africa. What we most need are food systems that do not cause knock-on damage to either the environment and wildlife, the climate, the oceans or to consumer health – and which ease tensions, so promoting peace, not conflict. These are described in Chapters 8 and 9.

Resource Scarcity

The average citizen of planet Earth today uses at least ten times the volume of resources used by their grandparents a century ago. Since the human population has also quadrupled over the same time, this means humanity's gargantuan appetite for minerals, metals, timber, water, food and energy has grown forty-fold in barely a hundred years. As the Global Footprint Network explains, we are presently using enough 'stuff' for 1.6 Earths, not just the one we have. We now outrun the Earth's natural ability to supply our needs in August each year.[9] As with the mining of groundwater, the decline and collapse of global resources like soil, water and phosphorus, is often imperceptible to the individual: people have simply no idea they are living on borrowed time and, with that, comes enormous risk.

To make the issue of resource consumption a little more personal: you (as an average individual citizen of the planet) will in your lifetime
- use 99,720 tonnes (i.e. 40 Olympic pools) of fresh water
- displace 750 tonnes of topsoil
- consume 720 tonnes of metals and materials
- use 80 billion joules of energy
- release 288 tonnes of CO_2
- release 320 kilograms of toxic chemicals
- waste 13.4 tonnes of food
- destroy 800 square metres of forest.

Because of the long, cryptic, industrial and international trade chains which hide it, most of us are unaware of the vast damage we do to the planet through our simple habit of shopping.

Yes, some of us have a notion that some of our purchases may be bad for gorillas in the Congo, orangutans in Borneo or flamingos in the Atacama – but we mostly have no true appreciation of the wider havoc we inflict on the Earth and its natural systems by the 'innocent' act of consumption, which business and governments try constantly to convince us is essential to 'growth and jobs'.

It should therefore come as no surprise that the world finds itself increasingly short of key resources like fresh water, soil, phosphorus, timber and certain minerals – and that these shortages are giving rise to tensions and even to conflicts. Indeed, resource scarcity has for some time been considered by strategic experts to be one of the most likely causes of war in the twenty-first century.[10]

However, people are not equally responsible for the devastation of Planet Earth. The diagram below (Figure 6.1), from

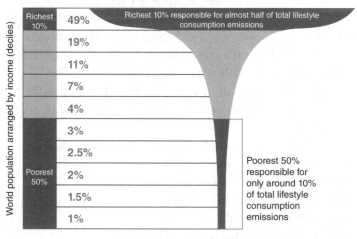

Figure 6.1. Consumption of material goods (expressed as carbon emissions) by income. Source: Oxfam, 2015.

Oxfam, illustrates how just one tenth of humanity consumes five times as much in the way of material resources (expressed here in the form of their carbon footprint) as the poorest *half* of the world population. The affluent are chiefly responsible for the destruction taking place on a global scale as they seek to sustain lifestyles that the planet can no longer afford or support.

The significance of this blind spot around consumption for global food security is very great. As described in earlier chapters, the world food system depends critically on soil, water, nutrients and a stable climate, to supply humanity's daily need for nutriment – and all of these essential resources are in increasingly short supply, chiefly because of our own mismanagement of them and our collective failure to appreciate that they are finite. On current trends, the existing food system will tend to break down, first regionally and then globally, owing to resource scarcity from the 2020s onward, and especially towards the mid century – unless there is radical change in the world diet and the means by which we feed ourselves. This will lead to increasing outbreaks of violence and war. Nobody, neither rich nor poor, will escape the consequences.

Weapons of Mass Destruction

Detonating just 50–100 out of the global arsenal of nearly 15,000 nuclear weapons would suffice to end civilisation in a nuclear winter, causing worldwide famine and economic collapse affecting even distant nations, as we saw in the previous chapter in the section dealing with South Asia. Eight nations now have the power to terminate civilisation should they desire to do so – and two have the power to extinguish the human species. According to the nuclear monitoring group Ploughshares, this arsenal is distributed as follows:
- Russia, 6600 warheads (2500 classified as 'retired')
- America, 6450 warheads (2550 classified as 'retired')
- France, 300 warheads
- China, 270 warheads
- UK, 215 warheads

- Pakistan, 130 warheads
- India, 120 warheads
- Israel, 80 warheads
- North Korea, 15–20 warheads.[11]

Although actual numbers of warheads have continued to fall from its peak of 70,000 weapons in the mid 1980s, scientists argue the danger of nuclear conflict in fact increased in the first two decades of the twentyfirst century. This was due to the modernisation of existing stockpiles, the adoption of dangerous new technologies such as robot delivery systems, hypersonic missiles, artificial intelligence and electronic warfare, and the continuing leakage of nuclear materials and knowhow to non-nuclear nations and potential terrorist organisations.

In early 2018 the hands of the 'Doomsday Clock', maintained by the Bulletin of the Atomic Scientists, were re-set at two minutes to midnight, the highest risk to humanity that it has ever shown since the clock was introduced in 1953. This was due not only to the state of the world's nuclear arsenal, but also to irresponsible language by world leaders, the growing use of social media to destabilise rival regimes, and to the rising threat of uncontrolled climate change (see below).[12]

In an historic moment on 17 July 2017, 122 nations voted in the UN for the first time ever in favour of a treaty banning all nuclear weapons. This called for comprehensive prohibition of "a full range of nuclear-weapon-related activities, such as undertaking to develop, test, produce, manufacture, acquire, possess or stockpile nuclear weapons or other nuclear explosive devices, as well as the use or threat of use of these weapons."[13] However, 71 other countries – including all the nuclear states – either opposed the ban, abstained or declined to vote. The Treaty vote was nonetheless interpreted by some as a promising first step towards abolishing the nuclear nightmare that hangs over the entire human species.

In contrast, 192 countries had signed up to the Chemical Weapons Convention to ban the use of chemical weapons, and 180 to the Biological Weapons Convention. As of 2018, 96 per cent of previous world stocks of chemical weapons had been destroyed – but their continued use in the Syrian conflict and in alleged assassination attempts by Russia indicated the world remains at risk.[14]

As things stand, the only entities that can afford to own nuclear weapons are nations – and if humanity is to be wiped out, it will most likely be as a result of an atomic conflict between nations. It follows from this that, if the world is to be made safe from such a fate it will need to get rid of nations as a structure of human self-organisation and replace them with wiser, less aggressive forms of self-governance. After all, the nation state really only began in the early nineteenth century and is by no means a permanent feature of self-governance, any more than monarchies, feudal systems or priest states. Although many people still tend to assume it is. Between them, nations have butchered more than 200 million people in the past 150 years and it is increasingly clear the world would be a far safer, more peaceable place without either nations or nationalism. The question is what to replace them with.

Although there may at first glance appear to be no close linkage between weapons of mass destruction and food, in the twentyfirst century with world resources of food, land and water under growing stress, nothing can be ruled out. Indeed, chemical weapons have frequently been deployed in the Syrian civil war, which had drought, agricultural failure and hunger among its early drivers. And nuclear conflict remains a distinct possibility in South Asia and the Middle East, especially, as these regions are already stressed in terms of food, land and water, and their nuclear firepower or access to nuclear materials is multiplying.

It remains an open question whether panicking regimes in Russia, the USA or even France would be ruthless enough to deploy atomic weapons in an attempt to quell invasion by tens of millions of desperate refugees, fleeing famine and climate chaos in their own homelands – but the possibility ought not to be ignored.

That nuclear war is at least a possible outcome of food and climate crises was first flagged in the report *The Age of*

Consequences by Kurt Campbell and the US-based Centre for Strategic and International Studies, which stated 'it is clear that even nuclear war cannot be excluded as a political consequence of global warming'.[15] Food insecurity is therefore a driver in the preconditions for the use of nuclear weapons, whether limited or unlimited.

A global famine is a likely outcome of limited use of nuclear weapons by any country or countries – and would be unavoidable in the event of an unlimited nuclear war between America and Russia, making it unwinnable for either. And that, as the mute hands of the 'Doomsday Clock' so eloquently admonish, is also the most likely scenario for the premature termination of the human species.

Such a grim scenario can be alleviated by two measures: the voluntary banning by the whole of humanity of nuclear weapons, their technology, materials and stocks – and by a global effort to secure food against future insecurity by diverting the funds now wasted on nuclear armaments into building the sustainable food and water systems of the future (see Chapters 8 and 9).

Climate Change

The effects of food and war on climate change as it is presently predicted to occur were described in Chapter 3: in brief, the stable climate in which agriculture arose over the past 6000 years is now becoming increasingly unstable as a result of the billions of tonnes of carbon that humans are injecting into the atmosphere and oceans, forming a colossal heat engine to drive more frequent, violent weather. This in turn impairs food production in regions of the world already facing severe stresses from population growth and resource depletion. Military analysts describe climate change as a 'threat multiplier', augmenting the tensions, conflict and instability which already exist. In reality it is a feedback loop, in which worsening climate conditions cause greater food insecurity, which is met by measures (like increased land clearing and use of fossil fuels and chemicals), which in turn worsen climate conditions, which worsen food security, which cause wars, which inflict more eco-damage...

Two degrees (2 °C) of global warming – described as the danger point for humanity – are predicted to occur well before 2050 because of our collective failure to curb our carbon emissions.[16] Those 2 °C of warming portend bad things for any food system that depends on the weather – but just how bad cannot easily be forecast as both the climate state and the response of the global food system are governed by human behaviour, which is fairly unpredictable. Current estimates suggest crop losses of the order of 20–50 per cent at the very time we are trying to raise food output by 50–70 per cent. What can be confidently predicted, however, is that there will be an increase in both the frequency and scale of harvest failures and agricultural disease outbreaks around the world as we approach the mid century – and that beyond 2 °C of warming it will become very hard indeed to maintain a stable outdoors, agriculture-based system to meet an anticipated doubling in world demand for food by the 2060s. The 'worst case' risk of this, as previously outlined, would be ten billion people having to subsist on enough food to feed only four billion.

That, however, is by no means the worst case of the climate story. There are ominous signs that humans have already unleashed planetary forces over which we have *absolutely no control* – and that these, should they become large enough, will take charge of the Earth's climate engine and drive it into a superheated condition of +9–10 °C or even higher.

Today, more people are aware that global warming may lead to complete melting of all glaciers and the polar ice-caps, thereby raising sea levels by 65 metres and inundating almost all of the world's seaboard cities, fertile river deltas and coastal plains.[17] This would clearly have a devastating effect on coastal food production. However, this process will probably take several centuries, allowing populations ample time to relocate inland. That sea levels previously rose by a similar quantum at the end of the last Ice Age, flooding part of Australia, severing Britain from Europe and America from Asia, is proof enough that such events occur as a regular part of the Earth's warming and chilling cycles.

The great existential threat to humanity lies in vast stores of frozen methane gas (CH_4) locked into the soils of the tundra regions of Canada and Siberia, in colossal deposits of frozen methane on the continental seabed surrounding the Arctic Ocean, and in massive stores of methane submerged in peat deposits and swamps in places such as the Amazon and the wet tropical forests of Southeast Asia and Africa. Methane is a gas with 20–70 times the climate-forcing power of carbon dioxide. These deposits are the accumulation of the slow decomposition of planet and animal matter in the Earth's sediments over several hundred million years – they are identical in origin to the gas bubbles that surface when we stir the bed of a pond or lake.

The actual volume of these methane deposits is still being assessed by science. Recent estimates suggest:

- seabed deposits – between 500–2500 billion tonnes of frozen carbon;[18]
- tundra deposits – potentially emitting 180–420 million tonnes of carbon a year by 2100; and
- tropical peat swamps – could emit 480–870 million tonnes of carbon a year by 2100.[19]

That carbon released from peat swamps, tundra and possibly the oceans can have a catastrophic effect on the Earth's climate is foreshadowed by an event known as the Palaeocene–Eocene Thermal Maximum (PETM), which took place some 55 million years ago, when Earth took a sudden fever and its temperature rocketed upwards by +5–9 °C. This 'heat spike' caused a lesser extinction event involving widespread loss of ocean life and a smaller toll of land animals.[20] However, the heating occurred over a much longer period – 100–200,000 years, compared with human-driven heating (50–100 years) – and is thought to have been mainly caused by the drying out and burning of tropical peat swamps as the climate warmed. However, the volume of carbon which caused this sharp planetary heat spike in the past is estimated to be barely a tenth of that released by humanity today.[21]

Today, human activity in clearing rainforests, draining swamps and burning the world's forests to open them up for farming and food production is releasing vast amounts of methane and CO_2. Explosion craters have been reported across Canada and Siberia as frozen methane deposits well up and erupt with the melting of the tundra. And scientists from Sweden, Russia, Canada and America have reported methane bubbling from the seabed of the Arctic Ocean, though not yet in massive volumes. The risk in all this is that, by warming the planet by only 1–2 °C, we have set in train natural processes that we are powerless to control, setting ourselves on an inescapable trajectory to a Hothouse Earth, 5–10 °C or more above today's levels.

Although it is hard to estimate, some scientists are of the view that fewer than one billion humans would survive such an event[22] – in other words, nine people out of every ten may perish in the cycle of famines, wars, heatwaves and pandemic diseases which global overheating would entail. This underlies the deadly urgency of ceasing to burn all fossil fuels, locking up as much carbon as possible and re-stabilising the Earth's climate. In that, food production can and will play a central role.

Poisoned Planet

'Earth, and all life on it, are being saturated with man-made chemicals in an event unlike anything which has occurred in all four billion years of our planet's story. Each moment of our lives, from conception unto death, we are exposed to thousands of substances, some deadly in even tiny doses and most of them unknown in their effects on our health and wellbeing or upon the natural world. These enter our bodies with every breath, each meal or drink, the clothes we wear, the products with which we adorn ourselves, our homes, workplaces, cars and furniture, the things we encounter every day. There is no escaping them. Ours is a poisoned planet, its whole system infused with the substances humans deliberately or inadvertently produce in the course of extracting, making, using, burning or discarding the many marvellous products on which modern life depends. This

explosion in chemical use and release has all happened so rapidly that most people are blissfully unaware of its true magnitude and extent, or of the dangers it now poses to us all as well as to future generations for centuries to come.'

This is a summation of the chemical crisis facing all of humanity, as well as all life on Earth, which I wrote in *Surviving the 21st Century*, and which is based on the extensive scientific research reported in *Poisoned Planet*.[23] It is a crisis with profound impact for everyone.

According to the medical journal *The Lancet*, nine million people – one in six – die every year from chemical pollution of their air, water, food and living environment.[24] A further 40 million die from the so-called noncommunicable or 'lifestyle' diseases (NCDs), cancer, heart disease, diabetes and lung disease, which are mostly diet-related.[25]

Food production, as we have seen, is deeply implicated in the chemical deluge. However, it is also an existential threat to human health, both in terms of infectious disease and the new 'lifestyle' diseases. No-one to my knowledge has compiled an accurate assessment of the total chemical effusion of humanity or presented a realistic impression of its true scale. Box 6.1 represents my own best estimate, drawn from various reliable sources.

From this it can easily be seen that the scale of humanity's chemical assault on ourselves and on the planet is many times the scale of our climate assault – yet this issue commands nowhere near the political or scientific priority that it should. It is arguably the most under-rated, under-investigated and poorly understood of all the existential threats to humanity.

The poisoning of the Earth by human activities has grave implications for the health and safety of the global food chain and its eight billion consumers. It is not only the use of chemicals in food production that is of concern, but also the contamination of water, soils and livestock by industrial pollutants from other sources, such as mining or manufacturing. It is also the disruption of vital services such as pollination by insects of a

---

Box 6.1 Estimate of gross anthropogenic chemical release

- 30 million tonnes of industrial chemicals and pesticides
- 161 million tonnes of nitrogen and phosphorus
- 400 million tonnes of hazardous wastes including 50 million tonnes of 'e-waste' from old computers, mobile phones, etc.
- 15 billion tonnes of fossil fuels leading to the release of:
  - 50 billion tonnes of carbon
- 335 million tonnes of plastic
- 72 billion tonnes of materials and metals
- 75 billion tonnes of topsoil
- 300–1000 billion tonnes of mining wastes
- 9 trillion tonnes of water, mostly polluted with the above

Source: data from Surviving the 21st Century *(Springer 2017)*
and references therein.

---

third of the world's food crops and 90 per cent of wild plants.[26] It is the contamination of up to three quarters of the world fish catch with microscopic plastic particles and clothing microfibres made by the petrochemical industry.[27]

The ending of this flood of poisons is a prerequisite for a safe, healthy and sustainable global food supply in future. And, since government regulation has largely failed to stem the worldwide flood, the task now falls to consumers – to choose foods which have been produced by safe methods and shun foods produced by unsafe methods. That is the only way that the food industry can be encouraged (and penalised) into doing the right thing by humanity and the planet: by consumers rewarding it for producing clean food and punishing it for toxic food. Otherwise it will continue to pollute as profitably as it can. It follows that the urgent global education of consumers about which foods are safe and which are toxic is also a pre-requisite.

Food Security

Our demand for food is set to double by the 2060s – potentially the decade of 'peak people', the moment in history when the irresistible human population surge *may* top out at around 10 billion. However, as we have seen, many of the resources needed to supply it agriculturally could halve and the climate for the growing of food outdoors become far more hostile.

Why food insecurity is an existential threat to humanity should, by now, be abundantly clear from the earlier chapters of this book: present systems are unsustainable and, as they fail, will pose risks both to civilization and, should these spiral into nuclear conflict, to the future of the human species.

The important thing to note in this chapter is that food insecurity plays into many, if not all, of the other existential threats facing humanity. The food sector's role in extinction, resource scarcity, global toxicity and potential nuclear war has already been explained. Its role in the suppression of conflict is discussed in the next chapter. Its role in securing the future of the megacities, and of a largely urbanised humanity, is covered in Chapter 8. And its role in sustaining humanity through the peak in population and into a sustainable world beyond is covered in Chapter 9.

Food clearly has a pivotal role in the future of human population – both as a driver of population growth when supplies are abundant and as a potential driver of population decline, should food chains collapse. It is no exaggeration to state that the fate of civilisation depends on it.

Pandemic Disease

Disease pandemics have been a well-known existential risk to humanity since the plague of Athens in 430 BC – itself linked to a war. However, a point that escapes many people nowadays is that, as humans have become so numerous – indeed the predominant lifeform on the planet – we have also become the major food source for many microbes. We are now the 'living compost heap' on which they must dine and in which they must reproduce, if they are themselves to survive.

As our own population grows, pandemics are thus likely to increase, as more and more viruses and bacteria are forced to take refuge in humans following the depletion or total extinction of their natural hosts, the wild animals we are exterminating. This process is greatly assisted by our creation of megacities, tourism and air travel, schools and child-minding centres, air-conditioned offices, night clubs, sex with strangers, pet and pest animals, insects which prosper from climate change or human modification of the environment (like mosquitoes), ignorance, poor public hygiene, lack of clean water, and deficient food processing and handling.

So, while humanity is confronted with an ever-expanding array of parasites, we are simultaneously doing everything in our power to distribute them worldwide in record time – and to seed new pandemics. The World Health Organisation has identified 19 major infectious diseases with potential to become pandemic: chikungunya, cholera, Crimean-Congo haemorrhagic fever, Ebola, Hendra, influenza, Lassa fever, Marburg virus, meningitis, MERS-CoV, monkeypox, Nipah, plague, Rift Valley fever, SARS, smallpox, tularaemia, yellow fever and Zika virus disease.[28] While none of these is likely to fulfil the Hollywood horror movie image of wiping out the human species – for the simple reason that viruses are usually smart enough to weaken to a sublethal state once comfortably ensconced in their new host – the apocalyptic horseman representing Pestilence and Death will nevertheless continue to play a synergetic role with his companions warfare, famine, climate change, global poisoning, ecological collapse, urbanisation and other existential threats.

Food insecurity affects the progression of pandemic diseases, often in ways that are not entirely obvious. First, new pandemics of infectious disease tend to originate in developing regions where nutritional levels are poor or agricultural practices favour the evolution of novel pathogens such as, for example, the new flu strains seen every year – which arise mainly from places where people, pigs and poultry live side-by-side and shuffle viruses between them – and also novel diseases like SARS and MERS. Second, because totally unknown diseases tend to arise first in places where rainforests are being cut down for farming and viruses hitherto confined to wild animals and birds make an enforced transition into humans. Examples of novel human diseases escaping from the rainforest and tropical savannah in recent times include HIV/AIDS, Hendra, Nipah, Ebola, Marburg, Lassa and Hanta, Lujo, Junin, Machupo, Rift Valley, Congo and Zika.[29] And thirdly, because the loss of vital micronutrients from heavily farmed soils and from food itself predisposes many populations to various deficiency diseases – for example, a lack of selenium in the diet has been linked with increased risk from both HIV/AIDS and bowel cancer.[30] A key synergy is the way hunger and malnourishment exacerbate the spread of disease, classic examples being the 1918 Global Flu Pandemic which spread rapidly among war-starved populations, or the more recent cholera outbreak in war-torn Yemen. In a fresh twist, Dr Melinda Beck of North Carolina University has demonstrated that obesity – itself a form of malnutrition – may cause increased deaths from influenza by both aiding the virus and suppressing the patient's immune response.[31]

At the same time, food is largely responsible for the fastest growing pandemic of all – the so-called 'lifestyle', chronic or noncommunicable diseases, such as cancer, heart disease, diabetes, obesity, kidney and liver failure and some mental conditions, all of which are diet-related. These are responsible for 71 per cent of deaths worldwide, killing around 42 million people a year.[32]

Food and dietary quality are therefore inseparable from worldwide efforts to prevent or contain new disease pandemics. Vaccines, public health and biosecurity alone are not enough. In an overpopulated world, people must be sufficiently well-fed to avoid becoming fertile soil for the germination of fresh plagues. Diseases must be prevented – not just 'cured', and the key to prevention lies in a healthy diet.[33]

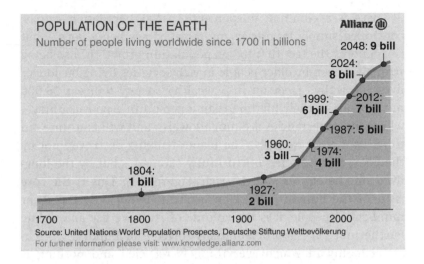

POPULATION OF THE EARTH

Number of people living worldwide since 1700 in billions

Allianz ⑪

2048: **9 bill**

2024: **8 bill**

1999: **6 bill** 2012: **7 bill**

1987: **5 bill**

1960: **3 bill** 1974: **4 bill**

1804: **1 bill**

1927: **2 bill**

| 1700 | 1800 | 1900 | 2000 |

Source: United Nations World Population Prospects, Deutsche Stiftung Weltbevölkerung
For further information please visit: www.knowledge.allianz.com

Figure 6.2. World population 1700–2050. Source: UN.

Population and Megacity Failure

Human numbers have expanded eightfold since the beginning of the nineteenth century. In my own lifetime they have tripled from 2.5 billion to 7.5 billion – from a level that was almost certainly sustainable, to one that is almost certainly unsustainable (Figure 6.2).

However, birth rates are now falling in almost all countries and regions of the world, except the very poorest. Women, whether supported by their menfolk or not, have decided to take the matter in hand and have reduced their fertility from 4.4 babies each in the 1970s to 2.4 babies in the 2010s. If this trend persists, the human population could peak at just over 10 billion by the late 2060s.

Within reason, population alone is not an existential risk. The real threat comes from the scale of our consumption, waste and poisoning of global resources – the resources we rely on to breathe, drink, feed, house, clothe, employ and entertain ourselves. Our present consumption of these is forty times what it was a century ago.

There is a common misperception that population can be controlled simply by preventing more babies being born – but this ignores the fact that today, population growth is also being strongly driven by older people in rich societies living far longer lives. Typically, a person in a wealthy society will eat 35,000 more meals in their lifetime than a person in a poor country – where life expectancies are much lower – and will consume ten times as many resources. The planet is being destroyed not by the poor, as is so often untruthfully claimed – but by the long-lived middle classes and the rich (Figure 6.1). This is the core issue of the human population boom: it is not only the sheer numbers of people, it is the volume of stuff we use and waste. Furthermore, it is a problem easily solved – by building a circular economy in which everything is recycled and nothing is wasted.[34] This will buy time for the necessary family planning to take effect. However, it is still essential to take the human population into a managed reduction as soon as possible, returning it to a state that is within the capacity of the planet to support it. What that exact number is depends upon the *per capita* resource consumption of each individual: at today's average rates of consumption, a sustainable population is probably close to the level of the mid twentieth century, 2–2.5 billion people. Because poverty and lack of food are linked to high birthrates, a vibrant circular food economy combined with universal family planning are the two main tools for achieving this.

Fiftyfive per cent of the world's population, around 4.5 billion people, already live in cities. By the mid century this is predicted by the UN to climb to almost 70 per cent – around 6.4–7 billion people.[35] However, this is a conservative estimate, as it depends on the rate at which humanity relocates from rural areas into cities. As we have seen in Chapter 4, a critical factor may be the rate at which agriculture is corporatised globally by huge agribusiness companies: left unchecked, this could throw as many as a billion smallholder farmers off their land, driving them and their families into cities. This would mirror at global scale the urban migration which occurred in Syria prior to the outbreak of civil war, or the US 'dustbowl' migration of the 1930s. In such an event, the mid-century world urban population could climb as high as 8 billion (out of 9.2 billion).

As will be explained in more detail in Chapter 8 these vast cities are disasters-in-waiting. They suffer from a range of vulnerabilities insufficiently acknowledged by urban planners and governments. These include the fact that not one of the world's great cities can feed itself – all rely on fragile transport chains to deliver their daily food. They are also intensely reliant on imported energy and water, and any large-scale failure of either would cause chaos. By virtue of their close-packed, cheerfully fornicating humanity and their function as global travel hubs, they are ideal bioreactors for breeding and distributing epidemic diseases and new plagues. Low-lying cities are especially susceptible to climatic impacts, such as exceptional floods, sea-level rise and superstorm damage. And finally, they present attractive targets to those wielding weapons of mass destruction, whether governments or terrorists. The more their populations grow towards the mid century, the more vulnerable these gigantic conurbations become, and the more likely that we will witness megacity collapses.

Megacity failure is hard to predict, though it is not hard to identify those cities which are more at risk than others. However, the timing of a collapse depends on so many variables – politics, weather, resources, wars – that it is difficult accurately to predict the onset of particular urban crises. Suffice to say that even a single megacity collapse nevertheless represents a significant existential risk to humanity at large, as the failure of one of these gigantic metropolises, consisting of tens of millions of people, would set off domino consequences for the global economy and all its neighbours in the form of collapsed borders and floods of refugees. It follows that every city on the planet should be planning to avoid such a contingency – and if it isn't, its city councillors should be fired.

From the perspective of food and war, megacity collapse is one of several probable outcomes of major failures in the global food system, the energy supply or any war which precipitated them. It is one for which few, if any, cities or their governments are prepared. The collapse of a major city or urban region would in turn send shockwaves through the entire global food system, causing prices in unaffected cities and regions to skyrocket and requiring the delivery of food aid on a hitherto unimagined scale and over a very short time-frame – mere days. Other existential outcomes such as disease pandemics and wars are likely. Food and conflict thus play into the risk of megacity collapse – and are also one of the unavoidable consequences. The solutions to this issue are dealt with in detail in Chapters 8 and 9.

Uncontrolled Supertechnologies

Humanity has recently developed several ultra-powerful new technologies, over which it presently has no control, and any of which could destroy it. These include artificial intelligence, killer robots and universal surveillance. A great many experienced and wise individuals – such as the late Professor Stephen Hawking, Tesla boss Elon Musk, Microsoft founder Bill Gates, solar pioneer Jeremy Leggett, Oxford University's Nick Bostrom, UK Astronomer Royal Martin Rees and others – have warned about the dangers of uncontrolled supertechnologies in the wrong hands being used for evil purposes. This threat is described more fully in *Surviving the 21st Century*, but here are the key issues.

– Artificial intelligence: machine thinking becomes so smart it not only replaces humans in most roles, but ultimately could decide autonomously that humans are redundant to its own needs.

– Killer robots and drones are widely used by militaries the world over. Some may already be armed with weapons of mass destruction. They are being trained to use 'swarm intelligence' which could, potentially, over-ride human directives, leading to the risk of real wars being started by what we would regard as a computer malfunction or inadequate programming. Or they could be instructed to seek and destroy people of a certain genotype.

- The advent of quantum computers and blockchain herald
  an age in which it will be possible to spy on every person
  on the planet for the whole of their lives, by mining the
  data that already exists in their bank accounts, mobile
  phones and computers, medical records, CCTV, employment
  history, etc. In the wrong hands, this could be used to
  influence or compel people to vote for dictators. In terms
  of human survival, it could be used to enforce beliefs –
  like climate denial – which threaten the very existence
  of humanity.
- Deliberate misuse and/or accidental disasters created by
  biotechnology and nanotechnology, such as the manufacture
  of uncontrollable new lifeforms which prove dangerous,
  or genetically altered humans.

The essential point is that there is no public or ethical oversight
of these ultra-powerful technologies, which are open to exploitation by anyone with the resources and who can afford the
expertise.

They are emerging and evolving far faster than legislators or
regulators can keep up. Without strong public oversight, they
can very easily be used to enslave humanity, silence dissidents or
to control or destroy by various means those whom their over-
seers want controlled or destroyed.

The connection between these supertechnologies and
twentyfirst-century warfare is evident. Most are being developed
as military technologies, not only by democracies where there is
little or no public scrutiny, but also by dictatorships and corporations where there is no public oversight at all. Links with food
include the deployment of artificial intelligence for managing
corporate super-farms (which may or may not be sustainable),
the use of robot swarms and cyber warfare to attack the food
systems of potential enemies, and the use of universal surveillance to silence or deter people who wish to produce food sustainably and who find themselves opposed to the dominance of
oil and coal companies, agribusiness corporates, their puppet
governments and other wielders of power.

The over-arching issue is that use of universal spying systems to subordinate and censor the whole society could very easily silence the warning voices who presently speak out about risks to our future. Such a development would increase the likelihood of human extinction.

Self-Delusion

'The human brain is a complex organ with the wonderful power of enabling man to find reasons for continuing to believe whatever it is that he wants to believe', the French philosopher Voltaire is said to have observed.

This capacity to see our world as we desire it, rather than as it truly exists, is among the greatest of existential dangers to humanity. The four great human belief systems – money, politics, religion and the narratives we tell about ourselves – all tend to ignore the reality of our state in favour of unevidenced belief. Even if we acknowledge threats such as those posed by nuclear weapons, climate change, extinction or famine, very often our beliefs get in the way of our doing enough to solve them. For example, many people who believe in money – a pure figment of the human imagination – tend to think it is more important than the real things which actually keep us alive, like food, soil, water, clean air, intact forests and so on. Since money, being imaginary, is also infinite, it follows that we will exhaust the Earth's finite resources long before we run out of money (unless monetary systems can be somehow brought to recognise this and to regenerate our resources).

By calling on his fellow Catholics to protect the Earth which sustains us in his encyclical *Laudato Si*, Pope Francis provided a shining example of how religious beliefs can be refocussed on human survival – an example many other leading faiths have since begun to adopt.

Similarly, Hollywood, and prominent actors like Leonardo DiCaprio, are using their star-power as well as the movies they make to alert humanity to the risks it now faces.

The real problem is politics. No political belief, no matter how ardent its followers, has ever produced a truly just, compassionate and sustainable society – and none ever will. While many governments have signed up to the Paris Climate Accord, far fewer have signed up to ban nuclear weapons, to clean up the toxic pollution that is engulfing the planet or to end the Sixth Extinction and ecological wipeout now taking place. Twentyfirst-century politics remains fiercely fixated on the small, the local and the trivial – while, for the most part, ignoring the very real threats that could bring down civilisation and the human species. No government, anywhere in the world, yet has a policy for preventing human extinction or ensuring human survival. This is a worry. It is further evidence the nation state has reached its use-by date, as a structure for human self-organisation,[36] and we may need to explore different structures of self-governance if we wish to survive.

Consequently, all ten of the existential risks that humanity now faces will remain unsolved unless human belief systems start to focus on the solutions – and we cease, as a species, to bury our heads in the sand.

In the context of food and war, one of the most obvious and dangerous of delusions is that, because the supermarkets are usually full of food, the global food system is secure and there is nothing to worry about. Anyone who has read this far would be aware from the evidence that this is certainly not the case, now or in the approaching future.

Solving the Risks

Solutions to all these risks exist. All of them are capable of being mitigated and brought under control, through concerted worldwide action and changes in human behaviour, beliefs and consumption habits. The solutions, both for society and each of us as individuals, are set out in *Surviving the 21st Century*.

However, these risks cannot be solved one at a time, as solving one often involves making another risk worse.

For example, if we try to solve the problem of food insecurity by burning more fossil fuels, clearing more land and using more chemicals – as many, including some scientists, advocate – then we will only make the climate risk, the extinction risk, the human health risk and, in the long run, the food security and conflict risks worse.

Therefore, the solutions to existential risk have to be *cross-cutting*. They must mitigate the threat in *all ten* of the main areas of danger. This is the missing element in the global debate. Our scientific habits encourage us to focus on one problem at a time, often to the exclusion of others – and very often the 'solution' turns out to have unforeseen and disastrous downstream consequences.

However, cross-cutting solutions do exist. They include building a circular world economy that wastes nothing, recycles everything, mines nothing anew and no longer pollutes. They include transferring half of global food production back into cities, recycling all their wasted water and nutrients – and then rewilding 25 million square kilometres of the planet to end the Sixth Extinction, under the stewardship of today's farmers and indigenous peoples. They include eliminating the use of all fossil fuels – which will not only reverse global warning, but also end the present poisoning of every child on the planet.

There are two essential solutions without which all others may be in vain.

First, the key to our survival in the twentyfirst century lies in our ability to think wisely, not just as individuals – but as a species.

In the second trimester of a baby's gestation a marvellous thing happens: the cells in the embryonic brain begin to connect – and a mind is born. An inanimate mass of tissue becomes a sentient being, capable of thought, imagination, memory, logic, feelings and dreams.

Today individual humans are connecting, at lightspeed, around a planet – just like the neurons in the foetal brain. We are crossing all the boundaries that formerly divided us.

We are in the process of creating a universal, Earth-sized 'mind'. Through thousands of organisations on the internet and social media, tens of millions of people are now joining hands and sharing ideas, information, values and solutions. Humans are learning to think at supra-human level by applying millions of minds simultaneously to the issues, in real time, by sharing our knowledge freely and by generating faster global consensus on what needs to be done to secure our future.

The citizens of Earth are starting to think and act together – albeit cautiously and often fractiously. But this is still a very wonderful thing. It is an evolution that will drive government, corporations, economic and social institutions as nothing ever has in the past. It is planetary democracy in practice. It will replace the failing nation states, the tyranny of transnationals, the fantasy of world government. It will be unstoppable – and it will decide the human future.

The second essential pillar for human survival is the question of who will lead. In writing previous books on the food crisis and the chemical deluge, it became abundantly clear that most of today's destructive behaviour is primarily by males. It is males, not females, who start wars. Who release the most carbon and toxic chemicals. Who clear-fell the forests, plunder and pollute the oceans, create deserts, slaughter wildlife. Men usually like to solve their problems quickly, using machines, weapons and chemicals – and to hell with the consequences. Men built modern society through the Bronze, Iron and computer ages, and that society is now at risk from its own success.

Women on the other hand, tend to be more cautious. They usually consider the needs of coming generations. They do not, as a rule, start wars or pillage the biosphere. They prefer to nurture, repair, preserve, heal, pacify and educate. This isn't gender stereotyping. It's an observation about how different kinds of humans think. To survive in the twentyfirst century, with ten billion people packed on a hot planet on which all resources and systems are stressed, we will all need to think more like women – and less like traditional males.

To secure the human future, women must lead – in business, politics, religion, society. Just as they have already led, without seeking male permission, by halving the world's birthrate. Instinctually, women understand the dangers of overpopulation and famine. Please note, this isn't an argument about feminism or gender equity. It's about the fundamental *rules for human survival* in this new and threatening world we are creating.

Survival is the one thing you'd imagine most people would agree on. But the issue is almost entirely absent from our political, economic and social discourse. It is as if we, and our leaders, simply do not care whether we survive or not. As a species, we are sleepwalking to disaster.

We need science and social media to alert humanity to the risks we face - and to the fact that there are practical solutions we can all adopt.

And to lead us to a place of safety, the world now needs the Age of Women.

7 FOOD FOR PEACE

Hunger and Conflict – Eco-wars – The Price of War –
Hunger and Peace – Swords into Ploughshares

'Hungry people are not peaceful people.'

Former US President Jimmy Carter

The nightly TV news brings us graphic images of conflicts raging
around the world to chill our blood. Yet the one or two fights
covered on the typical news bulletin are the merest tip of the
iceberg. In 2018, the Environmental Justice Atlas logged more
than 2500 current, separate conflicts – most not necessarily
hot wars – over resources[1], to present a far more detailed picture
of the capacity of humans to dispute over scarce materials,
especially food, land and water (Figure 7.1). There were about
40 actual wars in the first two decades of the twentyfirst
century. The average cost of conflict to the world economy in
this period was about $14 trillion a year – or $5 a day for every
one of us.[2]

A comprehensive study of internal armed conflicts for the
period 1946–2006 found a high percentage were linked to natural
resources: 39 per cent in the Middle East and North Africa, 44 per
cent in Sub-Saharan Africa, 56 per cent in South Asia, and 60 per
cent in East Asia and the Pacific. Of these, conflicts over natural
resource distribution (for example, land access and use rights, or
distribution of revenue) showed the steadiest increase.[3]

The point which can no longer be ignored is humans have
been fighting over food and its resources for at least 17,000 years
and this reflects human nature into the present day. The destiny
of our kind will be governed by it – unless we make radical
changes to the security of our global food system and the nature
of the modern diet, so as to prevent conflict.

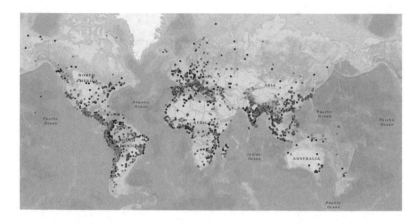

Figure 7.1. Resource conflicts. Source: Environmental Justice Atlas, 2018.

Hunger and Conflict

For decades the operating linear theory of human conflict was that war led to hunger – a monocular view heavily influenced by the experiences of World War I. Many food academics and military experts still cling to the war → hunger model and remain loath to accept the mounting evidence for hunger → war and its vital corollary – that many wars can be prevented by the relatively straightforward expedient of lowering the tensions created by hunger, by assuring equal access to food for all. Nowadays, much authoritative proof has amassed that the food/war equation works both ways. The FAO, for example, stated the following in its 2017 World Hunger Report.

- 'Food insecurity itself can become a trigger for violence and instability, particularly in contexts marked by pervasive inequalities and fragile institutions.'
- 'Sudden spikes in food prices tend to exacerbate the risk of political unrest and conflict, as witnessed in 2007–08 when food riots broke out in more than 40 countries.'
- 'Climate-related events, especially droughts, tend to jeopardize food security in terms of availability and access, which has been found to increase the risk of conflict. This is

particularly the case where deep divisions exist between
population groups or where coping mechanisms
are lacking.'

- 'Competition for natural resources can be detrimental to the
food security of vulnerable rural households, potentially
culminating in conflict.'[4]

Jimmy Carter, both a former US president and a farmer, was
among the first to note – in 1999 – that something big had
shifted in the world's geopolitical gravity field. Writing in the
International Herald Tribune, on the suite of conflicts then prevailing around the world and the contrasting lack of conflict in well-
fed countries, he observed 'The message is clear. There can be no
peace until people have enough to eat. Hungry people are not
peaceful people'.[5]

Carter was commenting on a groundbreaking report from the
Peace Research Institute of Oslo (PRIO) by Indra de Soysa and Nils
Petter Gleditsch, which found that, post the ending of the Cold
War and despite the high hopes for peace, the world was being
swept by a fresh form of conflict: 'the new internal wars,
extremely bloody in terms of civilian casualties, reflect subsistence crises – and are largely apolitical'.[6] In it they concluded:

> *Without cultivating development – a process highly dependent on
> favorable conditions for agricultural production and rural livelihood –
> there can be no sustainable peace. Enhanced productivity will provide
> the burgeoning food needs of a rapidly urbanizing world, especially
> the urban poor, who are easy conscripts of armed violence. The fight
> against hunger, scarcity, environmental pollution, and poverty can
> also convert hapless soldiers of violence into productive members of the
> global community. If prosperity for all is to be harvested in the 21st
> century, then the conditions fostering peace will have to be cultivated.*

One of the most compelling aspects of their report was a map
(Figure 7.2) which recorded the location of conflicts over the
1990s, superimposed on areas of food insecurity. Strikingly, *every*
conflict had taken place in an area of high, or very high, food
insecurity. Even more strikingly, there had been *no* wars at all in

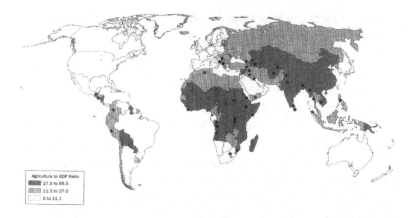

Figure 7.2. Food security and armed conflict in the 1990s. Credit: De Soysa and Gleditsch, 1999.

food-secure regions such as Western Europe, North America and Australasia. The coincidence of war and food insecurity supports both the war → famine and famine → war theories – but the *absence of war* in food secure regions is powerfully supportive of a view that a secure food supply pays off in the form of peace.

Reinforcing the argument was a remarkably similar map (Figure 7.3) produced by the British Ministry of Defence (MoD) a decade later, which showed the coincidence of conflicts in the early twentyfirst century with regions of the planet that were stressed by water scarcity, hunger, agricultural decline, over-population, flooding or all of the above. The reciprocal was also true: places unaffected by these stressors had far fewer conflicts, almost none in fact.

De Soysa and Gleditsch's report was written in a period when the prevailing expert view was that agricultural innovation could solve all the world's food problems – as it was supposed to have done with the Green Revolution in the 1970s – and all that was necessary was to throw more fossil fuels, fertilisers, pesticides, biotechnology and machinery at it. This was a time before the unsettling truth began to dawn that traditional agriculture-based food production is not going to feed ten billion mostly urban people reliably in a hot, climate-stricken world.

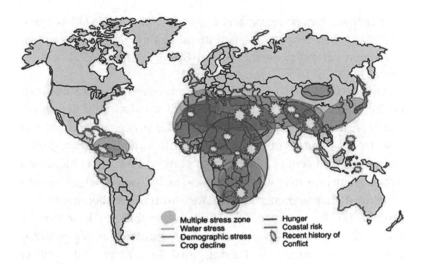

Figure 7.3. Coincidence of stress factors and human conflict.
Source: UK MoD, 2007.

A time before it was fully understood that unconstrained agricultural development devours the very ecosystems that keep it going.

Eco-Wars

The idea that food security and environmental security are intimately interwoven, and that both affect the risk of conflict, has gained wider acceptance in recent times, notably through the work of the UN's Global Environment Facility (GEF), a scientific body that tackles some of the world's most complex and intransigent issues of sustainability. In 1998, Dr Rodger Payne of the University of Louisville wrote a seminal paper for the GEF in which he explained: 'In recent years, a large and growing group of scholars has found that environmental degradation and/or resource scarcities can lead to violent conflict'. He continued:

> To date, global economic development has promoted far more environmental destruction than cleanup (UNEP 1997). Yet, failure to address ecological problems for whatever reason could prove

disastrous, because researchers expect environmentally-induced conflict to "jump sharply in the next decades as scarcities rapidly worsen in many parts of the world" (Homer-Dixon 1994).[7]

Two decades on, the sense of concern over the nexus between ecological collapse, food insecurity and war has only deepened. 'Environmental security views ecological processes and natural resources as sources or catalysts of conflict and barriers or limits to human well-being', a GEF report states.[8] The report identified four dimensions to environmental security, two of which lead to improved environments and greater human wellbeing and two which describe increased risk and vulnerability. These offer a frame through which we can identify countries or regions that are in most danger of lapsing into insecurity and conflict through the degradation of ecosystems, especially those surrounding food and water availability (Figure 7.4).

Although its focus was on delivering better outcomes from environmental restoration projects, especially in conflict-prone regions, the chief significance of this report lies in its recognition that successful and effective environmental restoration *can actually reduce the risk of war*. This is a view which has hitherto lain largely outside conventional military, strategic and resource

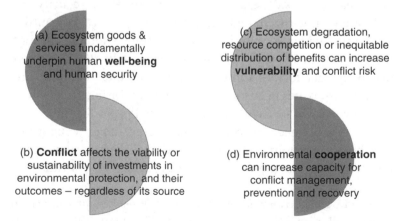

Figure 7.4. How environmental decline affects conflict risk and the converse. Source: Ratner B, GEF 2018.

thinking, which has clung to the old war ⟶ famine model. This preference for a simplistic war ⟶ famine model has led many policymakers to overlook or undervalue the scope for a secure environment and a secure food supply as key peacemakers in both local and international conflicts.

Some, however, take a broader view. Environmental scientist W. Douglas Smith, for example, has stated that from the early twentyfirst century 'Environmental degradation and disruption began to be recognized as a significant cause or magnifier of conflict and breaches in security'. These included impacts such as soil erosion, water scarcity, overfishing, deforestation, pollution (air, water, land), resource depletion and loss of species diversity:[9]

> *The degradation of the environment can cause conflict and a reduction in security; or conflict can destroy the resources and services provided by the environment, which also compromises security… Conflict influences the environment by direct damage as well as by disruption of productivity and responsible environmental and resource practices. Conversely, poor environmental and resource practices can increase vulnerability and the risk of conflict. In either case, the most severe expression of conflict is war.*

Furthermore, the UN's Environmental Cooperation for Peacebuilding Programme (ECPP) has provided solid evidence for the importance of good environmental and natural resources management as an explicit part of the peacemaking process, over an eight-year period from 2008 to 2016. Working from on-ground experience in 60 strife-afflicted countries, it described how sharing natural resources or common environmental threats can be built into a platform for dialogue, confidence-building and cooperation between divided communities or countries. Significantly, it also found the management of natural resources was a perfect way to empower women – the natural peacemakers in most conflict situations.[10] Though chiefly focussed on the use of resources as peace generators in post-conflict situations, the ECPP report also canvassed the role of resource scarcity in the lead-up to, and risk of, conflict.

The Price of War

Every year, on average, the world's taxpayers fork out around US $1.8 trillion with the express aim of killing someone else's taxpayers. That's the global arms budget. Divided equally among us, your personal annual contribution towards engines of violent death is about $230.[11]

If we contrast this with the effort the world puts into feeding itself better, the agricultural and food research budget – public and private – amounts to little more than $69 billion.[12] Or, for you personally, about $9.

That makes you the proud member of a species that devotes 25 times more fiscal effort to finding better ways to kill itself than it does better ways to feed itself.

Most likely, it will succeed.

While some may be inclined to point out that comparing arms spending with food research spending is a bit of an apples-and-oranges analogy, it is nevertheless a disturbing reflection of *Homo sapiens'* current sense of its priorities. Where, in history, can you find a time when the quest for superior killing machines so far outran society's efforts to secure and sustain its food supply?

Of course, the balance is not evenly distributed. In 2019 the USA headed the list of defence spenders with $716 billion a year, followed by China with $224 billion, Saudi Arabia with $70 billion and the UK, India and Russia with around $45–47 billion apiece. On the other hand, 120 countries lavish less than $1 billion each on their militaries.[13]

Just how this massive over-investment in engines of destruction will play out is the subject of much perfervid speculation in the grand strategy community. Various scenarios involving cyber warfare, killer robots, space weapons, artificial intelligence, biotechnology and sundry 'drones' on land, sea and air are gleefully dissected by the pundits – the essence being that atoms (in the form of soldiers, tanks, planes, ships, etc.) are being progressively replaced by electrons and photons as the tools of future war.[14] What this means, at core, is that the old idea of 'battlelines', 'fronts' and defined theatres of war will progressively be replaced by planet-wide combat between the contenders, even if they happen to be next-door neighbours. From now on, the whole Earth is the battleground. And if cyber war does not settle the issues, there are still nukes and conventional explosives to fall back on. What the consequences will be for civilians, innocent or participating, are still speculative – collapsed energy grids, water and food supplies are among the likely outcomes – but nothing good, that's for sure.

Military scholars are divided on the amount of conflict we can expect. Some project that, on the basis of trends since the ending of the Cold War, the number and scale of conflicts will continue to slowly diminish.[15] Others, like Canadian journalist Gwynne Dyer and German scholar Professor Harald Welzer, both of whom authored books entitled *Climate Wars*, anticipate that warfare in the twentyfirst century will escalate, primarily due to climate change, and over the shortages of water and food that will flow from it. Also, it will involve the biggest refugee crises in human history.[16]

Welzer, in particular, contends that the twentieth-century motivations of national territory, religion and economics will take second place to concerns about survival in the face of collapsing resources and food supplies, in a reversion to the brute survival struggles of the past. 'Ideology will always be a surface-level justification for conflict ... but if you look deeply at the source of future conflicts, I think you'll see a basic resource conflict at the bottom of it all', he said.[17] He told journalist Sean Illing:

> *The thesis is very simple: that you always have a higher potential for violent conflict when the survival conditions of groups of people are threatened. This is a very basic principle. My original question was: if all these scientists and climate researchers are right, or even close to right, what does it mean for greater potential for violent conflict? And I think the answers are not encouraging. You can see this when you look at events that are already happening, like land conflicts due to desertification, or various resource conflicts around the world. But it's important to remember that the causal links between climate and conflict are rarely direct.*

Violence, Welzer argues, is a constant in human affairs (at least, so long as men are in charge[18]). More resource conflicts will thus probably lead to a spike in violence.

As the world's foremost military spender, with almost a third of the global arms budget, America also devotes more thinktank time to predicting the future of conflict[19] – yet seems constantly to find itself wrongfooted by history. Over the past half-century it has regularly been embarrassed, if not actually defeated, by opponents far less well-accoutred but more agile and practiced in the arts of 'asymmetric warfare', as the David-and-Goliath contest is known among the pundits. The USA lost out to Vietnamese patriot zeal, stumbled into an Iraqi and terrorism quagmire significantly of its own making, was constantly frustrated by the religious fanatics of the Taliban, was briefly stymied by the Facebook warriors of ISIL and was, rather shockingly, confounded by an assault on its own democratic processes by Vladimir Putin's cyber punks. The explanation for all this self-inflicted humiliation may lie with the American dream of martial glory. Many of its sons grew up imagining themselves there, at the high tide of the Confederacy, as Pickett's ragged and desperate soldiery hurled themselves at the unwavering blue of the Union lines at Gettysburg. This warlike iconography was gilded by subsequent US conquests in Western Europe (World War I and World War II) and the Pacific, which were represented to Americans chiefly as national victories rather than the shared Allied successes they in fact were. The historical irony is that success in war engendered in America a strikingly similar militaristic fantasy to those that had brought both Germany and Japan undone – the conviction that sheer might and soldierly excellence made it invincible. It then spent the next half century being taught by tiny forces it despised that this was not so.

Consequently, American defence policy today is still founded squarely – and wastefully – on the same old delusion: the more arms you have, the more victorious you are. Desperate to relive the glories of yesteryear, the USA over-arms to fight a conventional war that will probably never be fought. Thus, it spends nearly three times the amount of its nearest rival, China, on armaments and 16 times that of its next rival, Russia. And its example is emulated, widely and pointlessly, by many other countries in terms of what is actually required for self-defence. America's overinvestment in armaments compels others to do likewise, and the economic and political clout of its weapons makers – Eisenhower's notorious 'military-industrial complex'[20] – both over the US Government itself and over the world trade in arms, is like a new Iron Curtain raised against world peace.

In time, perhaps when it ceases to prize military grandeur above other qualities, America may come to appreciate – as it has at other times in history – that peace is won, not by guns but by brains, fair trade and goodwill. This is an urgent lesson for all humanity, too, because the source of peace lies in food, not war. And America, when it avoids over-industrialisation, is very good at food.

Hunger and Peace

In 2014, the executive secretary of the UN Convention to Combat Desertification (UNCCD) Monique Barbut issued an exemplary statement of the case that food and environmental insecurity leads to war:

> *When land degradation reaches a level at which it seriously threatens people's livelihoods, it can turn into a security issue. This is because land is so closely linked to basic human needs, such as access to food and water. If land degradation interferes with the fulfilment of these needs, it can lead to conflicts over scarce land and water resources, spark food riots or turn smallholder farmers into refugees.[21]*

She continued:

> *It is striking that many of today's violent conflicts are taking place in countries with vulnerable dry ecosystems. Syria, Mali and Darfur are just a few examples. I believe that this issue urgently needs to be addressed – by national and international policy-makers and*

researchers alike. That's why I have put the investigation of the connection between land degradation and conflict high on the UNCCD's agenda.

But Barbut took her argument a significant step further. 'The Great Green Wall for the Sahara and Sahel Initiative is bringing a coordinated and harmonised response to food security and peace', she said.

When complete, The Great Green Wall is envisioned as the 'largest living structure on the planet'. Modelled on a parallel venture by China designed to repair years of deforestation during Mao Zedong's Cultural Revolution and obsession with steel making, the Great Green Wall of Africa was conceived by the African Union as a 7700 kilometre belt of trees, covering 50 million hectares and costing $4 billion to plant, in order to halt the inexorable southward march of the Sahara desert in the region known as the Sahel.[22] Researchers argue over both its design and execution, but generally acknowledge the fight against the world's largest desert to be worthwhile.[23]

Barbut in particular contends the Great Green Wall and projects like it are already delivering a peace dividend, pointing out that such solutions are far cheaper than fighting wars or coping with huge refugee crises:

Proactive solutions (e.g., sustainable land management and ecosystem restoration) that reduce the extent and degree of land degradation can often be cheaper and more effective than relying on crisis management, humanitarian relief, and military means to address the resulting challenges. Improving the well-being of the rural poor and other land-dependent communities will enhance overall human security and help ensure international stability today and in the future.[24]

An 'unassuming veterinary project' to improve the health of cattle belonging to violently feuding herders in the Ethiopia/South Sudan/Kenya/Uganda border region had helped bring peace and co-operation where years of efforts by government negotiators and well-meaning aid donors had failed, reported Blake Ratner and colleagues. They argued that collective action around shared natural resources can assist in transforming bitter competition and violence into peaceable and resilient societies and environments.[25] As the GEF's Blake Ratner and Virginia Gorsevski sum it up: 'In developing countries where access to, and use of, renewable resources essential to rural livelihoods are highly contested, improving cooperation in their management is increasingly seen as an important element in strategies for conflict prevention, confidence building and longer-term social-ecological resilience'.[26]

The GEF also noted that of more than 800 peace agreements forged since 1945, fewer than 15 per cent had addressed issues related to natural resources. 'Fortunately, in recent decades, these trends have improved. While roughly half of all peace agreements concluded between 1989 and 2004 (51 out of 94) contain direct provisions on natural resources, all major agreements from 2005 to 2014 contain such provisions', it says. This amounts to compelling evidence for a view that peacemakers around the world are now far more conscious of the connection between food, natural resources and war – and in their efforts to prevent future conflict are writing them into treaties and armistices. Words on paper, however, cannot alone do the job: that requires investment.

Swords into Ploughshares

'They shall beat their swords into ploughshares, and their spears into pruning-hooks; nation shall not lift up sword against nation, neither shall they learn war any more', quoth the Biblical book of Isaiah.

Likewise, the Roman dictator Lucius Quinctius Cincinnatus, summoned from his plough to give the troublesome Aequian tribe a good thrashing, promptly returned to his fields as soon as the fighting was over, bequeathing his name and example to the modern US city of Cincinnati. People in the ancient world clearly understood what to do with all that scrap metal once peace was restored – turn it into food. They also had a clear-eyed appreciation – because they mostly grew their own food and did not buy it in supermarkets – of which was the more

important application. This issue now lies at the very fulcrum of
the human destiny in the twentyfirst century: are we still smart
enough to do the same?

For most of the 2010s the Global Campaign on Military
Spending (GCMS) called for a 10 per cent reduction in military
expenditure in all countries.[27] 'Global military spending has
increased to $1739 billion in 2017, according to the Stockholm
International Peace Research Institute. This amount of
resources being directed to rearmament is morally bankrupt',
declared Annette Brownlie, Chair of the Independent and
Peaceful Australia Network, which supports the Global Campaign. 'Funds that are now spent in the military are urgently
needed to reduce inequalities, to increase worldwide cooperation, to remove energy injustices, to focus on the causes that
generate huge numbers of refugees and displaced people, to
implement people-based global market regulations and to build
a peaceful world.' The statement spoke of directing more government money away from military ends and towards human
needs. In particular, it urged greater investment in conflict
prevention – while noting, somewhat despairingly, that whenever there was a call for greater 'defence' spending, there was
seldom any real political debate or argument against it.

That such a reduction is well within the power of governments to achieve is amply substantiated in Figure 7.5, in which
SIPRI (Stockholm International Peace Research Institute) documents world arms spending in constant dollars. After a 32 per
cent drop to the mid 1990s, it rose again by at least 70 per cent
through the 2010s – for no tangible increase in world peace, as
the following figure suggests.

This second graph, Figure 7.6, shows that violent deaths in
conflict in fact increased in the 2010s, in parallel with the
increase in arms spending. At the very least, this undermines
the claim that more arms mean more peace. The opposite,
indeed. Taken together, both graphs indicate it is possible to
have more peace at a far lower level of arms spending, for that
is exactly what happened between 1990 and 2010.

Can it really be possible to achieve both goals – better defence
and greater human wellbeing?

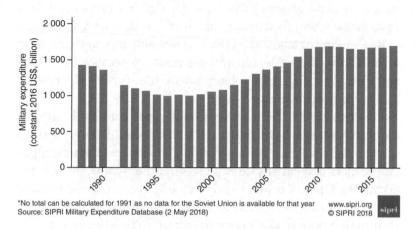

Figure 7.5. World military spending in US$ billions, 1988–2017. Source: SIPRI, 2018.

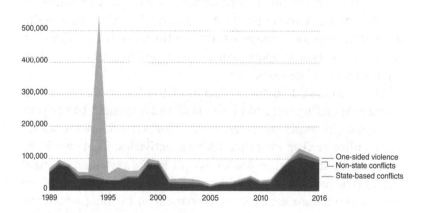

Figure 7.6. Violent deaths in conflict, 1989–2016. Source: UCDP/PRIO. (The spike is the Rwanda massacre.) Note: State-based conflict is between at least two named organisations, where at least one was the government of a state. Non-state conflict is between two named non-state organisations. One-sided violence is that between a named organisation and civilians, such as genocides.

The weight of the evidence advanced in this book is that such an aim is entirely achievable – by recognising investment in a sustainable global food supply as, in effect, defence spending.

By thinking of landscape repair, renewable food systems, food science, recycling of water and nutrients as weapons of peace and plenty, especially in a dangerously hot, turbulent, stressed and overcrowded world.

By thinking of them as legitimate, powerful, ethical and highly affordable ways to reduce the risk of conflicts ever getting started. As means for soothing public passions which unscrupulous leaders may otherwise exploit – in other words, as tools for taking the wind of popular support out of the sails of dictators, warlords, insurgents, terrorists and belligerent politicians by eliminating hunger as a major source of public discontent.

It is also important for the public to understand that the weapons which won World War II are not the type of weapons likely to bring peace in the twentyfirst century, any more than the muskets of the nineteenth century would have prevailed in the twentieth century. For that, humanity needs a new definition of 'weaponry' – one more akin to the ploughshare than the sword. These new weapons will be described in the two concluding chapters of this book.

Let us imagine that the ambition of the Global Campaign on Military Spending were to be realised and a modest 10 per cent cut made in world arms budgets. This would release about $174 billion a year for other human activities. That would be enough, for instance, to double world R&D investment in food and agriculture (from $70 billion to $140 billion), to meet the annual $80 billion net capital investment in farming which the FAO considers is necessary to make the world hunger-free[28], and still have $24 billion left over to develop novel, climate-proof urban food systems to feed the megacities.

While the peace-dividend from such an investment is not easy to predict, there is already a great deal of on-the-ground evidence from the work of UN and non-government aid agencies in conflict zones that it would be considerable – and certainly far more than the peace dividend from the same value in shiny new weapons.

Applied across the seven hotspot regions for likely future food wars described in Chapter 5, investing $174 billion a year in food, not war, would significantly reduce the risk of conflict in all seven – especially in South Asia, Africa, Central Asia and Latin America.

On the basis of recent military budgets America would have $70–80 billion to redirect towards agricultural and food science – a field in which it excels. It might build four fewer aircraft carriers, for example, but would experience significantly more peace and growth in commerce, along with reduced migration pressures, in its own hemisphere and Asia especially. China might field five fewer squadrons of jet fighter aircraft – but be able to plough $15 billion into ensuring a renewable high-tech food supply to its megacities in the mid century as well as taking its food pressure off Africa. India and Pakistan would have $6 billion a year extra to devote to making sure a nuclear war never breaks out between them over food and water. And the European Union would have $22 billion extra a year to invest in ensuring its member countries do not vanish beneath a tide of hundreds of millions of desperate African refugees, by helping Africans to secure their own food supplies in a climate-menaced world.

A cut of 20 per cent in world arms purchases would give global civilisation a third of a trillion dollars a year extra to spend on peace through food. For those who may be tempted to object that such a cut is too heavy, the timeline of world defence spending (Figure 7.3) makes it abundantly clear that a real cut of 32 per cent was achieved between 1995 and 2005 – and that this was accompanied by a global reduction in carnage. Cuts of 20–40 per cent in defence spending are, arguably, entirely feasible without loss of either global or national security.

The money saved at that time went back into most countries' general revenue, so its benefits are hard to trace. Under the *Food or War* initiative, proposed in this book, *all* monies saved from defence will be redeployed exclusively to aspects of peace-through-food (including environmental repair) – thereby serving both defence and food security aims.

A cut of a third of a trillion dollars is a fraction of the savings in arms spending by countries worldwide during the peaceful era from 1995 to 2005. It is the equivalent of around 0.4 per cent of world gross domestic product. It is just 2.5% of the annual cost of war. It is just $46 a year for each of us.

Surely $46 is a very small sum to invest in the survival of our grandchildren? Is there a rational parent on the planet who would not spend it, if assured the money would be devoted to that end?

Besides securing the world food supply, such a sum opens the way to solving one of the greatest existential threats confronting the whole of civilisation – extinction and environmental collapse. This threat was outlined in Chapter 6, and in more detail in Chapter 2 of *Surviving the 21st Century*. The essential challenge is described by Harvard biologist E. O. Wilson in his book *Half Earth*, in which he makes the case that 'if we conserve half the land and sea, the bulk of biodiversity will be protected from extinction'.[29] Setting aside half the planet for the other life we share it with would be sufficient to afford protection to 84 per cent of the Earth's species, Wilson and his fellow biologists project, on the basis of recent experience in managing large nature reserves.[30]

If 20 per cent of world arms spending were redeployed to solving this problem, we would have a very good chance of ending the Sixth Extinction, warding off ecological collapse, protecting the very ecological services that give us clean air and water, creating a climate-resilient food supply and reducing significantly the tensions between competing groups that lead to war.

Key solutions therefore include the following.

1. To transfer up to half of global food production back into cities, using their recycled water and nutrients and novel food production systems (Chapter 8), and introduce eco-agriculture in the remainder (Chapter 9).
2. To 'rewild' 25 million square kilometres of the planet's land area, under the stewardship of existing farmers and indigenous people, for the preservation and renewal of the

earth's terrestrial biosystems and their services, and the removal of carbon from the atmosphere.

3. To end the avalanche of toxic chemicals which humans currently release and which are poisoning ourselves, our children and all life on Earth (Chapter 6).

A major advantage of a 'peace through food' defence strategy over conventional thinking is that it offers huge spinoff benefits which weapons do not. These include economic and social development, environmental sustainability and, most importantly, the increased societal stability which creates a platform for sound governance in nations and regions prone to insurgencies and government failures.

Clearly, if $340 billion extra were made available every year for peace through food, there would be much debate on how best to spend it (Figure 7.7). Based on the evidence in this book, here is a notional allocation.

• Research into eco-agriculture and novel urban food systems, technology development and dissemination – $60 billion.

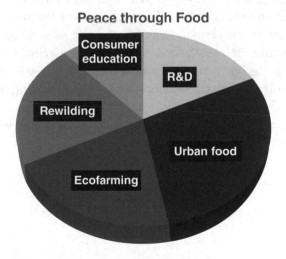

Figure 7.7. Proposed allocation of investment to Global Peace through Food Initiative. Source: J. H. J. Cribb, 2019.

- Capital investment in recycling of urban water and nutrients and development of urban food production units – $100 billion.

- Transition to regenerative eco-agriculture (and carbon storage) in the best areas of farming and grazing land worldwide – $70 billion.

- 'Rewilding' of marginal farming lands, hill country, etc., in all regions to conserve biodiversity, lock up carbon and reduce conflict. Funding of indigenous people and former farmers as Earth Stewards – $70 billion.

- Education of consumers worldwide to choose foods that are healthy *and* sustainable, including a Year of Food in every junior school on the planet – $40 billion.

This budget, it must be borne in mind, is *additional* to the world's existing investments in agriculture, conservation, food technology, nutrition and preventative healthcare – which would continue – and would supplement all of these activities from both government and private sources.

In military terms, this would achieve the most essential aim in all of human history – to place the *budget* for the survival, peace and sustenance of civilisation on a 'war footing'.

In more pacific terms, it would echo the scale of investment made during the 1960s and 1970s in the Green Revolution, which was designed to overcome a food crisis in which a third of humanity at the time went hungry. Reallocating a fifth of today's arms spending to peace through food would help bring on the 'double green revolution' which has long been spoken of.[31]

8 URBAN DREAMS AND NIGHTMARES

Homo urbanus – The Nutrient Crisis – Urban Food
Loops – Green Cities – Urban Permaculture – Stewards
of the Earth – Wise Consumers

*'Only by safeguarding Nature's resilience can we hope to have a
resilient form of food production and ensure food security in the long
term.'*

HRH Charles, Prince of Wales

By the start of the 2020s the world's cities were a ravenous mouth,
bolting down 14 quadrillion calories of food every single day. They
were a colossal throat gulping 1.5 trillion tonnes of water a year.

They then proceeded to throw it in the garbage, down the
sewer or drain. Enough nutriment and water to sustain
4,500,000,000 people, just thrown away.

People think of cities as vibrant centres of population, miracles of architecture and design, humming centres of industry
and culture, seats of government, places of entertainment, leis-
ure and learning. In fact, the modern city is an engine of colossal, mindless waste.

Unlike their predecessors through history, most cities cannot
feed themselves. Not even close.

Once upon a time, pigs, goats and chickens roamed the
streets, vegetable plots and rice paddies separated the buildings,
people grew fruit in their gardens and allotments, kept rabbits,
guinea pigs and bees. That is nearly all gone today, swept into
the dustbin of history by the sterile, concrete dreams of two
generations of urban planners, architects and developers.

The world's cities' food arrives daily, in a river of fossil-fuelled
trucks, ships and planes, on average from 2000 kilometres away.
A river which, should its flow ever falter or cease, would see tens

of millions starving by the end of the week, such is the just-in-time character of the twentyfirst-century food chain. This is a nightmare that few city governments have even contemplated – and for which none are prepared. Everyone just assumes the food and water will keep on flowing – come hell, climate-driven high water, war or oil shock.

What happens when it doesn't is evident in the 11 million refugees who quit the ruined cities of Syria in the wake of its civil war, half of whom fled the country sending shockwaves across Europe and the Middle East. It is evident in the horrendous events of the *Holodomor* in the Ukraine, Kazakhstan and parts of Russia in the 1920s and 1930s, and the outcome of the 1940s German Hunger Plan, the siege of Leningrad, the failure of Japan to feed its soldiers and the Soviet invasion of East Germany at the end of World War II, in all of which cannibalism was rampant among the starving populace.

This, however, is a risk which no modern city in the twentyfirst century needs to take, if it does not wish to.

For if they are vast devourers of nutrients and water, cities are at the same time equally vast wellsprings of these two most basic elements of human survival. They are food mines of the future.

If the millions of tonnes of raw nutrients – phosphorus, nitrogen, potash, minerals and other micronutrients – and the billions of tonnes of water now being squandered in landfills, drains and sewers were to be harvested, cleansed of toxins and pathogens, and then reused to generate new food, cities would become the basis for an entirely sustainable way of feeding themselves. One that can weather even an overheating climate.

Homo urbanus

More than anything, the twentyfirst century is the era of the city. Fiftyfive per cent of the human population are already urbanites. By the 2060s this is liable to grow to two thirds, or even three quarters – between seven and eight billion souls.

The largest megacity on the planet is the Pearl River Delta region around Guangzhou-Shenzen, in southern China, which harboured 58 million residents in its nine component 'cities' in 2015 according to the World Bank, and a total of 120 million residents in their combined greater metropolitan area, according to the UN Regional Settlements Programme.

By 2030, the UN forecasts that the world will have 41 megacities, each holding more than 10 million inhabitants. These will include:
– Mumbai, India, 42 million inhabitants
– Tokyo, Japan, 37 million
– New Delhi, India, 36 million
– Dhaka, Bangladesh, 35 million
– Kinshasa, DR Congo, 35 million
– Kolkata, India, 33 million
– Lagos, Nigeria, 32 million
– Karachi, Pakistan, 32 million
– Shanghai, China, 31 million
– Manila, Philippines, 30 million
– Beijing, China, 28 million
– Mexico City, 25 million
– New York, 25 million.[1]

Each of these vast conurbations is a disaster in waiting – some more so than others. And when it happens, a universally online humanity will be able to watch its horrors unfolding live, on our smart devices. It is an event such as this that may finally awaken us to take belated action on the existential threats that engulf us (Chapter 6). How belated remains to be seen.

However, cities are important for another reason: they concentrate humanity into a small area allowing more to be set aside to keep nature and the Earth system functioning. Provided, of course, that their footprint on the wider planet can also be constrained to that area – which is not the case today. Reusing all their wasted nutrients and water, as well as other resources, makes this possible.

The Nutrient Crisis

The world's cities hold answers to global hunger, climate instability and war but first they and their citizens need to decide whether they are part of the solution – or part of the problem. One of their greatest future roles in piloting humanity through the peak of human population – likely to occur in the late 2060s – is in the recycling of urban nutrients and water back into locally grown food.

The idea of re-using nutrients is scarcely new. In Homer's 3000-year-old tale, the Greek hero Odysseus, when he finally returns to his island home of Ithaca afters 20 years' absence at the Trojan war and wandering the seas, finds his old dog Argos dying on the 'heaps of mule and cow dung that lay in front of the stable doors till the men should come and draw it away to manure the great close'. Every mediaeval farmstead had its 'dunghill' in the yard, on which the cock so proudly crowed, consisting of animal and human manure, crop and kitchen wastes, composting quietly into fertility to be forked back onto the fields again come springtime. The Chinese, famously, had their 'night soil' collectors who carted urban ordure back to fertilise the rice paddies. Re-using nutrients is a thrifty human custom that probably dates back to Stone Age cave-dwellers and the very first farmers, when people would have noticed a more vigorous crop of wild grains sprouting on the rubbish dump at the mouth of the home cave. Thereafter, for the whole of history until the twentieth century, the idea of continually cycling fertility was the dominant paradigm. Human food, broadly, went round and round in a never-ending circle, reducing the amount that had to be gathered from the wild. In parts of the world, untouched by modern technical agriculture, it still does.

The development of industrial fertilisers and discovery of the Nobel prizewinning Haber–Bosch chemical process for fixing nitrogen from the air in the early 1900s put an end to all that. It ushered in the Age of Waste. An age when it was acceptable to mine the most important nutrients, distribute them in inefficient ways that squander up to 90 per cent of them, and pollute rivers, streams, lakes, the atmosphere and oceans with them. People nowadays recoil at the thought (and probable smell) of mediaeval cities, where a broad-brimmed hat was essential because householders were in the habit of flinging the contents of their chamber pots from upper-storey windows into the street where, if it missed pedestrians, it lay and festered until a downpour washed it away. Unfortunately, modern humanity is still doing much the same thing with its nutrients – but to an entire planet, where the consequences may be less noisome but are equally serious. In the Middle Ages the most common outcome was pestilence: today it is ecological collapse, caused by *eutrophia* – an overconcentration of nutrients.

In their famous papers on Planetary Boundaries – the Earth's limits we ought not to exceed for our own safety – Johan Rockstrom, Will Steffen and their 26 scientific colleagues from around the world used a simple traffic light diagram (Figure 8.1)

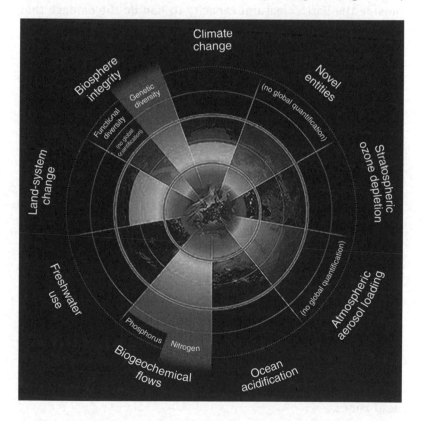

Figure 8.1. Safe Planetary Boundaries – humans have already crossed four of them. Credit: Felix Pharand-Deschenes/Globaia.

to illustrate how close we are to those limits – or how far beyond them we have already overshot. Those in the outer circles mean real danger, those in the middle circles, strong risk, those in the innermost circles mean we are probably still OK.[2]

Climate change, for example is halfway through the middle circle, meaning we are well outside the safe zone and halfway to a state where it is going to be difficult for the Earth to support human life, certainly at present levels. Likewise, land-system change – the deforestation, soil and water degradation and loss of ecological services discussed earlier – is well beyond safe.

Now look at the Extinction and Nitrogen/Phosphorus segments. These are far into the outer circle, meaning we are well outside the Earth's natural capacity to handle the damage that humans are doing to it. We are producing such an excess of nitrogen (N) from agriculture, livestock, use of fertilisers and burning fossil fuels as to risk poisoning our whole living environment. Likewise, phosphorus (P), mainly from modern fertilisers. On average we are pumping 150 million tonnes of N per year and 20 million tonnes of P into the Earth system, which would not be happening without human agency. This cosmic-scale excretion could double by the 2060s, if conventional agriculture was doubled to meet food needs – and is a salient reason why traditional agriculture *cannot* remain the sole source of human food: it simply leaks and wastes too many nutrients. Add to that 15 billion tonnes of carbon dioxide and 5 million tonnes of toxic pesticides from today's food system and the scale of its chemical impact on the planet becomes clearer.

N and P are nutrients essential to life. Every living cell in your body and all the microbes, plants and animals on Earth need them to survive. But when supplied in excess they tend to favour algae over animals or humans. Unchecked, they will slowly return the Earth system to its primordial slime-bath state, killing off life in the oceans, as their oxygen is stripped by bacteria. This is already happening in the world's 400+ aquatic dead zones.

The solution to such a vast act of nutrient pollution is plain: it is to stop releasing new N and P – and start re-using the old.

That's where cities come in. They are enormous collectors and traps for nutrients. Nearly two thirds of the nutrients used by humanity flow through our cities, mostly in the form of food and its wastes. These are then usually mixed with water and dumped back into rivers, lakes, aquifers and the ocean to create havoc with the local ecology, hurled into landfills together with toxic industrial wastes that make them unusable in future or else dried as biosolids. Often, they form stinking 'fatbergs', foul concretions of fats and kitchen sludge that clog and choke urban sewers.[3] Because human waste contains toxic heavy metals as well as disease-causing organisms, it is rarely used directly in modern agriculture any longer. Typically, according to the marvellously titled *Global Atlas of Excreta*, sewage sludge contains 4–7 per cent P, 2–4 per cent N and 0.5 per cent potash (K), plus a bundle of valuable micronutrients – meaning it is pretty useful as plant food, were it not for the toxins.[4] Then there is the one third of our food which is thrown away uneaten and which mostly goes to landfill – but which also contains vast amounts of N, P, K and micronutrients. In theory, then, the world's cities are processing around 70 million tonnes of nitrogen and 10 million tonnes of phosphorus a year as well as a host of other essential food elements, all of which can be reused to feed and sustain humanity, but which under present management are mostly squandered.

Since the P used in agricultural fertiliser is extracted from mines, which run out, and the N is extracted from the atmosphere using natural gas, which is also finite, the world supply of raw nutrients risks running into serious shortages by the mid century. At the very least, this means fertilisers will become so expensive that many farmers, especially in developing countries, may not be able to afford them, and the consequent yield losses will affect the price and supply of food for everyone. The report *Our Nutrient World* describes the dilemma:

> *Without swift and collective action, the next generation will inherit a world where many millions may suffer from food insecurity caused by too few nutrients, where the nutrient pollution threats from too much*

will become more extreme, and where unsustainable use of nutrients
will contribute even more to biodiversity loss and accelerating climate
change.[5]

The bottom line here is that cities contain one of the Earth's
most precious resources – a potentially inexhaustible supply of
nutrients from which to make new food. Provided we simply
recycle them.

Urban Food Loops

'Food is a metabolic circuit closer. Our urban waste streams,
when properly managed, could act as its feedstock', comments
Oscar Rodriguez FRSA, a British architect who runs an international discussion group on *LinkedIn* about novel urban food
production systems and building designs.

Inspired by trends in rooftop gardens, Rodriguez decided to
estimate how much of its own food London could produce if it
dedicated its combined 1572 square kilometres of roof space to
growing vegetables. The answers were intriguing. He found that
just putting planter boxes on available spare space on London
roofs could supply up to 6 per cent of the city's fresh fruit and
vegetable needs within a matter of days. If *all* of London's roof
space were farmed, it could supply 730,000 tonnes of fruit and
vegetables, or nearly two thirds of the city's needs, from a mix of
private and commercial horticulture. If this growing system
used modern hydroponics (see Chapter 9) it could furnish nearly
a million tonnes of fresh produce, around 84 per cent of the
city's needs. [6]

And finally, using the most advanced intensive food production methods currently available, Rodriguez projected that
London could – in theory – supply much of the fresh produce
required by the whole of England, about 5 million tonnes.

While theoretical yield projections tend to disappoint in reality, they nevertheless offer a target to aim for – and a strong
notion of what may be possible if the world's city planners,
scientists and food producers put their heads together on the

question of how best to reuse nutrients and water. Furthermore, the Rodriguez estimates are all based on conventional rooftop crop growing practices, and do not include the more high-tech forms of production such as vertical farms, biocultures and algae farming. With these, London's actual food yield could be considerably higher.

The main limitations to growing such enormous quantities of food in urban areas are twofold: light and nutrients. Since every city already imports enough food to feed itself and manages to waste at least a third of it, then it theoretically handles enough nutrients to meet 130 per cent of its food needs, provided it can recapture and reuse them all. In other words, every city on the planet can potentially feed itself, provided it recycles all its organic 'waste'. Furthermore, by ceasing to import much of its food and 'eating local', each city will reduce by 20 per cent or more its total greenhouse emissions, by cutting out much of the need for long transport, storage, re-handling and refrigeration chains.

Sunlight is a different matter. Cities, because of their limited area, can never receive as many solar photons as the extensive wheatfields of Canada, the Ukraine or Australia, or even East Anglia, so, since plants require light to grow and photosynthesise (to convert solar energy into food) other techniques must be employed. These may range from importing electricity for LED lighting of greenhouses from solar and wind farms (using HVDC powerlines), to growing plants on the sides as well as the roofs of buildings, to coating all building windows with solar films to generate power for extra lighting, to the use of 'light pipes' to transport photons within buildings direct to basement and multi-storey farms, to growing strategic mixes of C-3 and C-4 plants which make better use of available light, to more speculative scientific advances such as artificial photosynthesis (the direct chemical conversion of sunlight to hydrocarbons and carbohydrates, or edible calories[7]) or genetically modifying the natural photosynthetic reaction itself within food plants to augment its efficiency (which is very low). Urban 'farms' using artificial light are already taking off, especially in Scandinavia and northern Europe, where daylight is limited for half the year.[8] Suffice to say there are a great many promising options for improving the global yield of food from sunlight – and if the world were to put the same imagination and R&D effort into them as it has done into renewable energy, then the problem would soon be solved.

Water is a potentially limiting factor in the world's dry regions, but since cities even there discard enormous quantities of water daily, recycling offers a good solution, which can be supplemented by solar-powered desalination of saline ground-water or seawater, floating farms, greenhouses that catch and recycle plant-transpired water, or the use of fog catchers and evaporation traps. Since much urban food production is likely to take place indoors, the scope for recapturing the water used by plants and lost when they transpire it, and thus recycling their irrigation water, is high.

The chief objection to reincorporating human sewage sludge, biosolids or even effluent water into food chains is the risk of disease or of concentrating the toxic heavy metals that they contain, usually in trace amounts. Both issues can be overcome with advanced technologies. First, waste water can be filtered to exclude bacteria, viruses and chemical salts using basic solar desalination technology or treated by other means, such as ultraviolet light, to kill pathogens. Secondly, a wide array of methods is coming on stream to immobilise heavy metals such as mercury, cadmium and arsenic, including cleverly modified clays and filters which attract and lock up these toxins, or the use of particular strains of plants, algae or microbes to 'phytomine' – or preferentially extract – them. Furthermore, raw nutrients saved from urban waste streams do not have to be used directly in food production – but rather to feed long nutrient chains that start with algae and proceed up through crops and insects to meat and milk animals, poultry and fish. These chains can either dilute toxins to safe levels or else have built-in filtration stages. Also, importantly, human sewage con-tains valuable micronutrients – essential in the diet to prevent disease – and it is critical these are conserved for reuse and not wasted, since the world's heavily cropped soils are now becoming depleted in these substances. With a bit of creativity and inventiveness, the twentyfirst-century metropolis can readily redevelop itself as the high-tech equivalent of Odysseus' compost heap – a source of reliable nutriment for all time to come.

Importantly, cities which grow most of their own food can avoid the greatest threat of all – a climate disaster affecting the world grain harvest on several continents, like the one which sparked the French Revolution. In the modern era, such a severe event may threaten some cities with collapse in their food supplies, bread especially. However, with extensive greenhouse culture, 'protected cropping' and vertical farms, urban food is likely to be largely free from climatic impacts such as droughts, floods, heatwaves and insect plagues. It is an important way to keep 'farming' in the Century of Climate Change.

Green Cities

For much of the twentyfirst century, discussion and debate around 'green cities' has focussed on issues such as green spaces, aesthetics, social benefits and urban renewal. It is time those running the debate awoke to the fact that the survival of human civilisation is also on the line, not just its trimmings.[9]

The modern city is an amazing, wonderful place – but it is also a disaster waiting to happen, should its food or water supply fail, or warfare disrupt it. In the coming decades no city can legitimately lay claim to the descriptors 'green' or 'sustainable' unless it has also planned and built a renewable food supply and the reuse of nutrients and water, into its urban plan. Unless its streets and buildings – instead of being a sterile, windy, concrete-and-glass graveyard designed by people obsessed with geometry – become a functioning ecosystem in which the 'urban jungle' more closely resembles a real jungle, abundant with plant life, birds, insects and fresh food and the constant cycling of its resources. Unless the city pulls its weight in helping to curb human conflict by replacing scarcity with food security for all. And unless it makes a material contribution to ending the Sixth Extinction.

These qualities of the renewable city of the twentyfirst century are being delivered by an ever-growing band of 'urban
farmers' and intensive food producers, who are now working
to green our conurbations – often in defiance of hidebound city
councils and health departments who cling to the anachronistic
rules of the tiny cities of the twentieth century.

'Today's urban farmers don't just grow food to eat; they also
see urban agriculture as a way of increasing the diversity of
plants and animals in the city, bringing people from different
backgrounds and age groups together, improving mental and
physical health and regenerating derelict neighbourhoods' says
British architect Silvio Caputo.[10] 'Many new urban farming projects still struggle to find suitable green spaces. But people are
finding inventive solutions; growing food in skips or on rooftops,
on sites that are only temporarily free, or on raised beds in
abandoned industrial yards. Growers are even using technologies such as hydroponics, aquaculture and aquaponics to make
the most of unoccupied spaces.'

The World Economic Forum (WEF) in reviewing current
trends in urban farming concluded: 'Urban farms have the
potential to change the world's agricultural landscape. Granted,
we're probably not going to see a planet of supercities in which
all farming is done in high-rise buildings. But urban farms can
bring greater yields in smaller areas, increase access to healthy
options in urban food deserts, and mitigate the environmental
impact of feeding the world'[11], continuing:

*New technologies are. . . allowing people to grow food in places where
it was previously difficult or impossible, and in quantities akin to
traditional farms. Urban farms can be as simple as traditional
small outdoor community gardens, or as complex as indoor vertical
farms in which farmers think about growing space in three-
dimensional terms.*

*These complex, futuristic farms can be configured in a number of
ways, but most of them contain rows of racks lined with plants rooted
in soil, nutrient-enriched water, or simply air. Each tier is equipped*

with UV (ultraviolet) lighting to mimic the effects of the sun. Unlike the unpredictable weather of outdoor farming, growing indoors allows farmers to tailor conditions to maximize growth.

Above all, urban farms represent vast savings in soil and water compared to conventional systems – as well as considerable savings in fertilisers, energy and pest control. An example is a 'farm' in a 40-foot shipping container developed by a group called Local Roots for the US cities of Los Angeles and Laurel, Maryland. This modular setup, they say, can turn out the same amount of food as five acres of market garden in half the time, using 97 per cent less water and zero pesticides – for the same food prices as a traditional farm.[12]

Traditional farmers think in terms of hectares or acres. Urban farmers, increasingly, think in terms of cubic metres or cubic feet of growing space, with layers of crops stacked one atop the other, says Dave Haider, the president of Urban Organics, a company that operates urban farms based in St. Paul, Minnesota, USA. 'Urban Organics grows three varieties of kale, two varieties of Swiss chard, Italian parsley and cilantro, but uses the same water to raise Arctic char and Atlantic salmon – a closed-loop system often called aquaponics. Fish waste fertilizes the plants, which clean and filter the water before it goes back into the planters.'[13]

A similar setup is operated by Blue Smart Farms at Camden, Sydney, Australia, using a controlled environment to produce high-quality fresh herbs and sea bass (barramundi) fish for the supermarket trade. Fish waste is converted in a worm farm to ten times its value in organic fertiliser to grow herbs on a giant conveyor-belt production system. Integrated pest management avoids the need for pesticides; remote nutrient and environmental control maintains optimal growing conditions for both fish and plants, and stacking saves on space.[14]

Faced with a shortage of arable land, Miljogartnieret of Norway developed an industrial-scale hydroponic setup which produced 2200 tonnes of high quality tomatoes and peppers from a seven hectare indoor farm. Nutrients were reused, benign insects employed for pollination and pest control, space heating was supplied by waste heat from the local power station, crop hygiene was used to prevent disease, plants were individually monitored, and nutrients and water were recycled.

Following a call from its Mayor to make Paris greener, the city government responded in 2016 by launching *Parisculteurs*, a project to cover the city's rooftops and walls with 100 hectares (247 acres) of vegetation by 2020. A third of this green space will grow food. 'Paris not only intends to produce fruit and vegetables but also (plans to) invent a new urban model... Citizens want new ways to get involved in the city's invention and be the gardeners' said deputy mayor Penelope Komites. The Parisian plan has sparked a rush of emulators in cities around the world.[15]

Cities are also being turned into forests and fruit plantations. Milan, Italy, set the trend with its celebrated *Bosco Verticale* (vertical forest) – trees planted into the walls of high-rise apartment towers. Architect Stephano Boeri describes it as 'a model for a sustainable residential building, a project for metropolitan reforestation contributing to the regeneration of the environment and urban biodiversity without expanding the city...'. His two towers support 800 trees, 4500 shrubs and 15,000 flowering plants – the equivalent of two hectares of forest – and provide insulation, biodiversity and fresh oxygen to the urban setting.[16] Boeri has exported his idea to the Chinese cities of Beijing, Shanghai, Nanjing and Liuzhou, where it is also seen as an answer to urban air pollution, and has launched projects in Lausanne, Switzerland, Utrecht in the Netherlands, São Paolo in Brazil and Tirana in Albania.[17]

From Sydney, Australia, to Los Angeles and New York, USA, to Africa and Europe a movement known as "guerrilla gardeners" is planting flowers and vegetables on traffic islands, footpath borders, road verges, freeway underpasses and on urban waste land, inviting passers-by to linger, contemplate, inhale and gather food. Defined as 'starting a garden on land the gardener has no right to', this cheeky Australian idea has captured the imagination of urban citizenry planet-wide.[18]

Urban farms are rising at every point on the scale from lilliputian to macro-industrial.

In *The Edible Balcony*, Australian journalist Indira Naidoo preaches her philosophy of fresh food for the high-rise apartment-dweller, which she has spun off into a consultancy helping others to build these tiny oases of fresh food on their own vacant balconies.[19] Before it, she reflects

> *My world consisted of cars, gridlock, pollution, television studios, concrete towers, fluorescent lights, noisy bars, restaurants, manicures, drycleaners, high-rise apartments, concrete and steel. I could easily go a week without my feet touching a blade of grass, my hand brushing up against the bark of a tree or my nose taking in the scent of a flower. I was about as far removed from nature as any human being on the planet could be...*

Then she sampled a home-grown tomato at a grower's market stall:

> *The flavour detonation that followed stopped me in my tracks. It was like no tomato I had ever tasted – sweet and full-flavoured, its thin, delicate skin wrapped around a juicy, fruity centre. It was how I remember tomatoes tasting from my childhood. Little did I know that one tiny tomato was to be the catalyst for a food-gardening obsession that would change my life...*

Naidoo's discovery conjures the yearning of five billion urbanites for a lost world – a world of true freshness (as distinct from the dubious claims of supermarket advertisements), flavour, healthiness and freedom from the toxic swamp of ten thousand chemicals that is the modern food supply. It is an atavistic cry, reaching deep into the human experience to a time when we had tens of thousands of edible plants and animals to choose among – not the 12 major plants and animals and 200–300 total plants which represent the unbelievably narrow bounds of the modern industrial food supply.

The new, exploding field of 'agritecture' – a fusion of urban building design with food production, is gaining followers worldwide. The movement was inspired significantly by the thinking of US microbiologist Professor Dickson Despommier[20] who developed the concept of 'medical ecology' over a ten-year period from 1999, which embodied the idea of a healthy urban food supply resilient to extremes of climate – and of green cities which could contribute to solving both the climate and waste problems, instead of making them worse. 'We are the only animal on the planet that doesn't know what to do with its own waste', he observes, adding 'All the answers are in Nature. You just have to know which question to ask'. The result of Despommier's reflection was a series of eyecatching designs for indoor and vertical farms which have inspired architects and urban gardeners around the world and given birth to 'agritecture' both as a concept and as a profession.

In an echo of the clean energy revolution, agritecture projects, urban food gardens and 'sky farms' are booming planet-wide. Swedish agritecture firm Plantagon says it is building ten crowd-funded underground farms in Stockholm and exporting its vertical farming designs to food-insecure regions such as the Middle East.[21] In Singapore, architects SPARK have come up with a concept they call HomeFarm, a combination of high-rise retirement village and vertical farm to keep retirees healthy, active, well-fed and fit into old age by growing their own fresh food.[22] In desert-lapped Dubai, industrial engineer Omar Al-Jundi has created a pilot 850 square metre 'fertigation' complex where he grows 26 different crops under LED lighting, with one tenth the water use of a normal farm, with plans to scale up to indoor farms in Jeddah, Saudi Arabia and elsewhere.[23] In the USA, San Francisco startup Plenty – backed by Amazon billionaire Jeff Bezos – is prospecting China and Japan as part of its ambitious goal to replicate its vertical farms in each of the world's 500 largest cities and overcome the long transport routes, carbon emissions, pesticides and dowdy, tasteless produce that afflict modern food chains.[24] In Telangana, India, farmers like Yadav Bhavanth are moving their crops under cover into greenhouses to avoid the water losses and climatic extremes of open-air horticulture.[25] In Montreal, Canada, Lufa Farms has developed a rooftop hydroponic system at three sites supplying fresh produce, year-round, for online orders which are delivered direct to consumers' homes or local pick-up points.[26] The former industrial wastelands of Detroit, Michigan, are blooming with food and greenery through projects such as the Michigan Urban Farming Initiative, which not only grows fresh food but also addresses issues such as nutritional illiteracy and food deserts in the community.[27] In Brooklyn, New York, three companies have helped pioneer a global trend to urban 'aquaponic' farms, which grow fish and fresh vegetables together.[28]

In the densely-packed enclave of Gaza, Middle East, where two million people struggle to exist, the FAO has supplied homes with hydroponic equipment to create 200 model rooftop farms, while in nearby Tel Aviv, Israel, a company called LivingGreen has established an urban aquaponic farm on the roof of the city's oldest shopping mall.[29] In Dubai, airline Emirates has launched 'the world's largest vertical farm', a $40m venture to supply 225,000 airline meals per day.[30] In Denmark, HumanHabitat has designed a modified shipping container as an 'urban popup farm' capable of producing two to four tonnes of vegetables a year.[31] In New York, Brooklyn Grange has established roof-top soil-culture gardens turning out 20 tonnes of organic produce a year, while Urban Farm aspires to do the same for Dublin, Ireland.[32] The Boston Medical Centre, Massachusetts, USA, has established a rooftop farm to supply seven tonnes of fresh greens to its patients as part of their healing process and to spread the word in the wider community about how to prevent disease through diet.[33] In Hong Kong's densely packed suburbs, HK Farm is introducing rooftop food gardens for high-rise buildings old and new, producing vegetables, fruits, herbs and honey and composting waste.[34] In Berlin's Kreuzberg district, Prinzessinnengärten is demonstrating how to transform abandoned wasteland or empty building sites into temporary or permanent organic vegetable plots, to acclaim from locals and tourists alike.[35] In Tokyo, scores of new urban farms are sprouting from the largest to the smallest scales – showing urbanites how to grow rice, poultry, fruit and vegetables and keep bees atop skyscrapers, under the tutelage of former professional farmers driven from their land by development.[36]

While the field of urban farming is in its infancy, and failure rates among startups are high – as is common in both agriculture and high-tech – it has several advantages which clever entrepreneurs are taking advantage of. These include very low water, energy and chemical costs compared with conventional farming systems, short delivery chains in close proximity to customers, access to cheap nutrients from composted organic waste and hectares of 'free' space on the roofs of factories, malls, office buildings, apartments and homes. Against this, the capital costs of setting up are generally high, energy costs (for lighting) can be heavy, cultural techniques are often experimental, highly paid workers with advanced technology skills are needed for all but the simplest systems – and new marketing chains must be established, in a true mammals-versus-the-dinosaurs contest, in the teeth of bitter competition from some of the world's largest supermarket and food corporates. The global response to urban farms ranges across the scale from high enthusiasm to deep scepticism – just as it did for solar power in the 1990s. The urban food revolution is no different to the energy revolution – and its time will come, with proportional reward for early investors and innovators who go the distance.

The boom in alternative foods sourced from urban farms has not escaped the attention of the giants of the food world, the vast supermarket chains and food processing networks that span the planet and which, in individual cases, command wealth and power far beyond those of most countries. Facing prospective loss of market share for one of their most lucrative product categories to an array of agile, highly entrepreneurial local food suppliers, global supermarket chains are reacting with their own versions of urban food production. Some are introducing their own farms, using the hectares of vacant rooftop space in their retail stores and warehouses, or leasing it to grower companies who in turn sell to them direct.[37] Farms are even entering the shopping space, in the form of lighted hydroponic display cabinets where customers can harvest their own fresh vegetables.[38]

There are promising signs that city governments, too, are starting to awaken to the looming crises in water and food they will have to confront by the mid-century. In Tokyo's central Sumida City, for example, Dr Skywater – formerly civil servant Dr Makoto Murase – has inspired an urban revolution which compels all developers of large buildings to store rainwater falling on their site underground for use in showers, toilets, fire-fighting, as flood control and for irrigating greenery. So far, more than 600 large new buildings, including Tokyo's famous Sky Tree, have been constructed to save water and 'Sumida City has been changed from Drain City to Rain City', he proclaims. Dr Skywater, a person who thinks both big picture and small, has also taken his ideas about conserving rainwater to rural Bangladesh where over 3000 homes have been equipped with safe, clean household water supplies using the simplest and cheapest of technology – a roof, a steel chain and a large, sealed, clay pot. By such means he sees urban water as both a symbol and a tool to build peace, plenty and good health internationally: 'Japan is blessed with rain. But the origin of almost all our rain comes from Bangladesh, India and the western Pacific. We are all monsoon Asian people. We must help each other and make peace and happiness through friendship'.[39]

Urban Permaculture

Permaculture is a word originally coined by Australian innovators Bill Mollison and David Holmgren in the mid 1970s for 'consciously designed landscapes which mimic the patterns and relationships found in nature, while yielding an abundance of food, fibre and energy for local needs'.[40] The word means, literally, permanent or sustainable agriculture but embodies a far more complex weaving together of organic farming, agroforestry, recycling of water and nutrients, ecological building design, renewable energy, appropriate technologies, ethics, health and wellbeing. From an idea begun in Australia half a century ago, it has caught on around the world in a network of permaculturalists, mostly small, self-sustaining farmers and homesteaders. Its ethical principles are: Care of the Earth, Care of People and Fair Sharing. Unlike some alternative food systems, permaculture does not impose rigid rules, but rather encourages its adherents to innovate within the broad principles and ethics it espouses.

While the industrial food industry has been quick to dismiss permaculture as 'another greenie fad', in reality its principles of mimicking nature, recycling everything productively and sharing knowledge address many of the critical threats and limitations facing humanity and our vast, overgrown and deeply vulnerable cities of today. Typical claims about it are 'we can't all live like that', 'the economy would cease to function' and 'sustainable farming cannot feed the world'[41] – but, like climate denial, these can usually be sourced back to the industrial chemical, machinery and factory food lobby which has an unashamed financial interest in badmouthing alternative systems of food production that endanger its profits by not using its products.

Until now permaculture has largely been practiced at the small farm and householder level. The important question for the twentyfirst century is: can permaculture principles be applied to the design of cities and megacities? Can they, their buildings, water and waste systems, be redesigned on natural principles that reuse, rather than ones which waste and pollute? Can their citizens be persuaded to recycle instead of casting aside the essentials that support life?

It is the contention of this book that 'urban permaculture', on the largest as well as the smallest scale, will become a hallmark and a theme in the total redesign of the planet's cities as the century advances. Indeed, it may well come to be viewed as a *sine qua non* for megacity survival. However, for all the zeal of its pioneers and urban food investors, the main impulse to totally green the world's cities may well be the universal shock which will accompany the collapse of individual megacities or the wars which spring out of local failures in sustenance. Of course, one wishes it were otherwise – but humanity, as a rule, is slow to absorb new lessons and make essential changes, until the dangers become life-threatening.

In the future, as visionary individuals like Oscar Rodriguez, Stephan Boeri, Dr Skywater, Silvio Caputo and David Holmgren foresee, the city can become a permanent fount of renewal, regeneration and fresh food – instead of a doomed concrete tunnel of waste and insecurity.

Stewards of the Earth

As described in Chapters 6 and 7, the famed US biologist Professor E. O. Wilson has proposed the extension of nature reserves to half of the Earth's land and sea area as the only practical way to head off the Sixth Extinction of plants and animals and its disastrous consequences for humans.

We currently protect about 15 per cent of the land and 3 per cent of the oceans in nature reserves of one sort or another – and are losing species at rates from 100 to 1000 times greater than usual on Earth. Wilson proposes we expand the protected zone to 50 per cent of the planet by creating larger areas 'from large and small fragments around the world to remain relatively natural, without removing people living there or changing property rights'. On the basis of evidence from previous conservation reserves, this would probably save about 84 per cent of the Earth's species, he argues.

Where this proposition chiefly runs into difficulty is that the land alone which Wilson and his colleagues propose to conserve covers an area of 25 million square kilometres – the size of the continent of North America – and is presently extensively used for food production, by over a billion small, medium and large farmers, pastoralists and fishers. If such a vast area were to be taken out of agriculture, grazing or fishing, or even their intensity reduced by half, the result in our already overstressed and climate-menaced world would be global famine.

In order to solve the problems of extinction and ecological collapse, it is therefore necessary to solve the problem of food security.

At the same time, the Half Earth plan would probably entail nearly quadrupling the amount we currently spend on managing National Parks, training millions of rangers, ecologists, managers and the like, including in some of the poorest countries in the world, which can least afford big conservation budgets.

An alternative to such an approach is to progressively employ many of the world's farmers and indigenous peoples, who already live on, understand and care for this land and its species, as *Stewards of the Earth*, responsible for the progressive rewilding, forest and grassland restoration of their local area. This was first proposed in *Surviving the 21st Century*. This approach will address two problems – how to rewild half the Earth using local knowledge and expertise, and how to continue to employ hundreds of millions of smallholder farmers who will otherwise, inevitably, be ruined and driven from their lands by the giant supermarket and industrial food chains, whose only interest is profit and procuring 'food' at the cheapest possible prices.

The evidence for this claim lies in the wholesale decimation of family farms that has taken place in North America, Europe and Australasia over the past century, as 'agriculture' industrialised and the 'uncompetitive' millions of bankrupt small farmers were forced to sell up, walk off their farms or kill themselves.

Indigenous people and small farmers usually have an innate wisdom about their environment and how to tend or farm it sustainably, founded on generations of human observation, knowledge and accumulated experience. It is only when they are drawn into the industrial food system by money, and begin to force-feed their farming system with pesticides and fertilisers that it becomes unsustainable and they themselves become the unwitting fodder for a global economic machine. For decades, agriculture worldwide has been driven by the misguided economic theory of 'productivity' – trying to maximise the yields of crops like corn, rice or wheat to meet the steadily falling prices that the food industry was prepared to pay for them, while steadfastly ignoring all the external damage this causes to the farming environment, to people, animals and to the planet. The goal was to force as many tonnes of grain as possible from a single hectare of land – and this supposedly made industrial farmers of North America and Europe superior in 'efficiency' to their counterparts in Asia, South America and Africa, who have since been adopting the same measures. However, Indian Nobel laureate Amartya Sen, among his many contributions to the field of economics and social justice, also showed that small-holder farmers, while their yields of particular crops were lower than those of industrial farmers, actually grew *more food* per area of land, because their farming systems were more diverse and complex.[42]

In his book *Small Farmers Secure Food*, Professor Lindsay Falvey, a former Dean of Agriculture at Melbourne University, argued that modern development aid (and the science that supports it) has in fact increased the risks of starvation because it has erroneously presumed that 'broadacre farms are more efficient than small farms'. From a wealth of international experience Falvey challenges this assumption, contending that small farms have many advantages not captured by large farms: more intensive oversight of land, crops, animals and labour, detailed knowledge of a wider range of crops and livestock, greater empathy with animals and their environment, feeding their families and others on fresh, wholesome unprocessed food, low food losses and zero transport costs, ability to produce a wider diversity of niche foods, the preservation of strong local communities and so on. However, almost everywhere, government policy favours the 'big end of town', the large commercial operators, neglecting the 1.8 billion small farmers who feed themselves and half the world sustainably. He attributes this to a misguided belief that commerce and capital alone can deliver food solutions whereas, Falvey argues, the world needs many forms of production, large and small, to deliver true food security.[43]

Today millions of smallholder farmers are being thrown off their land worldwide by the brute economic might of supermarket giants, land-grabbing agribusiness transnationals, corporations and acquisitive big farmers.[44] This process, which echoes the ugly histories of the Irish Famine and Scottish Highland Clearances of the mid nineteenth century, the Soviet war on the Kulaks, the US 'dustbowl' of the 1930s, the postwar

Australian soldier-settler disasters and the Chinese Cultural
Revolution, is taking place in almost every country in the world.
British writer George Monbiot described how:

> Big business is killing small farming. By extending intellectual prop-
> erty rights over every aspect of production; by developing plants
> which either won't breed true or which don't reproduce at all, it
> ensures that only those with access to capital can cultivate. As it
> captures both the wholesale and retail markets, it seeks to reduce its
> transaction costs by engaging only with major sellers. If you think
> that supermarkets are giving farmers in the UK a hard time, you
> should see what they are doing to growers in the poor world. As
> developing countries sweep away street markets and hawkers' stalls
> and replace them with superstores and glossy malls, the most pro-
> ductive farmers lose their customers and are forced to sell up. The rich
> nations support this process by demanding access for their companies.
> Their agricultural subsidies still help their own, large farmers to
> compete unfairly with the small producers of the poor world.[45]

The greatest tragedy in this process is the loss of skills, wisdom
and human capital. The fact is that, despite all the propaganda
by pro-agribusiness economists, most small farmers actually
know what they are doing when it comes to producing a diversity of healthy nutritious food sustainably and managing their
local environment and its wildlife. There is sense, then, in trying
to retain their wisdom and experience on the land, to manage its
rewilding and regeneration as *Stewards of the Earth*, instead of
squandering it in the teeming slums of dangerously vulnerable
megacities. There is no obstacle to them, as Stewards engaged in
rebuilding the wild world, also continuing to operate as self-
sufficient farmers or graziers on the kind of small, mixed family
plots described by Sen, Falvey and others. It is simply a wise use
of human skills – instead of their complete loss.

Compelling evidence that such a stewardship programme can
succeed in restoring the natural world is to be found among the
laureates of the Rolex Awards for Enterprise[46], many whom
have been responsible for establishing regeneration projects for

forests, wilderness and rare wildlife using the skills and insights of indigenous people or local farmers and pastoralists who understand their own environment, through time, better than any scientist. Rolex laureates are, for example, engaged in conserving and restoring the Mata Atlantica, Brazil's once mighty but now almost-vanished eastern forest, the rainforests and seagrass meadows of Thailand, the mangrove forests of eastern Africa, the Sierra Gorda and Yucatan of Mexico, the rainforests of India, the fjords of Patagonia, the grasslands of Mongolia, the wetlands of the Brazilian Amazon and southern Africa. In many, if not most, cases, their campaigns are built around iconic species and the necessity to preserve or restore the wider habitat on which they depend – creatures such as the snow leopard, the Amur tiger, the Asian dugong, the hornbill, the whale shark, the Mongolian wild horse, the South American condor, the African crowned crane, the European vulture, the Philippines seahorse and the South American manta ray. Using these creatures as totems of renewal in projects carried out by local indigenous people and small farmers, fishers and foresters has the added benefit of restoring many other species that occupy the same environment. The introduction of *sustainable grazing* of cattle, sheep, camels and goats at low stocking rates across the world's grasslands, rangelands and savannahs, can not only hasten the recovery of wildlife, but also lock up millions of tonnes of carbon across 40 per cent of the planet's landmass – while returning a better income to pastoralists from the production of healthy meat, milk, wool and leather. For this reason, it is important that meat remain a part of the human diet.

A second example of restoration taking place at the global scale is the Bonn Challenge, a plan to restore 350 million hectares of forest and degraded land in participating nations by 2030.[47] Another is the 'Trillion Trees Partnership' led by the Worldwide Fund for Nature, the Wildlife Conservation Society and BirdLife International.[48] Restoring damaged landscapes can have a big economic payoff, argues the World Resources Institute: its study *The Economic Case For Landscape Restoration In Latin America*, found that restoring 20 million hectares of the continent's degraded lands by adding trees and improving farming practices could reap $23 billion in net benefits over 50 years, equal to about 10 per cent of annual food exports from the region.[49]

The cost of funding the biosecurity and human security such a stewardship plan would deliver can be met in at least two ways: by placing a small levy (say 5–10 per cent) on all food sold worldwide, to cover its true environmental cost and invest in repairing the damage it causes – or by paying the Stewards directly from the defence budget, as previously described, in recognition of their role as peace makers. For the very poor, a small increase in food prices can be offset by food subsidies or other social measures. The average family, however, can well afford it: the share of household income devoted to food has fallen from 30 per cent in the 1920s to about 10 per cent today. Thus, an increase of 1 or 2 per cent in household expenditure to cover the cost of a sustainable food supply is well within their means – though it may mean buying slightly fewer cosmetics, clothes, accessories or electronic gadgets. Put simply, that may be the price of human survival. The reason for using public funding for a worldwide stewardship programme is that the global supermarket and food corporates cannot be trusted to return the extra income to farmers.

In short, we need – and can easily afford – a global *Stewards of the Earth* programme that will:

- repair the damage caused by industrial agriculture worldwide, replant forests and grasslands especially in marginal areas, and help save most of the world's endangered plants and animals from extinction;
- employ up to a billion skilled indigenous people and smallholder farmers in planet-scale environmental repair and renewal, to restore the environmental services to humanity they provide, while still meeting their own food needs from small, sustainable holdings;
- help transition the world food system to a sustainable, climate-proof and largely urban model using recycled nutrients and water;

- help to lock up vast amounts of human-emitted carbon in the restored forests and grasslands and so turn the climate trend back to a more stable course; and
- serve as peacemakers for the planet through food and environmental security.

Wise Consumers

The person at the heart of the transition to a renewable food revolution taking place in green cities and on eco-farms around the world, is *you*. As a consumer you have the power, through the money you spend daily on food, to sustain the human future – or doom it to conflict and devastation. Passing the supermarket checkout is no longer a trivial moment in your day: it is your personal contribution to the destiny of civilisation and the fate of your grandchildren. Use it wisely.

If enough consumers buy wisely – for health, safety and sustainability – they will send a mighty monetary signal to farmers and to the food industry worldwide that this is the sort of food supply that we want: one that heals instead of sickens, one that sustains, recycles and restores rather than one that wastes, pollutes and destroys, one that leads to peace, not war. No farmer, fisher, food producer, supermarket or agribusiness tycoon can or will ignore such a powerful economic signal. Indeed, most genuine farmers and food producers will be delighted if you send it. It will encourage them and speed the transition.

If, on the other hand, you continue to spend your money on cheap, malnourishing industrially fabricated foods, chock full of toxins and chemicals, not only will you live sick and die years younger than you should from one or more of the lifestyle diseases, you will also condemn your children and grandchildren to a planet that has been strip-mined to produce this rubbish. You will send exactly the wrong signal to the global food enterprise, and to the farmers who are its financial prisoners. What you choose to eat will influence the fate of humanity in the twentyfirst century more profoundly, probably, than any-thing else you will ever do in your life – including your carbon emissions.

To take an example, researchers from Oxford University looked at the environmental impact of 40 different foodstuffs produced by 39,000 farms in 119 countries. Choosing a diet with significantly more plant foods and significantly less animal prod-ucts can have a dramatic effect in reducing greenhouse emis-sions, for example, they showed. In the USA, a switch from a meat-based diet to a plant-based diet would cut the food sector's greenhouse output by up to 61 per cent. It would also reduce rates of forest destruction, nutrient and soil losses. The same foodstuffs can have a dramatically different environmental impact depending on how they are produced, they added.[50]

All this goes to underline the point that informed consumers, who buy wisely and thoughtfully, can help build a sustainable world with every dollar they spend – whereas unwise, unin-formed consumers only invest in destroying the one we have today. So how to make consumers more aware and informed?

Since the publication of *The Coming Famine* in 2010, I have been urging the adoption of a *Year of Food* in every junior school on the planet. This is a year in which food informs the teaching of every subject in the school curriculum, from science and sport to art, languages, mathematics, literature and geography. It is a year when food not only provides the backdrop to the teaching of all subjects – in recognition of the fact that everyone must eat in order to live – but that all schools should have a small farm or food garden, where children can gain their own experience of growing, preparing and eating fresh foods. These principles are beautifully enunciated by Australian chef Stephanie Alexander, who has helped establish kitchen gardens in hundreds of schools in Australia and the USA, with the aim of giving children good food habits for life.[51] Teachers I have spoken with all say that teaching food in school, with hands-on projects, can engage even the most disruptive kids – and that most children will happily eat their greens if they grow them themselves.

If the coming generation of three billion children now growing up in the world's cities know nothing of food – how to choose between healthy and unhealthy, sustainable and unsustainable – then, like a swarm of locusts, they will devour the planet's food resource base and suffer the killer lifestyle diseases already rampant among them and their parents. If on the other hand, they purposefully seek out foods that give health, sustain the natural world and deliver peace, then they will unlock a Renewable Food Revolution to match and even surpass the Renewable Energy Revolution that has swept the planet.

So, because children also help educate their parents, it is essential that the children of tomorrow know how to eat – safely, healthily, thriftily and well. The food revolution starts in school.

Beyond that, there is a growing focus in social media, among culinary publishers and even celebrity chefs on food health and sustainability. Books like Lars Charas's *Food Forever: Recipes for a Healthy Planet*[52], Sue Radd's *Food as Medicine*[53], Mark Bittman's *The Food Matters Cookbook: 500 Revolutionary Recipes for Better Living*[54], Anne Lappé's *Diet for a Hot Planet*[55] and the shows of British TV chef Jamie Oliver[56] not only offer delicious cuisine for the new Age of Food but also challenge the chefs, cooks, dieticians, consumers and food producers of today to become change agents for the healthy, sustainable diets of tomorrow.

While convincing eight or ten billion people to eat more sustainably may appear a tall order, in fact rising awareness of the damage caused by lifestyle diseases and industrialised diets, as well as the effects of today's food system on the climate, water and wildlife of the planet, is already spreading at breathtaking speed among consumers, thanks to the internet and social media. As described in *Surviving the 21st Century*, humanity is now connecting at lightspeed around the planet, sharing knowledge, ideas and values, in the early stages of the formation of a universal, species-wide, consciousness – an Earth-sized 'mind'. We are learning to think as a species, as well as individuals. Developing a peaceful, sustainable and healthy diet for the future is an essential mission for humanity, which now needs to seriously engage in species-saving thought.

Food, besides being about sustenance, is also a fashion-driven industry – and nothing catches on faster than a new fashion. Through the internet, the food revolution will therefore be followed with unbounded interest and enthusiasm by hundreds of millions of youngsters and elders around the planet, even among those not well informed of the deeper existential threats that underpin it. Ideas for the Age of Food are already propagating like wildfire on social media.

As to the difficulty in choosing between a 'sustainable food' and an unsustainable one, a mass of mobile apps are becoming available that enable people to scan food for details about how it was produced, its health and sustainability rating. Likewise, apps that help reduce food waste and order only what we will eat are multiplying. In 2018, 4.1 out of 7.5 billion people were online. But the mid 2020s, the internet will be universal – and with it, sound, reliable information from trustworthy scientific sources, about food and diet, will also be available to all humanity for the very first time.

The sustainable food revolution will be driven largely by the informed inhabitants of the green cities of tomorrow – by you and me, spending our food money more wisely in a truly global, grassroots movement. Because we all eat, every day, this will be greater and more all-encompassing even than the green energy revolution. It will define the human future – and help to ease the tensions that lead to war. The next chapter explains how.

9   THE FUTURE OF FOOD

Ecological Farming – Aquafoods – The Urban Food
Revolution – Biocultures – Exploring an Unexplored
Planet – The Age of Food

*'If more of us valued food and cheer and song above hoarded gold, it
would be a merrier world.'*

J. R. R. Tolkien

Wilbur and Orville Wright did not begin by asking 'How do we
take a conventional pony and cart, and attach wings to them?'.
Likewise, Jonas Salk and Albert Sabin did not start from the
position 'How do we build a better iron lung?'. The brothers
Wright started by asking how they could construct an entirely
novel form of human transportation. And the polio vaccine
pioneers began by asking how they could eradicate a disease
that was paralysing tens of thousands of children worldwide
every year.

The challenge for the world food system, its scientists,
farmers and commercial managers is to kick the flying-pony/
better-iron-lung habit of thought. In the present context of 10
billion people packed on a hot, resource-stressed and conflicted
world, incremental improvement of last century's farming
systems will not succeed. As quickly as they are improved, fresh
vulnerabilities and failings will appear.

The challenge is to design a total world food system that is
safe, clean and reliable enough to see humanity through the
human population peak of the mid twentyfirst century, and
down the other side in a managed, voluntary reduction of our
numbers. A food system whose harvest includes world peace –
and which can withstand whatever extremes a rapidly changing
climate is going to throw at it. A food system that, instead of

feeding the degenerative diseases that now kill most people, actively prevents them.

Calls for a new world food revolution have been growing in volume for more than half a century. Eminent ecologist Paul Ehrlich, whose trailblazing book *The Population Bomb* warned in 1968 of the dangers inherent in unconstrained population growth coming up against the planet's finite resources, amplified his call in 2015 in an essay with John Harte entitled *Food security requires a new revolution*. They said:

> *A central responsibility of societies should be supplying adequate nourishment to all. For roughly a third of the global human population, that goal is not met today. More ominously, that population is projected to increase some 30% by 2050. The intertwined natural and social systems, that must meet the challenge of producing and equitably distributing much more food without wrecking humanity's life-support systems, face a daunting array of challenges and uncertainties. These have roots in the agricultural revolution that transformed our species and created civilization. Profound and multifaceted changes, revising closely-held cultural traditions and penetrating most of civilization will be required, if an unprecedented famine is to be avoided.[1]*

They concluded: 'What is obvious to us is, however, that if humanity is to avoid a calamitous loss of food security, a fast, society-pervading sea change as dramatic as the first agricultural revolution will be required – and one where the consequences will be carefully considered'.

Among the movers and shakers for a global food revolution is Danielle Nierenberg, whose lively online Food Tank project is challenging a range of sacrosanct bovines in the conventional food and agriculture space with conferences, opinion pieces, interviews with food thought-leaders and a focus on food innovation and food security. She explains 'We're building a global community for safe, healthy, nourished eaters. We aim to educate, inspire, advocate, and create change. We spotlight and support environmentally, socially, and economically sustainable ways of alleviating hunger, obesity, and poverty and create networks of people, organizations, and content to push for food system change'.[2] Another ardent campaigner for a fresh approach to food and diet is Jon Foley, former head of the California Academy of Sciences and self-styled 'GlobalEcoGuy', who warns 'There's a powerful narrative being told about the world's food system. The problem is, it's mostly based on flawed assumptions... What we choose to do about population growth, and especially what we do about diets, will determine how much food the world ultimately needs. Growing more crops is not the only way to get more food on the table'.[3]

Evidence that *no country* in the world is yet able to meet its own food needs in a manner consistent with global sustainability, presented by Daniel O'Neill of Leeds University and colleagues, shows just how far we have to go.[4] 'When we finished the analysis, which included 11 social indicators linked to the UN Sustainable Development Goals, and 7 environmental indicators linked to the planetary boundaries framework, the results were clear – but depressing. Of the 151 countries we analysed, no country achieved the basic needs of its citizens at a globally sustainable level of resource use', O'Neill stated. 'The challenge is substantial, however, as we must become two to six times more efficient at transforming resource use into human well-being if all people are to live well within planetary boundaries.'[5]

Thus, the challenge of feeding humanity is vast – maybe greater even than the challenge of stabilising the climate or population, and its importance is far less widely acknowledged by governments, policymakers or consumers. It is, literally, the defining issue of the human destiny. Doing nothing is not an option.

For all these reasons food is going to change – radically. What we eat a century from now, how we produce and consume it, its health value and composition will be as unfamiliar to us today as our own ancestors would find the modern diet in this, the era of cosmopolitan cuisine, cold storage, takeaway, manufactured food, celebrity chefs and cooking shows.

Innovations to food systems in practices, technologies, policies, markets and institutions will be critical to both human and planetary health argues Dr Shenggen Fan, Director General of the International Food Policy Research Centre. Some of these will be farmer-led, some driven by high-tech startups venturing out of electronics and into food, and many will be absolutely transformational, he says. 'Food can fix many problems, but we must fix food systems first. Innovations in technologies, policies, and institutions will be critical in reshaping food systems for nutrition, health, inclusion, and sustainability. To develop and implement these innovations to ensure no one is left behind, we must work together – across disciplines, countries, and sectors. Global cooperation will be key to ensuring that innovations in food systems are widely disseminated and contribute positively to global development.'[6]

Summarising the body of evidence presented in this book, the basics of a sustainable future human food system are as follows. It must:

- recycle or reabsorb water, all nutrients and all crop and animal wastes and end food waste;
- produce far more food from a far smaller area of land, using much less water and as few artificial chemicals and poisons as possible;
- be balanced from a nutritional standpoint, especially in terms of micronutrients;
- promote prevention and healing of the major lifestyle diseases that now kill most humans;
- be close to the main centres of population to minimise transport costs, greenhouse emissions and wastage; and
- be climate-proof and immune to heatwave, storm, flood, drought and pestilence.

It must not:

- destroy other species, landscapes or ecosystems;
- degrade the Earth's soil, water or climate;
- poison its consumers or its environment;
- leak nutrients, chemicals, soil or greenhouse gases;
- increase tensions, multiply threats or cause wars, government collapses and refugee tsunamis.

Ecological Farming

It is increasingly agreed among scientists, farmers and experts in world agriculture that the existing farming system must transition to one which produces enough nourishing food, with a great deal less harm to the environment and consumers. This is known as eco-farming, ecological agriculture or regenerative farming – and was the principal conclusion reached in my 2010 book *The Coming Famine*.

Its goal is not necessarily to achieve higher crop yields but rather to produce more *nutritious food* (as distinct from industrial commodities). The basic idea is that agriculture should more closely mimic the processes found in nature, and minimise the waste, pollution and other collateral damage that over-industrialised systems can cause. Beyond these broad concepts there is heated debate over what exactly eco-farming entails and how it will develop. However, certain key features may include:

- it is self-sustaining, eliminates soil and water loss, and maintains or improves soil fertility and structure;
- it accentuates better management of soil, water, plants, livestock and microbes to achieve a healthier food growing environment;
- it is diverse, including a much richer mixture of symbiotic plants and animals to yield a more balanced, resilient system (and human diet) than traditional single-crop broadacre farming;
- farm size should be kept small, to intensify the farmer's ability to manage it successfully;
- food yields measured by nutrient value (and input) rather than individual crop yields are its defining basis;
- it should focus on providing a safe, healthy local supply of food, rather than exporting over vast distances.[7]

'Farming the land as if nature doesn't matter has been the model for much of the Western world's food production system for at least the past 75 years', wrote sustainable farming expert Daniel Moss and food writer Mark Bittman in the New York Times. 'The results haven't been pretty: depleted soil, chemically fouled waters, true family farms all but eliminated, a worsening of public health and more. But an approach that combines innovation and tradition has emerged, one that could transform the way we grow food. It's called agroecology, and it places ecological science at the center of agriculture. It's a scrappy movement that's taking off globally.'[8]

UK-based scientists Nina Moeller and Michel Pimbert concur.

> *Throughout the world, small-scale farmers are uniting under the banner of agroecology. They do so not only to produce healthy and nutritious food, enhance biodiversity and adapt to climate change, but also to improve their income and working conditions by developing short food chains and local markets. Local ecologies and economies are being regenerated from below through an insistence on food sovereignty (community control over the way food is produced, traded and consumed) and transformative agroecology (as opposed to more watered down versions of agroecology, such as "climate-smart" or "conservation" agriculture).*[9]

Many of these principles are echoed in the fast-developing urban food systems, as the previous chapter illustrated.

The case for eco-farming has been increasingly pressed by eminent international figures like José Graziano da Silva, director-general of the UN Food and Agriculture Organisation. Bearing in mind the limitations of the Green Revolution and its industrial technologies, he told a meeting of 70 countries in Rome: 'It is time to innovate again. This time, innovation means increasing the resilience and sustainability of our food systems, especially in the face of climate change. We need to put forward sustainable food systems that offer healthy, nutritious and accessible food for all, ecosystem services, and climate resilience. The emerging field of agroecology can offer several contributions in this regard'.[10] He continued:

> *A tailored combination of both science and cultural wisdom, agroecology's core elements comprise a strong emphasis on diversity, synergies, recycling, efficient use of resources, ecological and socio-economic*

resilience, the co-creation and sharing of knowledge, and the link between human values and sustainable livelihoods. It also includes the role of culture in food traditions and the important role that responsible governance mechanisms – covering issues ranging from tenure to the way that public subsidies are used – must play to support long-term investments in sustainability.

By the mid century it is therefore likely that intensifying resource scarcity and climate stresses, shifting consumer demand and technological advances will split the current largely agriculture-based world food system into three dominant and mutually supporting streams.

1. The conversion of half of all conventional farmland to eco-agriculture, occupying the best soils and most favourable climatic and environmental conditions, so enabling the rewilding of the other half of the land.
2. The development of a thriving urban food system that recycles city nutrients and water and provides half, or more, of the food needed by huge cities.
3. The development of worldwide deepwater aquaculture of fish, aquatic creatures, microalgae and seaweeds, on a scale several times larger than today.

With urban production and aquaculture able to supply the low-cost end of the food spectrum – the pies, sausages, dim sum, snackfoods and fresh vegetables, if you like – and so keeping food affordable to consumers, eco-farmers will receive a better price for sustainably grown grains, fruit, vegetables, meat, dairy and other livestock products from the upper end of the market, enabling them to afford the higher costs involved in repairing, protecting and maintaining the farming environment. For eco-farming to succeed, it is imperative that farmers be adequately recompensed for the skill, care, ecological and capital costs involved – instead of being screwed-over by giant supermarket chains, as is the current practice. Thus, with enhanced investment, agriculture can remain a mainstay of the human food system – one which sustains, rather than erodes it.

For this to happen there must be an end to the nonsensical ideological warfare between 'high tech' agriculture and sustainable farming, eloquently portrayed by Charles Mann in his book *The Wizard and the Prophet*, in which he illustrates this struggle in the persons and life's work of two great twentieth-century scientists, Norman Borlaug and William Vogt.[11] Just as there is no barrier to the use of sound ecological principles in conventional farming, there is equally no barrier to the use of high technology in eco-agriculture. Tools such as gene editing, farm robotics, artificial intelligence, blockchain, nanotechnology, remote sensing and advanced pest control can and must be committed (wisely) to the sustainable food system, rather than serving an unsustainable one dominated by corporations with only a narrow, short-term self-interest in view. To feed humanity well in a resource-stressed, climate-stricken world, high-tech farmers must embrace ecological thinking and sustainability, and eco-farmers must embrace appropriate advanced technologies.

Scientific 'moonshots' – visionary research projects that envisage major leaps in technology – offer potential benefits for both conventional and eco-agriculture, provided they are well and cautiously managed – and not regarded as panaceas. An example is the C4 Rice Project, described by its proponents as 'one of the scientific "Grand Challenges" of the 21st Century'. The aim of this research is to genetically endow rice, a crop with a C3 photosynthetic pathway, with a C4 pathway (found in corn and sugarcane) enabling it to turn sunlight into rice with greatly improved efficiency – enough, it is claimed, to feed a billion more people.[12] Potentially, its supporters assert, this could produce more rice from a much smaller area, using relatively less water and fertiliser.

A second 'moonshot' proposes that food crops and trees be equipped with extra genes (from coastal grasses) to form a waxy, cork-like substance known as suberin in their roots, enabling them to extract and lock up far more carbon from the air, thus helping to soak up human carbon emissions faster and so slow the rate of global warming. This could, potentially, benefit both perennial crop agriculture and rewilding, using enhanced native plants which can turn the pollutant carbon dioxide into food as well as sequestering it in the soil.[13]

Another is the growing use of nanotechnology in food production. 'Several nanoproducts could potentially contribute to global environmental benefits', the UN's Global Environmental Facility said, continuing:

> For example, nanomaterials may be used in pest control, precision agriculture, delivery of fertilisers and soil enhancers, and detection of plant diseases. These could increase agricultural productivity, and reduce dependence on harmful chemicals, including pesticides. . . Biodegradable nanomaterial from wood, with enhanced insulating properties, could replace existing insulators and provide energy-efficient buildings with climate benefits. Nanoscale desalination of water using less energy compared to traditional methods could help to provide freshwater.

Another 'moonshot' is the use of CRISPR biotechnology to 'edit' the bacteria in the stomachs of cows, sheep and goats, so they produce less of the climate-warming gas, methane. The advantage of this is that, instead of releasing excess carbon through their mouths, the animals obtain more energy from their feed for producing meat, milk or fibre. This in turn means a reduction in the number of animals needed to produce the same outputs, leading to more sustainable grazing industries.

However, with bitter experiences like coal, nuclear technology, cancer-causing chemicals and thalidomide to go on, humanity needs to be cautious of any self-proclaimed, one-shot 'technofixes', as most technologies prove with experience and widespread adoption to have downsides and shortcomings, which then need to be corrected. It is therefore essential for civil society to take a precautionary oversight of scientific 'moonshots' in any field, including food and agriculture, to ensure they do not exacerbate any of the ten existential threats to humanity described in Chapter 6 and lower our chances of survival. We need to make sure, in particular, they meet the needs – and do not harm – sustainable eco-farming, urban food production and aquaculture, as the pillars of a healthy world food supply and diet in the twentyfirst century. The core science of these technologies must remain in public hands, since commercial interests often skew the R&D focus to their own financial interests and sometimes promote dangerous products – like tobacco, pesticides and certain cosmetics – for profit, regardless of the human or environmental harm they cause.

Essential to the production of healthy food, which can reverse the lifestyle diseases that beset modern humanity, is a clean growing environment and healthy living soils, argues Dr Martin Stapper, a scientist who works on 'biological farming', a variant of eco-farming.[14] He says:

> In healthy soils, plants have a symbiotic relationship with soil microbes. Soil microbes protect and feed a plant, while the plant feeds them with a carbon source that leaks from the roots. Plants communicate to soil microbes the need for them to solubilise the minerals required to make strong cell walls and chemical compounds, as the plant's protection against attackers. Such compounds ... are important for the health of humans and grazing animals. All terrestrial life is thus dependent on healthy soils for health and wellbeing; they make up the skin of planet Earth.

And, as Lindsay Falvey has it, room must be left for the billion or so small farmers who comprise the present majority of food producers; they must not be destroyed by a mindless corporate agribusiness system for the sake of monetary profit.[15]

Aquafoods

After more than 7000 years of farming the land, the twentyfirst century will herald the widespread farming by humans of the Earth's waters, fresh and salt.

A generation ago most of the seafood we ate originated in wild catches from the oceans, from lakes or rivers – that harvest peaked in 1995 and has been declining, slowly, ever since (Figure 9.1).[16] In view of this contraction, it is highly unlikely

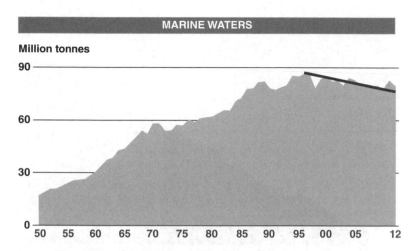

Figure 9.1. World wild fish harvest – in decline. Source: FAO 2016.

that wild fish catches can increase in line with the growth in human food demand – which is serious both from a food supply and a health perspective, as aquafoods are regarded, in many cases, as an essential component to a healthy global diet to reduce the burden of preventable disease.

From the 2020s on, therefore, more than half of the world's fish supply will come from farms, supplemented by millions of tonnes of edible water plants. Aquaculture, or the growing of fish, other aquatic animals like prawns, oysters, mussels, lobsters and sea cucumbers and the culture of algae both large (seaweeds) and small (microalgae) has, in barely two decades, emerged as the fastest growing food industry on Earth.

Aquaculture is expected to triple, even quadruple, in scale by the mid-century, providing 140 million tonnes of a global aquatic consumption of 220 million tonnes, according to the World Resources Institute (Figure 9.2). At this point, aquafoods could potentially contribute 40 per cent or more of the world's projected protein needs (about 550 million tonnes, according to the FAO).

One of the main reasons favouring the production of fish in farms, over cattle, sheep, pigs or other livestock, is that fish turn

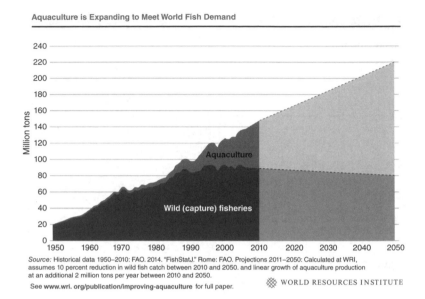

Figure 9.2. Projected growth of world aquaculture 1950–2050. Source: World Resources Institute.

feed into meat much more efficiently. For example, it typically takes 1.1–1.5 kilograms (kg) of feed (mostly made from grains, fish and food wastes) to produce 1 kg of fish – whereas it takes on average 2 kg of feed to produce 1 kg of chicken meat, 3 kg of feed to produce 1 kg of pig meat, 5 kg of feed to produce 1 kg of sheep meat and 6 kg of feed to produce 1 kg of beef. Thus, producing half the world's protein needs from fish instead of land animals could save the planet more than half a billion tonnes of grain a year. Indeed, it could save a great deal more.

The reason is that fish do not naturally eat grains, which are the seeds of grasses. They eat algae, or water plants. Even carnivorous fish eat algae and plankton when they are very small. The farming of algae can potentially feed most of the creatures which produce meat for humanity – and at the same time be used to harvest and reuse currently wasted nutrients. For this reason, algae farming – on land, in coastal areas and at sea – is likely to boom in the twentyfirst century. Through the 2000s and 2010s, the world harvest of water crops grew steadily from less than 10 million tonnes a year to more than 30 million tonnes[17] – but this is only a fraction of its potential, as farmers master the techniques and the value of algae, large and small, is more widely appreciated by industry, governments and consumers. Indonesia alone, for example, increased its seaweed production from less than a million to over ten million tonnes in barely a decade.

Many researchers consider that marine algae will become both a staple part of the human diet and a feed for fish and livestock by the mid-century – with species such as *Nannochloropsis* or 'Nanno', potentially using 75 times less area and 7400 times less water to produce the same amount of nutrition as steak.[18] Because they have never before been domesticated, algae have large potential for rapid, even dramatic, improvements in their yield of oils, carbohydrates and proteins – as shown by a scientific team who managed to double the lipid content of Nanno.[19]

However, algae do not just produce food for humans and feed for fish and animals. They can also produce renewable solar fuel for the transport industry, biodegradable plastics and textiles, fertilisers and green chemicals as well as perform valuable roles like cleansing polluted water and recycling nutrients. They offer a pathway of huge potential for turning urban organic waste back into food. They can also end the pollution of the world's oceans with plastics made from petroleum, by substituting bioplastics which break down much more quickly.[20]

Various species of algae contain 25–75 per cent oil – oil which can be converted to transport fuels as readily as fossil petroleum (which mostly came from algae in the first place) and without any net release of carbon dioxide – because the next crop of algae absorbs the carbon released when the last was consumed as fuel or food. Indeed, scientists have calculated most of the needs of the world transport industry could be supplied from marine algae farms producing clean, renewable liquid fuel from sunlight.[21] At current yields, the entire world oil industry could, in theory, be replaced by an area of algae farms the size of Brunei.

Driven by rising global demand for clean, renewable supplies of food, stockfeed, fuel, plastics and fertiliser, observers see an increasingly bright future for algae culture both on land and at sea. The World Economic Forum argues that aquaculture is inherently more efficient than land farming, because it produces plants and fish in three dimensions, instead of two, and thus has a much smaller footprint. Also, the temperature of water varies a lot less than temperature on land, leading to higher productivity and less vulnerability to climate shocks. With seafood grown in or near most cities using novel cultural methods such as aquaponics, the immense 2000-kilometre transport chains typically involved in supplying cities with their food can be greatly shortened.[22] Conducted in a sustainable way, aquaculture can help to end the global destruction of forests, farm lands and wildlife, reduce greenhouse emissions and supply a healthier diet, the WEF contends.

Sustainable is the operative word. Aquaculture is no help if it simply repeats the mistakes humans have made on land. It must control its own nutrient flows with utmost care, recycling wherever possible. It must avoid toxic chemical solutions as far as possible, to keep its product and the environment healthy. It must not pollute surrounding water. These are large technical challenges – but far from insoluble. One answer, for instance, is deepwater aquaculture – carried out in large sunken pens several miles offshore, thereby avoiding the problems of water fouling with fish waste and parasites, which have plagued coastal and estuarine fish farms, and disruption by bad weather. This type of farming – though costlier – has the support of environmentalists because it dissipates aquaculture's ecological impact into ocean currents while at the same time helping to protect wild fish stocks by offering an alternative supply of fresh, clean seafood.[23]

Furthermore, the WEF argues, aquaculture is 'pro-poor', offering a better living to people in poor and malnourished countries along with more protein in the diet. In Bangladesh, for example, the amount of farmed fish sold grew from 80,000 tonnes to over 2 million tonnes in a decade. A similar transformation is taking place in other Asian countries and in Africa.[24]

The Urban Food Revolution

The UN Food and Agriculture Organisation argues that urban food production will be an essential part of the green city of the future, helping to ensure 'food security, decent work and income, a clean environment and good governance for all citizens'.[25] Several hundred million 'urban farmers' are already hard at work growing food in Africa and South America, it says, and more than 20 countries have sought help to train future producers. As this and the examples described in Chapter 8 show, urban food production is advancing in a wide range of styles and technologies, from the apartment balcony to the corporate vertical farm, and from high-tech to low.

Urban farms: the simplest urban farms use traditional soil culture, with crops grown in beds, planter boxes and pots on spare land, in allotments or on the roofs and sides of buildings. Techniques range from conventional agriculture and horticulture using artificial fertilisers and chemicals to fully organic and permaculture systems. Besides fruit and vegetables, urban agriculture often encompasses the husbandry of small and large animals, poultry, fish, trees, urban beekeeping and insect farming, and some specialised grain production.[26] Fertile soils are usually created by composting urban organic waste or vermiculture (worm farms).

Sky farms: otherwise known as vertical farms, these are purpose-designed or redeveloped multi-storey buildings which grow crops in vertical stacks, usually under artificial lighting and with recycled irrigation water. Because of their size and cost (up to $50 million or more) such enterprises are usually corporate ventures. A variant is 'integrated agriculture' which takes place within large buildings, integrated around their other purposes as offices, manufacturing, retailing or residential structures. The technique of integrating food production with living and working space in a building is known as 'agritecture' and is a new industry shaping the urban food revolution.[27] Vertical farming has already caught the eye of defence planners, who argue it will be as important to protect these essential urban food sources from war and terrorism as sea lanes and transport hubs which deliver food to concentrated populations.[28]

Hydroponics: also known as 'fertigation', is the growing of plants in a liquid solution of minerals and nutrients. This can either be organic (i.e. extracted and concentrated from composted wastes) or inorganic (using synthetic fertilisers). The plants are generally grown in channels or piping filled with an inert growing medium such as rockwool or perlite, which supports their roots and ensures a steady supply of nutrient-enriched water, which is then adjusted for fertility and recycled. Provided there is adequate light, plants can be grown in far higher densities or stacked vertically, reducing space needs by up to 90 per cent compared with crops grown in a field.[29] Hydroponics is used at every scale from balcony and back-yard to large industrial complexes growing bulk crops of tomatoes, strawberries, peppers, lettuces and other food plants. Their salient feature is a closed nutrient loop that avoids waste and contamination of the wider world.

Aquaponics: is the integrated production of fish and vegetables in large tanks, with the vegetables floating on rafts, their roots dangling in the water, nourished by waste produced by the fish.[30] Fish grown include tilapia and barramundi, various types of carp, trout, shrimps and edible water snails. Typical crops include: lettuce, kale, watercress, arugula, decorative flowers, mint, herbs, okra, spring onions and leeks, radishes, spinach, bok choy and other small leafy vegetables. Its advantages include high yields of both plants and fish from a small area and the recycling of water and nutrients in a closed system. Sound water chemistry and hygiene are of paramount importance.

Aeroponics: is the enclosed culture of leafy green vegetables without soil, their roots dangling in a nutrient-enriched mist. This saves up to 95 per cent of the water, compared to field farming, as well as using minimal amounts of nutrients or fertilisers. Advanced systems use variable LED lighting which can be tuned to suit each type of crop to maximise its yield. In fully enclosed systems, pests are avoided by high levels of crop hygiene, so no pesticides are required. Such systems are often fully automated with computer monitoring of plant growth and nutrient delivery rates.[31]

Entomoculture: is the farming of insects, either as food for people or as feed for livestock like fish and poultry. Long practised throughout Asia and India, where insects are popular street food, it usually involves the culture of edible species of crickets, grasshoppers and locusts, mealworms, waxworms, cockroaches, silkworms and honeybees. Its main advantage in the green city is a high yield of protein, carbohydrate and micronutrients from very little land and water, and the ability to recycle crop and food wastes as insect feed. Besides being sold whole and fresh-cooked, insects are also made into high-protein flour for use in a variety of breads, snackfoods and sweets. Some beetles are farmed to produce specialty textile dyes and wood lacquer.[32]

Protected agriculture: also known as 'controlled environment agriculture' (CEA) usually takes place under some form of climatic protection, be it a shade house, a greenhouse, a shipping container, an old building or a purpose-designed sky farm. The main aim is to minimise or eliminate the variation in crop yields caused by weather and plant pests, leading to much more reliable food yields year-round. It is particularly useful in cities and in hot, dry regions of the world where irrigation water is scarce, for recycling transpired water. It is a major technology for climate-proofing the global food supply and can be coupled with any of the types of urban food system above.[33]

Floating farms: first developed by the ancient Aztecs of Mexico on floating beds of reeds, the technique of floating farms

extends the area for growing small crops to the surface of
lakes, rivers and the sea near large cities. Modern concepts
employ solar desalination to irrigate multi-storey farms on
floating pontoons to supply fresh vegetables and fish for
littoral cities such as Singapore, Tokyo, Jakarta, Shanghai
and Mumbai.[34]

Desert farms: offer food security to some of the world's most
climate-threatened regions, in Africa, South and Central
Asia, the Middle East and Central America. Their many
variants include shade and greenhouse culture of fruits and
vegetables, the supply of solar-desalinated groundwater or
seawater, the recycling of precious nutrients and the
production of camel and goat dairy products and meat.

Biocultures: see below.

Online markets: just as supermarkets drove the local corner food
store out of business, the burgeoning online food delivery
market is likely to drive the bulk supermarket to revise its
business model. Cooked food or fresh produce ordered
online from your favourite restaurant or grower's market
via smart device and delivered to the point of consumption
by electric van, scooter, cycle, robot vehicle or even drone is
revolutionising the urban food scene, especially for local
food startups who are challenging the predominance of
giant supermarket chains. Technologies like Blockchain are
expected to further enhance the sourcing and delivery
of food.

At the other end of the spectrum, expanding farmers' markets,
street stalls and 'slow food' movements offer the food-conscious
consumer or 'locavore' a better eating experience. The widespread use of apps reporting consumer reviews and experiences
with food is likely to drive the trend towards health and sustainability, changing demand signals all along the global food
chain.[35]

These and variant technologies comprise the coming urban
food revolution which will recycle our waste, bring food security
to the great cities of the world, improve human diets through
fresh, clean food, generate new and enjoyable work, combat

climate change, reduce the risk of war and help to end the Sixth Extinction of life on Earth.

Biocultures

Bioculture – or 'cellular agriculture' as it is sometimes known – is an emerging technology for producing food products from cultures of the cells from plants, animals, fungi and microbes. It is the commercial realisation of the tissue cultures which have been used in agricultural, biological and medical research since the technique was discovered by Wilhelm Roux in 1885. In the twentyfirst century it will furnish humanity with safe, healthy and nutritious foods or food ingredients in large volumes that require minimal inputs of land, water and energy.

Among the eyecatching advances under way are cowless meat and milk products, chickenless eggs and meat, pigless bacon and fishless fish. These are not substitutes made from vegetable material like soy – they are indeed true meat cultivated by carefully feeding embryo stem cells with the right nutrients to turn them into muscle fibre. The only thing missing is the animal in the middle of the process – which goes direct from living embryo to meat product at a speed and with an efficiency no animal can match. The technique was demonstrated by Professor Mark Post at Maastricht University when, in 2011 he produced the world's first 'test-tube sausage' followed a couple of years later by the first hamburger.[36] This breakthrough in food production has since been followed by biotech and food startups around the planet, in what some experts consider may become a technology boom to rival or exceed solar energy.

The UN Global Environment Facility explains why: 'Analyses show that producing 1000 kg of cultured meat requires approximately 99% less land, 82–96% less water, 78–96% less greenhouse gas emissions, and 7–45% less energy compared to conventionally produced European livestock', it said.[37] 'Research is [also] focusing on: creating meat substitutes from plant-based protein; engineering microbes to produce dairy products like milk; and making other products such as leather, fur, and wood. Cellular agriculture could help to achieve a more sustainable food production system, and significantly reduce the environmental impacts of the current system.'[38]

'Cellular agriculture could also improve food safety and transparency, animal welfare, the nutritional composition of food, and lead to increased product shelf life. Moreover, if scaled-up and made widely accessible, cellular agriculture could help reduce the protein nutritional deficit in developing countries', it added.

The first cultured hamburger, a research product, cost $325,000 to produce in Professor Post's university laboratory. Two years later a company called Future Meat Technologies said it had the cost down to $325 a pound and was aiming for $2–3 a pound by the early 2020s.[39]

Cultured meat is controversial. On the one hand it offers meat which is free from cruelty (to either animals or humans) and meets contemporary ethical standards with a much lower environmental footprint than conventional meat from animals.[40] On the other hand, its critics claim it is 'not real meat' and that its climate credentials may not be as good as natural grazing of animals (which, if done sustainably, can lock up large amounts of carbon). However, since the cultures are raised in bioreactors, they are immune to the impacts of weather and climate that afflict livestock systems. On the dietary side, it is likely they can offer a meat alternative that is designer-profiled to the needs of consumers with particular health problems, at an affordable price.

Meat is far from the only new food product that can be produced from biocultures. There is also milk made from yeast cells, vegetarian 'meat' and eggs made from plant cells. With gene editing, it may become possible for bio-factories to make new medical drugs, biofuels, bioplastics and green chemicals, even insulation, textiles and construction materials.

Carolyn Mattick of the American Association for the Advancement of Science assesses it as 'a technology that presents opportunities to improve animal welfare, enhance human health, and decrease the environmental footprint of meat production. At the same time, it is not without challenges. In particular, because the technology largely replaces biological systems with chemical and mechanical ones, it has the potential to increase industrial energy consumption and, consequently, greenhouse gas emissions'.[41]

The big question is: will consumers eat biocultured food? The answer, it appears, is that today's consumers do not know what is in a sausage, a pie, a chicken nugget, a dim sum or a crab stick anyway – and will probably eat it provided the price is right and the food is tasty and safe. In support of this view is the fact that, in the 1950s nobody on Earth wore synthetic fabrics made from petroleum – and today almost everybody does, suggesting that novel technologies can be universally embraced provided they meet consumer needs, wishes and budgets. This suggests the big opportunities for cultured foods will be at the lower end of the market price range, and in specialty health or ethical foods.

A major challenge facing this very new technology is how it will be received by the highly complex system of food law and regulation, institutions, commercial networks, healthcare policies, technical factors and social mores that influence the modern food supply.[42] These have posed no real obstacle to the introduction of genetically modified foods, and so may be expected not to do so for biocultured foods. However, the issue will be decided, in the end, by consumer preferences.

Another big question is: what effect will cultured meat have on the 60 billion animals which are slaughtered every year to feed humanity – and on the hundreds of millions of people who raise and process them? Since livestock now represent 65 per cent by weight of all the vertebrate land animals on Earth, clearly an alternative way to grow meat could potentially replace many of these – and so help to restore the ecosystems which humans have destroyed or damaged in trying to raise and feed so many livestock, allowing wild animal numbers to recover. However, it is likely that many consumers will still prefer their meat 'natural', in the same way that many people still choose to wear cotton, linen or wool over synthetic textiles, or build their homes from wood instead of concrete. This means there will

still be a large market for meat from livestock reared sustainably
on eco-farms or grazed sustainably in the rangelands – and that
animal meat, as an up-market product, will command a pre-
mium price, delivering the farmer a better return which she or
he can use to restore and preserve the natural and farming
environments. It is the intensive livestock industries, with their
high use of compound feeds, drugs and chemicals, their pollution and disease issues and questionable ethical practices that
stand to be supplanted by cultured meat, at the low-cost end of
the market. In other words, cultured meat can help to restore
the wild world (including the oceans) by supplanting the industrially produced product which causes so much pollution, greenhouse emissions and land cleared for feedgrain production
(which amounts to nearly two thirds of the total world area
farmed for grains). Former livestock producers will find fresh
opportunities in the biocultures sector – and others as eco-
farmers or Stewards of the Earth, helping to rewild the planet.

Coupled with biocultures, potentially, is another food technology revolution in 3D printing of food from raw ingredients,
or even from basic nutrient materials produced in biocultures.
Food printers have a range of possible applications, from
printing out hamburgers, pizza, donuts and snackfoods in fast
food outlets and vending machines, to automated production of
airline meals, to the sculpting of unique and beautiful designer
desserts in elite restaurants. In the home they can be used to
print out novel processed foods from raw, healthy ingredients,
thus sidestepping the unhealthy chemical dyes, additives and
preservatives and excess salt, sugar and fat of the industrial food
chain.[43] Dozens of different food printers are already on the
market, and hundreds of tech startups and major corporate
players are forecast to be distributing them by the 2020s.[44]

According to the GEF, biocultures can thus assist in mitigating
climate change, land degradation, deforestation, chemical and
waste pollution, over-fishing and biodiversity loss by diverting
livestock production from the current resource-intensive
system.

Also, according to the evidence presented in this book, biocultures have the potential to deliver a major peace dividend in the form of a safe, reliable supply of nutritious food to regions of the world beset with resource scarcity, instability and war. They can help materially in overcoming both hunger and poverty and in stabilising the local food supply, and hence government, in developing regions. Biocultures are thus an important, and highly affordable, 'weapon of peace' for the twentyfirst century.

Exploring an Unexplored Planet

Today the average consumer eats fewer than 200 different plants as food. Yet there are, according to Australian agronomist Dr Bruce French, no fewer than 30,500 edible plants on the Earth.

Dr French gained the first inkling to this stunning insight in the 1970s, when he was working in the highlands of Papua New Guinea, teaching the locals about modern farming methods. Instead the locals – who had been farming for around 12,000 years – taught him a thing or two about the richness, variety and nutritional value of a diet still substantially based upon a wild harvest and native crops. In 2005 Bruce gave a talk to his local Devonport Rotary Club about what he'd observed in Papua New Guinea, and how he thought this hidden indigenous knowledge could help ease world hunger. In less than two years he had teamed up with Rotary International to compile a world catalogue of plants[45] that are good to eat, drawing heavily on the rapidly eroding store of knowledge of native peoples still living on their land around the globe. This, plus an accompanying education programme called Learn*Grow, has since been shared with over 35 partner countries.[46]

The aim of the *Food Plant Solutions* project was to produce an online database of useful edible plants from all continents, and how to grow and prepare them as food, for countries struggling with hunger and poverty – but, in the event, Dr French should probably also be cast in bronze by the World Chefs' Association for identifying tens of thousands of novel ingredients their members, the best chefs on the planet, had never even heard of. Thanks to an observant eye and a flash of insight, Bruce French has reshaped the human culinary destiny, the future of food and of farming.

The take-home message from the life's work of Bruce French is that modern humans, while dreaming of settling the Moon or Mars, have yet to explore the Earth. At least in terms of what is good and healthy to eat. We have, for generations, ignored what is under our very noses – especially in the modern age, whose oppressively narrow food boundaries are defined for us by a handful of gigantic food and supermarket corporations. The freedom of choice enjoyed by all our ancestors, and the few remaining indigenous people scattered around the world, has been denied us, and with it the health benefits. An act of oblivion, inflicted by the industrialisation and corporatisation of food, has reduced the number of the plants humans once ate by over 99 per cent. Yet, somewhere, in the deeper recesses of our souls, we know we're missing out – and the urban food revolution, with its worldwide following on social media, is the first universal sign of it.

In Australia, where the European (and, latterly, American and Asian) diet has reigned for 250 years, Dr French has identified no fewer than 6100 edible native plants used by the continent's Aboriginal peoples for food and medicine for tens of thousands of years. So far, only about five of these foods have found their way into even the regular Australian diet, let alone the world diet – the macadamia nut being the best-known example. If one considers the impact of native American plants like the potato, tomato, pepper, maize and avocado on the world diet and cuisine post-Columbus, it offers some notion of the phenomenal potential scale of the food revolution to come. And that is only land-based plants. We should also consider unfamiliar livestock, marine organisms, algae and insects – not to mention entirely novel and unheard-of foods which may be invented as a result of technologies like biocultures and gene editing.

Since the plants in Dr French's database are mainly vegetables, they are ideally suited to the expanding world horticulture industry, and especially to climate-proof urban food production – being grown in a fraction of the time and with a fraction of the resources used to grow grain or large animals. They guarantee that the transition to a new global diet will be spectacularly diverse, tasty and healthy – making today's most interesting and exotic salad or vegetable dish look plain and wan by comparison.

With the recycling of urban nutrients – especially micronutrients – this prodigious diversity offers great potential for preventing lifestyle diseases through diet, a general improvement in human health and reduction of healthcare costs. To take one example, the bitter melon or bitter gourd, grown throughout Asia, India, Africa and Latin America but still unfamiliar in the western diet, has been scientifically shown to lower blood sugar levels and reduce the appetite of diabetics as effectively as any medical drug[47], and there are many similar plants with medicinal qualities in ethnic diets around the world that are presently neglected by a western medicine driven chiefly by the profitability of drug companies. The *Food Plant Solutions* database unfolds the prospect of thousands of new diet-based preventatives and health enhancers, subject to scientific proof that they work.

The abiding lesson of Dr French's work is that the human diet can be vastly more interesting, delicious and healthy than the narrow, industrialised feed we consume today, provided we first take the time and the care to explore our own planet and appreciate more fully what it has to offer.

The Age of Food

Human progress is defined by our technologies and the cultures they procreate: stone, bronze, iron, computers. Just as the 1970s were the age of rock 'n roll, and the 1990s the era of the internet, we are entering the Age of Food.

Never has world cuisine been so spectacularly diverse – or so far short of its true potential.

Never have the opportunities offered by food been so many or so great – to restore the planet and its climate, to end the Sixth

Extinction, to bring peace and plenty to all lands and societies, and to give rise to novel technologies and rewarding and useful employment and self-employment in megacities, on farms, in the oceans and in the world's rewilded lands.

Food can give full rein to humanity's imagination, dreams and ideas. It can prevent war and secure our future in the time of our greatest peril.

Food is one of the most creative acts which we humans perform.

How well we do it will shape and define the future of our civilisation, now and forever.

10 CONCLUSION: KEY RECOMMENDATIONS OF THIS BOOK

1. Develop a sustainable, nourishing and resilient global food system suited to conditions in the twentyfirst century and founded on:
    (a) ecological or regenerative farming,
    (b) aquaculture, and
    (c) urban food production.
2. Replan all of the Earth's cities so that they
    (a) recycle all their nutrients and water back into food production and fertile soil,
    (b) have a sustainable, climate-proof local source of food year-round, and
    (c) are based on permaculture principles.
3. Re-allocate 20 per cent of world military spending to 'peace through food'. Understand that sustainable food investment is defence spending, can reduce tensions and so
    (a) prevent many wars from starting in the first place, and
    (b) avoid vast movements of refugees which may otherwise overwhelm other regions, countries and cultures.
4. Rewild half the planet through a global movement led by small farmers, former farmers and indigenous peoples, known as *Stewards of the Earth*, to end the Sixth Extinction of life on Earth.
5. Raise a new generation of food-aware children, who understand how to eat healthily and sustainably, through a *Year of Food* in every junior school on the planet.
6. Put women in charge of business, politics, government, religion and society for the sake of human civilisation and its survival in the century of its greatest peril.

THE AUTHOR

Julian Cribb is an Australian author and science writer. He is a Fellow of the UK Royal Society for the Arts, the Australian Academy of Technological Science and Engineering (ATSE) and the Australian National University Emeritus Faculty.

His career includes appointments as scientific editor and editor of several newspapers and president of national professional bodies for agricultural journalism and science communication.

His published work includes over 9000 articles and ten books. He has received 32 awards for journalism. His internationally acclaimed book *The Coming Famine* (2010) explored the risks facing the global food supply in the century of peak population. His book *Poisoned Planet* (2014) examines the contamination of the Earth system and humanity by anthropogenic chemicals and how to prevent it. His book *Surviving the 21st Century* (Springer 2017) tackles the ten huge threats now facing civilisation and what we can do about them.

ENDNOTES

Chapter 1

1 The Four Horsemen, from The Apocalypse. https://www
.metmuseum.org/toah/works-of-art/19.73.209/

2 Barb Spearmen. http://www.bradshawfoundation.com/bradshaws/
description30.php.

3 Williams A *et al.*, Sea-level change and demography during the
last glacial termination and early Holocene across the Australian
continent, *Quaternary Science Reviews*, 182, 15 February 2018,
pp. 144–54. https://www.sciencedirect.com/science/article/pii/
S0277379117305267

4 Rickard J (9 October 2009), First Gallic Invasion of Italy, 390 B.C.,
http://www.historyofwar.org/articles/wars_first_gallic_invasion_
italy.html

5 Hallward B L, 1930. The Siege of Carthage. *Cambridge Ancient History*
Vol. VIII. Cambridge University Press.

6 McMichael A, 2017. *Climate Change and the Health of Nations*. Oxford
University Press.

7 For an excellent account, see Harper K, 2017. *The Fate of Rome:
Climate, Disease, and the End of an Empire*. Princeton University Press.
https://press.princeton.edu/titles/11079.html

8 Christian C and Elmore L, 2017. Droughts of Dismay: Rainfall and
Assassinations in Ancient Rome, Working Papers 1703, Brock
University, Department of Economics. https://ideas.repec.org/p/brk/
wpaper/1703.html

9 Haywood J, 1999. *The Vikings*. Sutton Press.

10 See Chapter 2 on *Lebensraum* as a primary motive for World War II.

11 'Man is the wolf of man', a Latin proverb.

12 http://archaeobotanist.blogspot.com.au/2010/07/arrival-of-wheat-in-
china.html

13 http://ricepedia.org/culture/history-of-rice-cultivation

14 In contrast with the highly urbanised Guangzhou-Shenzen region
on the Pearl River delta, where an estimated 120 million now reside.

15 https://www.theguardian.com/world/2013/jan/01/china-great-
famine-book-tombstone

16 http://www.circleid.com/posts/20141001_infographic_where_in_
  the_world_do_chinese_people_live/
17 https://www.foreignaffairs.com/reviews/capsule-review/china-s-second-
  continent-how-million-migrants-are-building-new-empire-africa
18 Brautigam D, 2015. *Will Africa Feed China?* Oxford University Press.
19 https://www.pri.org/stories/2013-01-03/china-and-worst-ever-man-
  made-gender-gap
20 Lal N, 2017. Hunger in a Time of Plenty. The Wire. https://thewire
  .in/54809/chronic-hunger-lingers-in-the-midst-of-plenty/
21 De Waal A, 2017. The Nazis Used It, We Use It. *The London Review of
  Books.* https://www.lrb.co.uk/v39/n12/alex-de-waal/the-nazis-used-it-
  we-use-it
22 De Waal A, 2017. *Mass Starvation* Wiley. https://www.wiley
  .com/en-au/Mass+Starvation%3A+The+History+and+Future+of
  +Famine-p-9781509524662
23 *Gale Encyclopaedia of Medicine,* 2006. Starvation. https://www
  .encyclopedia.com/medicine/diseases-and-conditions/pathology/
  starvation
24 UNHCR, 2018. Forced displacement at record 68.5 million. UNHCR,
  June 19, 2018. http://www.unhcr.org/en-au/news/stories/2018/6/
  5b222c494/forced-displacement-record-685-million.html
25 United Nations, 2017. International Migration Report. http://www
  .un.org/en/development/desa/population/migration/publications/
  migrationreport/docs/MigrationReport2017_Highlights.pdf

Chapter 2

1 http://www.history.com/topics/thirty-years-war
2 Daudin P, The 30 Years War: the first Modern War?, ICRC,
  http://blogs.icrc.org/law-and-policy/2017/05/23/thirty-years-war-
  first-modern-war/
3 Oosthoek K J, The Little Ice Age, Environmental History Resources,
  2015. https://www.eh-resources.org/little-ice-age/
4 Pfister U, The Population History of Germany, Max Planck Institut,
  2010. http://www.demogr.mpg.de/papers/working/wp-2010-035.pdf
5 Cohen J, 2012. Little Ice Age, Big Consequences. History, January 31
  2012. https://www.history.com/news/little-ice-age-big-consequences
6 Llewellyn J and Thompson S, Harvest failures, Alpha History, 2015,
  accessed January 2017, http://alphahistory.com/frenchrevolution/
  harvest-failures/

7 Kaplan SL, The Famine Plot: Persuasion in 18th Century France, *Transactions of the American Philosophical Society*, 1982.

8 Harcave S, 1970. *The Russian Revolution*, London: Collier Books.

9 Figes O, 2017. The women's protest that sparked the Russian Revolution, The Guardian. https://www.theguardian.com/world/2017/mar/08/womens-protest-sparked-russian-revolution-international-womens-day

10 Lo que separa la civilización de la anarquía son solo siete comidas.

11 Slezkine Y, 2017. *The House of Government*. Princeton University Press.

12 Conquest R, 1986. *The Harvest of Sorrow*. Oxford University Press.

13 Slezkine Y. op cit.

14 Vardy S B and Vardy A H, 2007. Cannibalism in Stalin's Russia and Mao's China. *East European Quarterly*, XLI, No. 2 June 2007. http://www.paulbogdanor.com/left/cannibalism.pdf

15 Slezkine Y op cit.

16 This anti-science episode has unpleasant modern parallels in the efforts of the US Trump regime to suppress climate science and all reference to climate in US government documents and websites. The cost of ignorance is likely to be similar.

17 Collis B, 2001. A Rice God Named Harry, The Australian Weekend Magazine.

18 Simkin J, 1997. Trench Food. Spartacus Educational. http://spartacus-educational.com/FWWtrenchfood.htm

19 University of Sussex, Food During the First World War, http://www.eastsussexww1.org.uk/food-first-world-war/

20 Cornish P, Rationing and Food Shortages During the First World War, Imperial War Museum, 5 January 2018. https://www.iwm.org.uk/history/rationing-and-food-shortages-during-the-first-world-war

21 Peterson H C,1939. *Propaganda for War. The Campaign against American Neutrality, 1914–1917*. University of Oklahoma Press.

22 UK National Archives, The blockade on Germany. Spotlights on History, accessed 28 Jan 2018. http://www.nationalarchives.gov.uk/pathways/firstworldwar/spotlights/blockade.htm

23 Kriegsbrot – made of dried potato, oat and barley husks, even straw.

24 UK National Archives. Op cit.

25 Meyer G J, 2006. *A World Undone*. Random House Publishing Group, p. 415.

26 Vincent C P, 1985. *The Politics of Hunger: The Allied Blockade of Germany, 1915-1919*. Ohio University Press.

27 Cribb J H J, 2017. Jimmy Perry: A Soldiers' Life. Published privately.

28 Mernagh R, 2015. Why did Germany lose in World War I?, Quora. https://www.quora.com/Why-did-Germany-lose-in-World-War-I

29 Friedrich O, 1972. Before the Deluge: A Portrait of Berlin in the 1920s. Harper Perennial.

30 Onion R, 2014. A Post–World War I "Hunger Map of Europe", Slate. http://www.slate.com/blogs/the_vault/2014/07/31/history_of_famine_in_europe_after_wwi_a_hunger_map_for_american_kids.html

31 Kershaw I, 1998. Hitler. Allen Lane, Penguin, p. 153.

32 Messerschmidt M, 1990. "Foreign Policy and Preparation for War", Germany and the Second World War, Volume I, Clarendon Press: Oxford, UK.

33 Gerhard G, 2009. Food and Genocide: Nazi Agrarian Politics in the Occupied Territories of the Soviet Union. Contemporary European History, 18(1), 45–65. doi:10.1017/S0960777308004827

34 International Military Tribunal, Nuremberg, 1948.

35 https://en.wikipedia.org/wiki/Hunger_Plan

36 The 1930s and War Economy. Japan National Graduate Institute for Policy Studies. Accessed 31 Jan 2018. http://www.grips.ac.jp/teacher/oono/hp/lecture_J/lec09.htm

37 McDowell, K, Japan in Manchuria: Agricultural Emigration in the Japanese Empire, 1932–1945, Eras Journal, Monash University. http://artsonline.monash.edu.au/eras/1094-2/

38 Subsequently, most were murdered at the end of World War II by the invading Russian and Chinese armies.

39 Collingham E, 2011. The Taste of War: World War Two and the Battle for Food. Penguin New York.

40 Collingham, 2011 op cit.

41 Bacque J, 2010. Crimes and Mercies: The Fate of German Civilians under Allied Occupation, 1944–1950. Talon Books. http://talonbooks.com/books/crimes-and-mercies

42 Hill K et al., 2008. The Demographic Impact of Partition in the Punjab in 1947. Population Studies, 62(2), 155–170.

43 Schmidt J J J, 2018. Personal communication.

44 Wernaart B, 2013. The Enforceability of the Human Right to Adequate Food: A Comparative Study. Wageningen Academic Publishers.

45 Cribb J H J, 2017. Surviving the 21st Century, Springer, Switzerland.

Chapter 3

1   For example: https://www.google.com.au/search?q=empty+shelves
    +in+supermarkets&sa=X&tbm=isch&tbo=u&source=univ&ved=
    2ahUKEwiGp8Xk4tncAhVEvbwKHZ-6AEsQsAR6BAgBEAE&biw=
    1536&bih=716

2   UN Water, 2018. Water Facts. http://www.unwater.org/water-facts/?
    utm_content=buffer23e46&utm_medium=social&utm_source=
    twitter.com&utm_campaign=buffer

3   Gleick P and Iceland C, 2018. Water Security and Conflict. World
    Resources Institute/Pacific Institute. http://pacinst.org/wp-content/
    uploads/2018/08/Water-Security-and-Conflict_Aug-2018-2.pdf

4   World Water Council, 2000. The Use of Water Today. http://www
    .worldwatercouncil.org/fileadmin/wwc/Library/WWVision/
    Chapter2.pdf

5   Worldwatch Institute, 2012. http://www.worldwatch.org/global-
    irrigated-area-record-levels-expansion-slowing-0

6   UN Water, 2016. The United Nations world water development
    report, 2016: Water and jobs: facts and figures. http://
    unesdoc.unesco.org/images/0024/002440/244041e.pdf

7   Hoekstra A Y and Mckonnen M, 2010. The Water Footprint of
    Humanity, *PNAS* 109 (9) 3232–3237. http://www.pnas.org/content/
    109/9/3232.full

8   Mekonnen M M and Hoekstra A Y, 2016. Four billion people facing
    severe water scarcity. Science Advances, 12 Feb 2016. http://
    advances.sciencemag.org/content/2/2/e1500323

9   UNESCO, 2018. World Water report 2018. http://unesdoc.unesco
    .org/images/0026/002614/261424e.pdf

10 Schuster-Wallace C J and Sandford R, 2015. Water in the World We
    Want. United Nations University Institute for Water, Environment
    and Health, 2015. https://inweh.unu.edu/wp-content/uploads/2019/
    03/Water-in-the-World-We-Want.pdf

11 Howard B C, 2016. 8 Mighty Rivers Run Dry from Overuse, *National
    Geographic*. https://www.nationalgeographic.com/environment/
    photos/rivers-run-dry/

12 International Rivers, 2018. The State of the World's Rivers.
    https://www.internationalrivers.org/rivers-in-crisis

13 Qureshi W A, 2017. Indus Waters Treaty: An Impediment to the
    Indian Hydrohegemony, Denver Journal of International Law and
    Policy.

14 Ravilious K, 2016. Many of world's lakes are vanishing and some
    may be gone forever, New Scientist. https://www.newscientist.com/
    article/2079562-many-of-worlds-lakes-are-vanishing-and-some-may-
    be-gone-forever/
15 Izhitskiy A S et al., 2016. Present state of the Aral Sea: diverging
    physical and biological characteristics of the residual basins. *Nature
    Sci. Rep.* 6, 23906; doi: 10.1038/srep23906. http://www.nature.com/
    articles/srep23906
16 UN News 2017. Lake Chad Basin crisis is both humanitarian and
    ecological – UN agriculture agency. https://news.un.org/en/story/
    2017/04/555172-lake-chad-basin-crisis-both-humanitarian-and-
    ecological-un-agriculture-agency
17 Peryman L, 2012. Unchecked industry reduces land of a thousand
    lakes to a struggling few. https://journal.probeinternational.org/
    2012/07/20/unchecked-industry-reduces-land-of-a-thousand-lakes-
    to-a-struggling-few/
18 Weiss K R, 2018. Some of the World's Biggest Lakes Are Drying Up.
    Here's Why. *National Geographic*, March 2018.
19 UN Water, 2018. World Water Development Report 2018.
20 Lakenet, 2018. http://www.worldlakes.org/climatechange.asp
21 Van der Gun J, 2012. *Groundwater and Global Change: Trends,
    Opportunities and Challenges*. UNESCO, 2012. http://unesdoc.unesco
    .org/images/0021/002154/215496e.pdf
22 IGRAC, 2010. *Groundwater depletion leads to sea level rise*. International
    Groundwater Resources Assessment Centre (IGRAC), 2010.
    https://www.un-igrac.org/news/global-groundwater-depletion-leads-
    sea-level-rise
23 NASA, 2015. Study: Third of Big Groundwater Basins in Distress,
    July 2015. http://www.nasa.gov/jpl/grace/study-third-of-big-
    groundwater-basins-in-distress
24 American Geophysical Union, 2016. Groundwater resources
    around the world could be depleted by 2050s. AGU100,
    December 15, 2016. https://news.agu.org/press-release/agu-fall-
    meeting-groundwater-resources-around-the-world-could-be-
    depleted-by-2050s/
25 UN Water, 2016. The UN World Water Development Report 2016.
    UNESCO. http://unesdoc.unesco.org/images/0024/002440/244041e
    .pdf

26 Rodell M *et al.*, 2018. Emerging trends in global freshwater
    availability. *Nature*, 16 May 2018. https://www.nature.com/articles/
    s41586-018-0123-1#Abs1
27 Johnston I, 2017. The Earth Is Losing Its Ice. The Guardian, 11 May
    2017. https://www.independent.co.uk/environment/earth-ice-
    melting-glaciers-disappearing-glacier-los-glaciares-national-park-us-
    geological-survey-a7730466.html
28 NASA, 2018. Glaciers. Global Climate Change: Vital signs for the
    planet. https://climate.nasa.gov/interactives/global-ice-viewer/#/1
29 Choudhary A A, 2018. SC: Wake up or you'll have zero groundwater
    by 2020. *Times of India*, July 12, 2018. https://m.timesofindia.com/
    city/delhi/sc-wake-up-or-youll-have-zero-groundwater-by-2020/amp_
    articleshow/64953385.cms?_twitter_impression=true
30 Guterres A, 2018. Remarks at Launch of International Decade for
    Action "Water for Sustainable Development" 2018–2028. March 22,
    2018. https://www.un.org/sg/en/content/sg/speeches/2018-03-22/
    decade-action-water-sustainable-development-remarks
31 Gleick P, 2018. https://www.worldwater.org/water-conflict/
32 Gleick P and Iceland C, 2018. Water Security and Conflict. World
    Resources Institute/Pacific Institute. http://pacinst.org/wp-content/
    uploads/2018/08/Water-Security-and-Conflict_Aug-2018-2.pdf
33 Engelke P and Sticklor R, 2015. Water Wars: The Next Great Driver
    of Global Conflict? The National Interest. http://nationalinterest.org/
    feature/water-wars-the-next-great-driver-global-conflict-13842
34 World Economic Forum 2018. The Global Risks Report. https://
    www.weforum.org/reports/the-global-risks-report-2018
35 Da Silva, 2018. UN News. https://news.un.org/en/story/2018/03/
    1005362
36 Sengupta S, 2018. *Warming, Water Crisis, Then Unrest: How Iran Fits an
    Alarming Pattern*. New York Times, Jan 18, 2018. https://www.nytimes
    .com/2018/01/18/climate/water-iran.html?smid=tw-nytclimate&
    smtyp=cur
37 UN FAO 2015, Status of the World's Soil Resources. http://www.fao
    .org/3/a-i5228e.pdf
38 Leahy S, 2018. 75% of Earth's Land Areas Are Degraded. *National
    Geographic*, March 26, 2018. https://news.nationalgeographic.com/
    2018/03/ipbes-land-degradation-environmental-damage-report-spd/?
    beta=true

39 Watts J, 2018. Land degradation threatens human wellbeing, major report warns. *The Guardian*, 27 March 2018. https://www.theguardian.com/environment/2018/mar/26/land-degradation-is-undermining-human-wellbeing-un-report-warns.

40 UNCCD 2017. Global Land Outlook. https://www.unccd.int/sites/default/files/documents/2017-09/GLO_Full_Report_low_res.pdf

41 Wilkinson B H and McElroy B J, 2007. The impact of humans on continental erosion and sedimentation, *Geological Society of America Bulletin*, January/February, 2007, 119 (1-2), 140–56.

42 Cameron D, Osborne C, Horton P and Sinclair M, 2015. *A sustainable model for intensive agriculture*, University of Sheffield. 2 December 2015.

43 Crawford J, 2012. What If the World's Soil Runs Out? *TIME.* 12 December 2012. http://world.time.com/2012/12/14/what-if-the-worlds-soil-runs-out/

44 Alexandratos N and Bruinsma J, 2012. World Agriculture Towards 2030/2050. UN FAO. ESA working paper 12-03.

45 World Bank, 2017. https://data.worldbank.org/indicator/AG.LND.AGRI.K2?end=2016&start=1961

46 UN 2012. Land and Conflict. http://www.un.org/en/land-natural-resources-conflict/pdfs/GN_Land%20and%20Conflict.pdf

47 De Soysa I and Gleditsch N P, 1998. *To Cultivate Peace: Agriculture in a World of Conflict*, PRIO, 1999.

48 Chatham House, 2017. Chokepoints and Vulnerabilities in Global Food Trade. https://www.chathamhouse.org/publication/chokepoints-vulnerabilities-global-food-trade

49 UN FAO, 2016. Climate change and food security: risks and responses. http://www.fao.org/3/a-i5188e.pdf

50 Betts A *et al.*, 2018. Changes in climate extremes, fresh water availability and vulnerability to food insecurity projected at 1.5°C and 2°C global warming with a higher-resolution global climate model. *Philosophical Transactions of the Royal Society*, April 2, 2018. http://rsta.royalsocietypublishing.org/content/376/2119/20160452

51 Jiang D *et al.*, 2018. Climate change of 4°C global warming above pre-industrial levels. *Advances in Atmospheric Sciences*, July 2018, 35 (7), 757–70. https://link.springer.com/article/10.1007/s00376-018-7160-4

52 Zhu C *et al.*, 2018. Carbon dioxide (CO_2) levels this century will alter the protein, micronutrients and vitamin content of rice with potential health consequences for the poorest rice-dependent countries. *Science Advances*, 23 May 2018. http://advances.sciencemag.org/content/4/5/eaaq1012

53 Carrick D, 2013. Climate change poses grave threat to security, says UK envoy. *The Guardian*. https://www.theguardian.com/environment/2013/jun/30/climate-change-security-threat-envoy

54 US DoD 2014, Quadrennial Defence Review. http://archive.defense.gov/pubs/2014_Quadrennial_Defense_Review.pdf

55 US DoD 2015, Response to Congressional Inquiry on National Security Implications of Climate-Related Risks and a Changing Climate. http://archive.defense.gov/pubs/150724-congressional-report-on-national-implications-of-climate-change.pdf?source=govdelivery

56 Stavridis J, 2018. *America's Most Pressing Threat? Climate Change*. Bloomberg. https://www.bloomberg.com/view/articles/2018-01-11/america-s-no-1-enemy-climate-change

57 US Department of Defense, 2018. The 2018 National Defense Strategy. https://www.defense.gov/Portals/1/Documents/pubs/2018-National-Defense-Strategy-Summary.pdf

58 Coats D, 2018. Worldwide threat assessment of the US intelligence community. https://www.intelligence.senate.gov/sites/default/files/documents/os-dcoats-021318.PDF

59 Hartley J, 2018. *World Food and Water Crisis*. Future Directions International.

60 IPCC, 2018. Global Warming of 1.5° C. Summary for Policymakers. October 2018. http://report.ipcc.ch/sr15/pdf/sr15_spm_final.pdf

61 Thomas V, 2017. *The Climate Crisis*. Brookings Institution. https://www.brookings.edu/blog/future-development/2017/06/05/the-climate-crisis/

62 World Meteorological Office, 2018. State of Climate in 2017 – Extreme weather and high impacts. WMO, 24 March, 2018. https://public.wmo.int/en/media/press-release/state-of-climate-2017-%E2%80%93-extreme-weather-and-high-impacts

63 UN FAO *et al.* 2018. Global Report on Food Crises 2018. http://www.fsincop.net/fileadmin/user_upload/fsin/docs/global_report/2018/GRFC_2018_Full_report_EN_Low_resolution.pdf

64 UN FAO, 2018. The impact of disasters and crises on agricultural and food security. http://www.fao.org/3/I8656EN/i8656en.pdf

65 Cotterell R S *et al.*, 2019. Food production shocks across land and sea. *Nature Sustainability* 2, pp 130–7, 28 January 2019. https://www.nature.com/articles/s41893-018-0210-1

Chapter 4

1 The Lancet, 2017. The Lancet Commission on Pollution and Health. http://www.thelancet.com/commissions/pollution-and-health
2 CO2 Earth, 2018. https://www.co2.earth/global-co2-emissions
3 Alders R *et al.*, 2018. A planetary health approach to secure, safe, sustainable food systems: workshop report. *Food Security*, February 2018. https://link.springer.com/article/10.1007%2Fs12571-018-0780-9
4 Willett W *et al.*, 2019. Food in the Anthropocene: the EAT–Lancet Commission on healthy diets from sustainable food systems. *The Lancet*, 16 January, 2019. https://www.thelancet.com/commissions/ EAT
5 Moeller N and Pimbert M, 2018. Why food production needs to change to avoid a crisis. *The Independent*. https://www.independent .co.uk/life-style/food-and-drink/food-production-farming-agriculture-needs-change-avoid-crisis-population-nine-billion-2050-a8275646.html?amp&__twitter_impression=true
6 Ehrlich P and Harte J, 2018. Pessimism on the food front. *Sustainability* 2018, 10(4), 1120. http://www.mdpi.com/2071-1050/10/ 4/1120/htm
7 Weulle G, 2017. Indigenous rock shelter in Top End pushes Australia's human history back to 65,000 years. http://www.abc.net .au/news/science/2017-07-20/aboriginal-shelter-pushes-human-history-back-to-65,000-years/8719314
8 Snir A, Nadel D, Groman-Yaroslavski I, Melamed Y, Sternberg M, Bar-Yosef O and Weiss E. The origin of cultivation and proto-weeds, long before Neolithic farming. *PLOS ONE*, 2015; 10 (7), e0131422. DOI: 10.1371/journal.pone.0131422
9 Universitaet Tübingen. "Farming started in several places at once: Origins of agriculture in the Fertile Crescent", *ScienceDaily*, 5 July 2013. www.sciencedaily.com/releases/2013/07/130705101629.htm.
10 Da Silva J G, 2017. Climate change puts millions of people in vicious cycle of food insecurity, malnutrition and poverty. UN FAO. http://www.fao.org/news/story/en/item/1062612/icode/
11 Brent Z *et al.*, 2018. Will 'climate smart agriculture' serve the public interest – or the drive for growing profits for private corporations? Transnational Institute. https://www.tni.org/en/article/will-climate-smart-agriculture-serve-the-public-interest-or-the-drive-for-growing-profits
12 See for example Jiang D *et al.*, 2018, op cit.

13 Da Silva J G, 2017. Climate change puts millions of people in vicious cycle of food insecurity, malnutrition and poverty. FAO News, November 14, 2017. http://www.fao.org/director-general/newsroom/news/detail/en/c/1062683/

14 Goodall J, 2006. *Harvest of Hope: a guide to mindful eating*. Grand Central Publishing.

15 US NIH, 2018. Ch 8: Food Additives, Contaminants, Carcinogens, and Mutagens; from Diet Nutrition and Cancer. US National Academy of Science. https://www.ncbi.nlm.nih.gov/books/NBK216714/

16 Statista, 2018. https://www.statista.com/statistics/311943/agrochemical-market-value-worldwide/

17 Herz-Picciotto I, 2018. Organophosphate exposures during pregnancy and child neurodevelopment: Recommendations for essential policy reforms. *PLOS Medicine*, October. https://www.scribd.com/document/391463803/OP-Pesticide-Paper-PLOS-Medicine#from_embed

18 USDHHS, 2017. National Report on Human Exposure to Environmental Chemicals. https://www.cdc.gov/exposurereport/index.html

19 For a breakdown of these emissions, see the main text in this book and *Surviving the 21st Century* Ch 6, p. 105.

20 Grandjean P et al., 2014. Neurobehavioural effects of developmental toxicity, *The Lancet Neurology* 13 (3), 330–8. http://www.thelancet.com/journals/laneur/article/PIIS1474-4422(13)70278-3/abstract

21 Duff J, 2014. Why the Increase in Autism (ASD), ADHD and Neurodevelopmental Disorders? http://www.autism-adhd.org.au/autism_prevalence

22 Weisskopf M et al., 2013. Perinatal air pollutant exposures and autism spectrum disorder in the Children of Nurses' Health Study II participants. *Environ. Health Perspect.* 2013 Aug; 121(8), 978–84. https://www.ncbi.nlm.nih.gov/pmc/articles/PMC3734496/

23 EWG, 2005. The Pollution in Newborns. https://www.ewg.org/research/body-burden-pollution-newborns#.WsLIMREUmpo

24 WHO/UNEP, 2017. Results of the global survey on concentrations in human milk of persistent organic pollutants by the United Nations Environment Programme and the World Health Organization, Stockholm Convention Report, Geneva. http://wedocs.unep.org/bitstream/handle/20.500.11822/19392/UNEPPOPSCOP6INF33 English_%281%29.pdf?sequence=1&isAllowed=y

25 Levine H, 2017. Temporal trends in sperm count: a systematic review and meta-regression analysis. *Human Reproduction Update.* https://www.ncbi.nlm.nih.gov/pubmed/28981654

26 Birney M *et al.*, 2017. Atrazine induced epigenetic transgenerational inheritance of disease, lean phenotype and sperm epimutation pathology biomarkers. PLOS, September 20, 2017. https://journals.plos.org/plosone/article?id=10.1371/journal.pone.0184306

27 WHO, 2017. Depression and other common mental disorders: global estimates. https://www.who.int/mental_health/management/depression/prevalence_global_health_estimates/en/

28 Hidaka B H, 2013. Depression as a disease of modernity: explanations for increasing prevalence. *J. Affect. Disord.* https://www.ncbi.nlm.nih.gov/entrez/eutils/elink.fcgi?dbfrom=pubmed&retmode=ref&cmd=prlinks&id=22244375

29 Gunnars K, 2017. 11 Graphs That Show Everything That is Wrong With The Modern Diet. Healthline. https://www.healthline.com/nutrition/11-graphs-that-show-what-is-wrong-with-modern-diet

30 WHO, 2018. Obesity and overweight Fact Sheet. http://www.who.int/mediacentre/factsheets/fs311/en/

31 Heindell J J, 2015. Endocrine disruptors and obesity. *Nat. Rev. Endocrinol.* 2015 Nov; 11(11), 653–61. https://www.ncbi.nlm.nih.gov/pubmed/26391979

32 Andrews R, 2017. All about endocrine disruptors. Precision Nutrition. https://www.precisionnutrition.com/all-about-endocrine-disruptors

33 UN Human Rights Council, 2017. Report of the Special Rapporteur on the right to food. UN. https://reliefweb.int/sites/reliefweb.int/files/resources/1701059.pdf

34 Carvalho F P, 2017. Pesticides, environment, and food safety. *Food and Energy Security.* John Wiley and Sons. https://onlinelibrary.wiley.com/doi/epdf/10.1002/fes3.108

35 UNHRC, 2017. Op cit.

36 Stapper M, 2018. The Link Between Healthy Food and Biological Farming. *Future Directions International*, June 28, 2018. http://www.futuredirections.org.au/publication/dr-maarten-stapper-link-healthy-food-biological-farming-part-one/

37 Pearce F, 2018. Can the World Find Solutions to the Nitrogen Pollution Crisis? Yale Environment 360. https://e360.yale.edu/features/can-the-world-find-solutions-to-the-nitrogen-pollution-crisis

38 Queste B *et al.*, 2018. Physical controls on oxygen distribution and denitrification potential in the north west Arabian Sea. Geophysical research Letters, April 2018. https://agupubs.onlinelibrary.wiley .com/doi/abs/10.1029/2017GL076666

39 Scripps Institution, 2015. Earth Has Crossed Several 'Planetary Boundaries,' Thresholds of Human-Induced Environmental Changes. https://scripps.ucsd.edu/news/earth-has-crossed-several-planetary-boundaries-thresholds-human-induced-environmental-changes

40 Smil V, 2002. Harvesting the Biosphere: the Human Impact. http:// vaclavsmil.com/wp-content/uploads/PDR37-4.Smil_.pgs613-636.pdf

41 See http://www.nature.com/articles/nature22900

42 Ceballos G *et al.*, 2016. Accelerated modern human-induced species losses: Entering the sixth mass extinction, Science Advances 1.5. https://www.ncbi.nlm.nih.gov/pmc/articles/PMC4640606/

43 WWF, 2018. Living Planet Report. https://wwf.panda.org/ knowledge_hub/all_publications/living_planet_report_2018/

44 Fey S B *et al.*, 2015. Recent shifts in animal mass mortality events. *Proc. Natl Acad. Sci.* Jan 2015, 112 (4), 1083–88; DOI: 10.1073/ pnas.1414894112 https://www.pnas.org/content/112/4/1083

45 IUCN, 2018. Red List: Summary Statistics. https://www.iucnredlist.org/resources/summary-statistics

46 Newbold T *et al.*, 2016. Has land use pushed terrestrial biodiversity beyond the planetary boundary? A global assessment. Science 15 Jul 2016, 353 (6296), 288–91; DOI: 10.1126/science.aaf2201 http:// science.sciencemag.org/content/353/6296/288

47 Klein S *et al.*, 2017. Why bees are so vulnerable to environmental stressors. *Trends Ecol. Evol.* 2017, 32, 268–78. https://www.ncbi.nlm .nih.gov/pubmed/28111032?dopt=Abstract

48 Gabbatiss J, 2018. 'Shocking' decline in birds across Europe due to pesticide use, say scientists. *The Independent*, 21 March 2018. https:// www.independent.co.uk/environment/europe-bird-population-countryside-reduced-pesticides-france-wildlife-cnrs-a8267246.html

49 IPBES, 2018. Regional assessments of biodiversity and ecosystem services for the Americas, Asia and the Pacific, Africa, Europe and Central Asia. https://www.ipbes.net/news/media-release-biodiversity-nature%E2%80%99s-contributions-continue-%C2% A0dangerous-decline-scientists-warn

50 Diaz S *et al.*, 2019. IPBES Global Assessment Report on Biodiversity and Ecosystem Services, IPBES, May 2019. https://www.ipbes.net/ news/Media-Release-Global-Assessment

51 See Chapter 9 and http://foodplantsinternational.com/plants/

52 Shand H, 2018. *Biological Meltdown: The Loss of Agricultural Biodiversity*. Reimagine. http://www.reimaginerpe.org/node/921

53 FAO Commission on Genetic Resources for Food and Agriculture Assessments, 2019. The State of the World's Biodiversity for Food and Agriculture. FAO, Rome, 2019. http://www.fao.org/3/CA3129EN/CA3129EN.pdf

54 For a range of arguments, see Debating Europe, 2018. http://www.debatingeurope.eu/focus/arguments-gmos/#.Ws0-lBEUlD8

55 WHO, 2017. NCD mortality and morbidity. http://www.who.int/gho/ncd/mortality_morbidity/en/

56 Gorsevski V, 2018. *Environmental security: dimensions and priorities*, UNGEF, 2018.

57 Pollan M, 2007. *The Omnivore's Dilemma: A Natural History of Four Meals*, Penguin. https://michaelpollan.com/books/the-omnivores-dilemma/

58 Smil V, 2013. *Should we Eat Meat?* Wiley-Blackwell.

59 FAO, 2017. Livestock Commodities. http://www.fao.org/docrep/005/y4252e/y4252e05b.htm

60 FAO, 2013. Global Meat projections to 2050. Image source: https://ourworldindata.org/grapher/global-meat-projections-to-2050

61 Carrington D, 2018. Avoiding meat and dairy is 'single biggest way' to reduce your impact on Earth. *The Guardian*, June 1, 2018. https://www.scientificamerican.com/article/should-humans-eat-meat-excerpt/

62 Smil V, 2013. Should Humans Eat Meat? *Scientific American*. https://www.scientificamerican.com/article/should-humans-eat-meat-excerpt/

63 Savory A, 2013. How to fight desertification and reverse climate change. TED talks. https://www.ted.com/talks/allan_savory_how_to_green_the_world_s_deserts_and_reverse_climate_change

64 Grace D *et al.*, 2018. The influence of livestock-derived foods on nutrition during the first 1,000 days of life. ILRI Policy Brief, June 2018. https://www.slideshare.net/ILRI/anh-first-1000-days/

65 Millman O and Leavenworth S, 2016. China's plan to cut meat consumption by 50% cheered by climate campaigners. *The Guardian*. https://www.theguardian.com/world/2016/jun/20/chinas-meat-consumption-climate-change

66 Loria J, 2018. *Going Vegan Is the Best Thing You Can Do for the Planet, New Study Proves*. Ecowatch. https://www.ecowatch.com/vegan-climate-change-2558286917.amp.html?__twitter_impression=true

67 Heller M C, 2018. Greenhouse gas emissions and energy use associated with production of individual self-selected US diets. *Environmental Research Letters*. http://iopscience.iop.org/article/10.1088/1748-9326/aab0ac

68 Tree I, 2018. If you want to save the world, veganism isn't the answer. *The Guardian*, August 25, 2018. https://www.theguardian.com/commentisfree/2018/aug/25/veganism-intensively-farmed-meat-dairy-soya-maize

69 These include grain traders Archer Daniels Midland (ADM), Bunge, Cargill and Louis Dreyfus, food corporates Nestle, Pepsi, Coca-cola and Kraft-Heinz, supermarket chains like Aldi, Carrefour, Walmart, Tesco, China Resources Vanguard, Lianhua and Reliance (India).

70 These include chemical firms like Monsanto, Bayer AG and DuPont, machinery conglomerates like Deere & Co, CNH Industrial, Claas and Kubota, fertiliser giants PotashCorp, Mosaic, Uralkali, Belaruskali and Eurochem.

71 Lawrence G, Sippel S R and Burch D, 2015. The financialisation of food and farming, in *Handbook on the Globalisation of Agriculture*. Edward Elgar Publishing, 2015.

72 For a more detailed exposition of this argument and the risk posed by common human delusions, see Cribb J H J, *Surviving the 21st Century*, Springer 2017. https://www.springer.com/us/book/9783319412696

73 FAO, 2018. Key facts on food loss and waste you should know. FAO Global Initiative on Food Loss and Waste Reduction. http://www.fao.org/save-food/resources/keyfindings/en/

74 The Land Institute, 2017. Why Farming is broken (and always has been). https://landinstitute.org/video-audio/why-farming-has-always-been-broken/

75 Holmgren D, 2017. About Permaculture. https://holmgren.com.au/about-permaculture/

76 Salatin J, 2018. Polyface Farms. http://www.polyfacefarms.com/principles/

77 Savory A, 2018. Savory Institute: Our Strategy. https://www.savory.global/institute/

78 Tirado R, 2009. Defining Ecological Farming. Greenpeace. https://www.greenpeace.org/archive-international/Global/international/publications/agriculture/2011/Defining-Ecological-Farming-2009.pdf

79 FAO, 2018. Climate Smart Agriculture. FAO. http://www.fao.org/climate-smart-agriculture/en/

80 Brent Z et al., 2018. Will 'climate smart agriculture' serve the public
    interest – or the drive for growing profits for private corporations?
    The Ecologist. https://theecologist.org/2018/jan/19/will-climate-smart-
    agriculture-serve-public-interest-or-drive-growing-profits-private
81 Martin H, 2009. Introduction to Organic Farming. Ontario Ministry for
    Agriculture, Food and Rural Affairs, Canada. http://www.omafra.gov
    .on.ca/english/crops/facts/09-077.htm
82 Reaganold J P and Wachter J M, 2016. Organic agriculture in the
    twenty-first century. Nature Plants. http://www.nature.com/articles/
    nplants2015221
83 https://en.wikipedia.org/wiki/Biodynamic_agriculture
84 Holmgren D, 2017. About Permaculture. https://holmgren.com.au/
    about-permaculture/
85 University of Oxford, 2017. Sustainable Intensification. Oxford
    Martin Programme on the Future of Food. http://www.futureoffood
    .ox.ac.uk/sustainable-intensification and Garnett T et al., 2012.
    Sustainable Intensification in Agriculture. Food Climate Research
    Network, University of Surrey. http://www.futureoffood.ox.ac.uk/
    sites/futureoffood.ox.ac.uk/files/SI%20report%20-%20final.pdf
86 Petersen B and Snapp S, 2015. What is sustainable intensification?
    Views from experts. Elsevier Land Use Policy. https://www.science
    direct.com/science/article/pii/S0264837715000332
87 Soils for Life, 2018. http://www.soilsforlife.org.au/about/
    index.html

Chapter 5

1 Epic of Gilgamesh, 4100 BPA, summary: http://www.ancient-
   literature.com/other_gilgamesh.html
2 Kravik M et al., 2008. Water for the Recovery of the Climate – A New
   Water Paradigm. Krupa Print. http://www.waterparadigm.org/
   download/Water_for_the_Recovery_of_the_Climate_A_New_
   Water_Paradigm.pdf
3 Fountain H, 2015. Researchers Link Syrian Conflict to a Drought
   Made Worse by Climate Change. The New York Times. https://
   www.nytimes.com/2015/03/03/science/earth/study-links-syria-
   conflict-to-drought-caused-by-climate-change.html
4 Al Jazeera, 2018. Syria's civil war explained from the beginning.
   https://www.aljazeera.com/news/2016/05/syria-civil-war-explained-
   160505084119966.html

5 McKernan B, 2017. Syria civil war: Harrowing pictures of starving
   baby show horrors of the brutal conflict. *The Independent*. https://
   www.independent.co.uk/news/world/middle-east/syria-civil-war-
   starving-baby-pictures-photos-hamouria-east-ghouta-assad-rebels-
   regime-a8015211.html
6 Kelley C P *et al.*, 2015. Climate change in the Fertile Crescent and
   implications of the recent Syrian drought. *PNAS*, March 17, 2015.
   http://www.pnas.org/content/112/11/3241
7 Issa P, 2016. Syrian civil war: Five ways the conflict has changed the
   world. *The Independent*. https://www.independent.co.uk/news/world/
   middle-east/syrian-civil-war-isis-how-it-changed-the-world-refugee-
   crisis-a6928796.html
8 Barbut M, 2015. *Land degradation Is a Growing Threat to Global Security*.
   UNCCD Press release. https://www2.unccd.int/news-events/land-
   degradation-growing-threat-global-security
9 Barbut M and Alexander S, 2016. *Land Degradation As A Security
   Threat Amplifier: The New Global Frontline*. UNCCD. http://catalogue
   .unccd.int/761_Barbut_Alexander_2015_Chapter1.1_Elsevier_Land_
   Restoration.pdf
10 Barbut M, 2016. Interview with Ms. Monique Barbut,
   Executive Secretary of the United Nations Convention to
   Combat Desertification. A New Climate for Peace (website). https://
   www.newclimateforpeace.org/blog/interview-ms-monique-barbut-
   executive-secretary-united-nations-convention-combat
11 Engelke P and Sticklor R, 2015. Water Wars: The Next Great Driver
   of Global Conflict? The National Interest. http://nationalinterest.org/
   feature/water-wars-the-next-great-driver-global-conflict-13842?
   page=2
12 Wilford J N, 1997. *On Ancient Terraced Hills, Urbanism Sprouted With
   Crops. The New York Times*. https://www.nytimes.com/1997/09/02/
   science/on-ancient-terraced-hills-urbanism-sprouted-with-crops
   .html
13 Mundy M, 2017. The war on Yemen and its agricultural sector.
   Elikadura 21. http://elikadura21.eus/wp-content/uploads/2017/04/
   50-Mundy.pdf
14 Mundy M, 2017. The War on Yemen and its Agricultural Sector. The
   London School of Economics and Political Science. https://
   blogs.lse.ac.uk/mec/2017/06/19/empire-of-information-the-war-on-
   yemen-and-its-agricultural-sector/

15 De Waal A, 2017. The Nazis Used It, We Use It. *London Review of Books*. https://www.lrb.co.uk/v39/n12/alex-de-waal/the-nazis-used-it-we-use-it

16 Mundy M, 2017. Op cit.

17 Steinfeld H, *et al.* 1997. *Livestock-Environment Interactions: Issues and Options*. FAO. Ch 3, Box 3.4. http://www.fao.org/ag/againfo/resources/documents/Lxehtml/tech/ch3b.htm

18 Elmi A, 2010. *Understanding the Somalia Conflagration*. Pluto Press. https://www.twn.my/title2/resurgence/2011/251-252/cover04.htm

19 Gilkes P and Barry T, 2005. The War Between Ethiopia and Eritrea. Foreign Policy in Focus. http://fpif.org/the_war_between_ethiopia_and_eritrea/

20 Sikainga A, 2009. 'The World's Worst Humanitarian Crisis': Understanding the Darfur Conflict. *Origins*, 2, 5. http://origins.osu.edu/article/worlds-worst-humanitarian-crisis-understanding-darfur-conflict

21 Sova C, 2017. *The First Climate Change Conflict*. UN Food Programme. https://wfpusa.org/articles/the-first-climate-change-conflict/

22 Ki-Moon, 2007. *A Climate Culprit in Dafur*. Washington Post. http://www.washingtonpost.com/wp-dyn/content/article/2007/06/15/AR2007061501857.html

23 Coats D R. Worldwide Threat Assessment of the US Intelligence Community 2019. US Senate Select Committee on Intelligence, 29 January 2019. https://climateandsecurity.files.wordpress.com/2019/01/worldwide-threat-assessment_dni_2019.pdf

24 USGS, 2016. Groundwater depletion. USGS. https://water.usgs.gov/edu/gwdepletion.html

25 Little J B, 2009. The Ogallala Aquifer: Saving a Vital U.S. Water Source. *Scientific American*. https://www.scientificamerican.com/article/the-ogallala-aquifer/

26 Stewart D R et al., 2013. Tapping unsustainable groundwater stores for agricultural production in the High Plains Aquifer of Kansas, projections to 2110. *PNAS* August 26, 2013. http://www.pnas.org/content/early/2013/08/14/1220351110

27 Colgan J D, 2013. Oil, Conflict, and U.S. National Interests. International Security. https://www.belfercenter.org/sites/default/files/legacy/files/colgan-final-policy-brief-2013.pdf

28 FAO, 2017. The State of Food Security and Nutrition in the World. http://www.fao.org/3/a-I7695e.pdf

29 FAO, 2017. http://www.fao.org/americas/noticias/ver/en/c/1037375/

30 FAO, 2017. *Panorama of Food and Nutritional Security in Latin America and the Caribbean 2017*. FAO. http://www.fao.org/americas/publicaciones-audio-video/panorama/en/

31 FAO, 2016. Food and nutrition security and the eradication of hunger. https://www.cepal.org/en/node/37928

32 USDA, 2010. Food Security and Nutrition in Mexico. USDA Foreign Agricultural Service. https://gain.fas.usda.gov/Recent%20GAIN%20Publications/Food%20Security%20and%20Nutrition%20in%20Mexico_Mexico_Mexico_7–9-2010.pdf

33 Climate reality project, 2017. How Climate Change is Affecting Mexico. https://www.climaterealityproject.org/blog/how-climate-change-affecting-mexico

34 Veetil B K and de Souza S F, 2017. Study of 40-year glacier retreat in the northern region of the Cordillera Vilcanota, Peru, using satellite images. *Remote Sensing Letters*, 8, 2017. https://www.tandfonline.com/doi/full/10.1080/2150704X.2016.1235811

35 Blair L, 2018. The ecological catastrophe that turned a vast Bolivian lake into a salt desert. *The Guardian*, 4 Jan 2018. https://www.theguardian.com/world/2018/jan/04/the-ecological-catastrophe-that-turned-a-vast-bolivian-lake-to-a-salt-desert

36 Maddocks A *et al.*, 2015. *Ranking the World's Most Water-Stressed Countries in 2040*. World Resources Institute. https://www.wri.org/blog/2015/08/ranking-world-s-most-water-stressed-countries-2040

37 Kislinger L, 2017. The Venezuela Climate Change Will Leave Us. *Caracas Chronicles*, June 24, 2017. https://www.caracaschronicles.com/2017/06/24/the-venezuela-climate-change-will-leave-us/

38 Nobre C A *et al.*, 2016. Land use and climate change risks in the Amazon. *PNAS* September 27, 2016. http://www.pnas.org/content/113/39/10759.full

39 Draper F C *et al.*, 2014. The distribution and amount of carbon in the largest peatland complex in Amazonia. *Environmental Research Letters*. 15 December 2014. http://iopscience.iop.org/article/10.1088/1748-9326/9/12/124017

40 https://en.wikipedia.org/wiki/List_of_guerrilla_movements

41 Friedman G, 2017. 4 Maps That Signal Central Asia Is at Risk of War. *Mauldin Economics*. April 20, 2017 http://www.mauldineconomics.com/editorial/4-maps-that-signal-central-asia-is-at-risk-of-war

42 Qobil R, 2016. Will Central Asia fight over water? BBC, 25 October
    2016. http://www.bbc.com/news/magazine-37755985
43 Rosenberg M, Why Is the Aral Sea Shrinking? ThoughtCo,
    March 17, 2017. https://www.thoughtco.com/is-the-aral-sea-
    shrinking-1434959
44 Linn J F, 2008. *The Impending Water Crisis in Central Asia: An Immediate
    Threat.* Brookings Institution. https://www.brookings.edu/opinions/
    the-impending-water-crisis-in-central-asia-an-immediate-threat/
45 King E, 2017. Solving Central Asia's Water Crisis. *International Policy
    Digest*, 25 May 2017. https://intpolicydigest.org/2017/05/19/solving-
    central-asia-s-water-crisis/
46 Shahbazov F, 2017. Will Central Asia Fight Over Water Resources?
    Forbes Magazine. February 26, 2017. https://www.forbes.com/sites/
    realspin/2017/02/06/will-central-asia-fight-over-water-resources/
    #157c0e244c1f
47 Shenkkan N, 2016. A Perfect Storm in Central Asia. *Foreign Policy*,
    January 22, 2016. http://foreignpolicy.com/2016/01/22/a-perfect-
    storm-in-central-asia/
48 Crisis Group, 2017. Central Asia's Silk Road Rivalries. Crisis Group,
    July 27, 2017. https://www.crisisgroup.org/europe-central-asia/
    central-asia/245-central-asias-silk-road-rivalries
49 World Bank, 2017. Adaptation to Climate Change in the Middle East
    and North Africa Region. 2017. http://web.worldbank.org/WBSITE/
    EXTERNAL/COUNTRIES/MENAEXT/0,,contentMDK:21596766
    ~pagePK:146736~piPK:146830~theSitePK:256299,00.html
50 World Bank, 2017. Beyond Scarcity: Water Security in the Middle
    East and North Africa. https://www.worldbank.org/en/topic/water/
    publication/beyond-scarcity-water-security-in-the-middle-east-and-
    north-africa
51 Joffe G, 2017. A worsening water crisis in North Africa and the
    Middle East. *The Conversation.* September 1, 2017. https://the
    conversation.com/a-worsening-water-crisis-in-north-africa-and-the-
    middle-east-83197
52 UNDP, 2018. Climate change adaptation in the Arab states. UNDP,
    July 2018. https://reliefweb.int/sites/reliefweb.int/files/resources/
    Arab-States-CCA.pdf
53 Cooke K, 2016. Saudi agricultural investment abroad – land grab or
    benign strategy? *Middle East Eye*, October 5, 2016. https://www
    .middleeasteye.net/opinion/saudi-agricultural-investment-abroad-
    land-grab-or-benign-strategy

54 Sadoff C W, 2017. Game-changing water solutions for the Middle East and North Africa. The World Bank, November 22, 2017. http://blogs.worldbank.org/water/game-changing-water-solutions-middle-east-and-north-africa

55 See, for example, *Sputnik International*, 2017. Why Turkish Dams Could Push the Region Toward New Conflict. https://sputniknews.com/middleeast/201707201055733658-turkish-dams-could-result-in-conflict/

56 BBC, 2018. The 'water war' brewing over the new River Nile dam. February 24, 2018. http://www.bbc.com/news/world-africa-43170408

57 Brown L, 1995. *Who Will Feed China?* Worldwatch Institute. http://www.worldwatch.org/bookstore/publication/who-will-feed-china-wake-call-small-planet

58 Rosenberg M, 2018. China's Former One-Child Policy. *ThoughtCo*, January 31, 2018. https://www.thoughtco.com/chinas-one-child-policy-1435466

59 Parton C, 2018. *China's acute water shortage imperils economic future.* Financial Times, 22 February 2018. https://www.ft.com/content/3ee05452-1801-11e8-9376-4a6390addb44

60 Liu J et al., 2011. Sustainability of Groundwater Resources in the North China Plain. Chapter from *Sustaining Groundwater Resources*, Springer 2011. https://www.researchgate.net/publication/226084438_Sustainability_of_Groundwater_Resources_in_the_North_China_Plain

61 Westcott B and Wang S, 2017. Can China fix its mammoth water crisis before it's too late? CNN, 2017.

62 Hoekstra A Y and Mekkonen M M, 2012. The water footprint of humanity. *PNAS* February 28, 2012. http://www.pnas.org/content/109/9/3232

63 See for example http://www.abc.net.au/news/2014-08-10/agricultural-giant-says-climate-change-absolutely-real/5659058

64 Parton C, 2018 op. cit.

65 Lai E C-Y, 2011. Climate Change Impacts on China's Environment: Biophysical Impacts. Wilson Centre, July 2011. https://www.wilsoncenter.org/publication/climate-change-impacts-chinas-environment-biophysical-impacts

66 Bloomberg, 2017. Farming the World: China's Epic Race to Avoid a Food Crisis. Bloomberg News May 22, 2017. https://www.bloomberg.com/graphics/2017-feeding-china/

67 Walsh B, 2018. The State of China's Agricultural Research. *Future Directions International.* April 3, 2018. http://www.futuredirections .org.au/publication/state-chinas-agricultural-research/

68 National Intelligence Council, 2008. China: The Impact of Climate Change to 2030. https://www.dni.gov/files/documents/climate2030_ china.pdf

69 See for example Campbell K M *et al.*, 2007. The Age of Consequences. The Foreign Policy and National Security Implications of Global Climate Change. https://csis-prod.s3 .amazonaws.com/s3fs-public/legacy_files/files/media/csis/pubs/ 071105_ageofconsequences.pdf

70 UN Population Division, 2017. https://esa.un.org/unpd/wpp/ publications/Files/WPP2017_KeyFindings.pdf

71 FAO, 2018. Op. Cit.

72 Chow L, 2018. Climate Change, Conflict Leave 224 Million Undernourished in Africa. Ecowatch, February 20, 2018. https:// www.ecowatch.com/africa-malnutrition-climate-change- 2537161073.amp.html?__twitter_impression=true

73 Cole M J *et al.*, 2014. Tracking sustainable development with a national barometer for South Africa using a downscaled "safe and just space" framework. *Proc. Natl. Acad. Sci. USA* 111, E4399–4408. https://www.ncbi.nlm.nih.gov/pmc/articles/PMC4210279/

74 Butsic V *et al.*, 2015. Conservation and conflict in the Democratic Republic of Congo: the impacts of warfare, mining, and protected areas on deforestation. *Biological Conservation* 191, 266–73. http://luclab.berkeley.edu/wp-content/uploads/2015/08/ congo.pdf

75 World Bank, 2018. Climate Change Could Force Over 140 Million to Migrate Within Countries by 2050: World Bank Report. https:// www.worldbank.org/en/news/press-release/2018/03/19/climate- change-could-force-over-140-million-to-migrate-within-countries- by-2050-world-bank-report

76 Connor P, 2018. International migration from sub-Saharan Africa has grown dramatically since 2010. Pew Research Centre, February 28, 2018. https://www.pewresearch.org/fact-tank/2018/02/28/ international-migration-from-sub-saharan-africa-has-grown- dramatically-since-2010/

77 Cherfurka P, 2008. Africa in 2040: The Darkened Continent. *PlanetThoughts*, 2008. http://www.planetthoughts.org/?pg=pt/ Whole&qid=1873#contributor

78 Population forecasts for South Asia vary widely, but here is one median interpretation: http://www.worldometers.info/world-population/southern-asia-population/

79 Biswas A J *et al.*, 2017. India is facing its worst water crisis in generations. *Quartz India*, March 15, 2017. https://qz.com/931878/india-is-facing-its-worst-water-crisis-in-generations/

80 Op cit. Choudhary A A, 2018. SC: Wake up or you'll have zero groundwater by 2020. *Times of India*, July 12, 2018. https://m.times ofindia.com/city/delhi/sc-wake-up-or-youll-have-zero-groundwater-by-2020/amp_articleshow/64953385.cms?__twitter_impression= true

81 Salopek P, 2018. Historic water crisis threatens 600 million people in India. *National Geographic*, October 19, 2018. https://www.national geographic.com/people-and-culture/water-crisis-india-out-of-eden/? cmpid=org=ngp::mc=social::src=twitter::cmp=editorial::add= tw20181022culture-watercrisisoutofeden::rid=&sf200566131=1

82 American Geophysical Union, 2016. Groundwater resources around the world could be depleted by 2050s. AGU100, December 15, 2016. https://news.agu.org/press-release/agu-fall-meeting-groundwater-resources-around-the-world-could-be-depleted-by-2050s/

83 Shiao T *et al.*, 2015. 3 Maps Explain India's Growing Water Risks. WRI, February 26, 2015. https://www.wri.org/blog/2015/02/3-maps-explain-india%E2%80%99s-growing-water-risks

84 Im E-S *et al.*, 2017. Deadly heat waves projected in the densely populated agricultural regions of South Asia. *Science*, August 2, 2017. http://advances.sciencemag.org/content/3/8/e1603322

85 Betts R *et al.*, 2018. Changes in climate extremes, fresh water availability and vulnerability to food insecurity projected at 1.5°C and 2°C global warming with a higher-resolution global climate model. *Philosophical Transactions of the Royal Society A.* April 2, 2018. http://rsta.royalsocietypublishing.org/content/376/2119/20160452

86 Subramanian S, 2018. India food crisis likely if climate change continues: report. *The National*, January 30, 2018. https:// www.thenational.ae/world/asia/india-food-crisis-likely-if-climate-change-continues-report-1.700310

87 Wester P *et al.*, 2019. *The Hindu Kush Himalaya Assessment*. Springer 2019. https://link.springer.com/content/pdf/10.1007%2F978-3-319-92288-1.pdf

88 Walsh B, 2017. Climate Change, Food and Water Security in South Asia 2030: Change is Inevitable and the Region Must Prepare for it.

Future Directions International. May 4, 2017. http://www.future
directions.org.au/publication/climate-change-food-water-security-
south-asia-2030-change-inevitable-region-must-prepare/

89 Armed Forces.eu, 2018. https://armedforces.eu/compare/country_
India_vs_Pakistan

90 Quereshi WA, 2018. Dispute Resolution Mechanisms: An Analysis
of the Indus Waters Treaty. *18 Pepp. Disp. Resol. L.J.* 75 (2018).
https://digitalcommons.pepperdine.edu/drlj/vol18/iss1/4

91 Sharma S, 2018. *Emerging Crisis of Climate Refugee: An Unfolding Tale
of South Asia.* International Political Science Association.

92 Harvey F, 2018. Climate change soon to cause movement of 140m
people, World Bank warns. *The Guardian*, March 20, 2018. https://
amp.theguardian.com/environment/2018/mar/19/climate-change-
soon-to-cause-mass-movement-world-bank-warns?__twitter_
impression=true

93 Debate.org, 2017. Will India collapse?, http://www.debate.org/
opinions/will-india-collapse?ysort=1&nsort=5

94 Hegre H *et al.*, 2011. Predicting Armed Conflict, 2010-2050.
PRIO 2w011. http://folk.uio.no/hahegre/Papers/PredictionISQ_
Final.pdf

95 Robock *et al.*, 2007. 5 million tons of smoke created by 100
Hiroshima-size nuclear weapons. http://www.nucleardarkness.org/
warconsequences/fivemilliontonsofsmoke/

96 Conn A, 2016. Nuclear Winter with Alan Robock and Brian Toon.
Future of Life Institute, October 31, 2016. https://futureoflife.org/
2016/10/31/nuclear-winter-robock-toon-podcast/

97 Helfand I, 2016. Nuclear Famine: 2 Billion People at Risk? *World
Tribune*, 2016. https://www.worldtribune.org/2017/08/nuclear-
famine-2-billion-people-risk/

98 UNHCR, 2018. http://www.unhcr.org/en-au/news/stories/2018/6/
5b222c494/forced-displacement-record-685-million.html

99 World Economic Forum, 2016. Nearly 1 in 100 people worldwide
have been driven away from their homes. WEF. https://
www.weforum.org/agenda/2016/11/nearly-1-in-100-people-
worldwide-have-been-displaced-from-their-homes-by-war-and-
persecution/

100 United Nations, 2017. International Migration Report. http://
www.un.org/en/development/desa/population/migration/
publications/migrationreport/docs/MigrationReport2017_
Highlights.pdf

101 World Bank, 2017. International tourism, number of arrivals. https://data.worldbank.org/indicator/ST.INT.ARVL

102 The US alone had 16 million recreational boats in 2016.

103 World Bank, 2018. Climate Change Could Force Over 140 Million to Migrate Within Countries by 2050: World Bank Report. http://www.worldbank.org/en/news/press-release/2018/03/19/climate-change-could-force-over-140-million-to-migrate-within-countries-by-2050-world-bank-report

104 UN FAO, 2017. The State of Food Security and Nutrition in the World. http://www.fao.org/3/a-I7695e.pdf

105 World Economic Forum, 2018. The Global Risks Report 2018. WEF. http://www3.weforum.org/docs/WEF_GRR18_Report.pdf

106 Sandel M, 2018. Right-wing populism is rising as progressive politics fails – is it too late to save democracy? *New Statesman*, 21 May, 2018. https://www.newstatesman.com/2018/05/right-wing-populism-rising-progressive-politics-fails-it-too-late-save-democracy

107 World Food Programme, 2017. At the Root of Exodus: Food security, conflict and international migration. WFP. https://docs.wfp.org/api/documents/WFP-0000015358/download/?_ga=2.68562385.1142658458.1525057484-1603554657.1525057484

Chapter 6

1 Cribb J H J, 2017. *Surviving the 21st Century: Humanity's Ten Great Challenges and How We Can Overcome Them.* Springer 2017. https://www.springer.com/us/book/9783319412696

2 Cribb J, 2018. Op. cit. https://www.springer.com/us/book/9783319412696

3 WWF, 2016. The Living Planet Report 2016. Worldwide Fund for Nature. https://wwf.panda.org/wwf_news/?282370/Living-Planet-Report-2016

4 WWF, 2015. Living Blue Planet Report 2015. Worldwide Fund for Nature 2015. https://www.wwf.or.jp/activities/data/20150831LBPT.pdf

5 Glancy J, 2014. *EO Wilson: king of the ants has the gigantic task of saving us all. The Sunday Times*, 9 November 2014. http://www.thesundaytimes.co.uk/sto/newsreview/features/article1480929.ece

6 Ceballos G *et al.*, 2010. The Sixth Extinction Crisis: Loss of Animal Populations and Species. *Journal of Cosmology*, 8, 1821–31. http://journalofcosmology.com/ClimateChange100.html

7 Williams M *et al.*, 2015. *The Anthropocene Biosphere*. The Anthropocene Review, Sage Publications, 2015. http://journals.sagepub.com/doi/abs/10.1177/2053019615591020

8 Stavridis J G and Bergenas J, 2017. The fishing wars are coming. *Washington Post*, September 13, 2017. https://www.washingtonpost.com/opinions/the-fishing-wars-are-coming/2017/09/13/05c75208-97c6-11e7-b569-3360011663b4_story.html?noredirect=on Also Welch C, 2018. Climate Change May Spark Global 'Fish Wars'. *National Geographic*, June 14, 2018. https://news.nationalgeographic.com/2018/06/climate-change-drives-fish-wars-science-environment/

9 GFN, 2018. https://www.footprintnetwork.org/our-work/

10 Klare MT, 2001. Resource Wars: The New Landscape of Global Conflict. Foreign Affairs, May/June 2001. https://www.foreignaffairs.com/reviews/capsule-review/2001-05-01/resource-wars-new-landscape-global-conflict. For current conflicts see Environmental Justice Atlas, https://ejatlas.org/

11 Ploughshares, 2018. World Nuclear Weapon Stockpile. https://www.ploughshares.org/world-nuclear-stockpile-report

12 Bulletin of the Atomic Scientists, 2018. https://thebulletin.org/2018-doomsday-clock-statement

13 UN, 2017. UN conference adopts treaty banning nuclear weapons. https://news.un.org/en/story/2017/07/561122-un-conference-adopts-treaty-banning-nuclear-weapons

14 Organisation for the Prohibition of Chemical Weapons, 2018. https://www.opcw.org/

15 Campbell K M *et al.*, 2007. The Age of Consequences. The Foreign Policy and National Security Implications of Global Climate Change https://csis-prod.s3.amazonaws.com/s3fs-public/legacy_files/files/media/csis/pubs/071105_ageofconsequences.pdf

16 Watson R *et al.*, 2016. *The Truth About Climate Change*. Universal Ecological Fund FEU-US, September 2016. https://www.ledevoir.com/documents/pdf/the_truth_about_climate_change.pdf

17 Jones N, 2013. How Fast and How Far Will Sea Levels Rise? *Yale Environment* 360, October 21, 2013. https://e360.yale.edu/features/rising_waters_how_fast_and_how_far_will_sea_levels_rise

18 Milkov A, 2004. Global estimates of hydrate-bound gas in marine sediments: how much is really out there? *Earth Science Reviews*, August 2004. https://www.sciencedirect.com/science/article/pii/S0012825203001296

19 Zhang Z *et al.*, 2017. Emerging role of wetland methane emissions in driving 21st century climate change. *PNAS*, September 5, 2017. http://www.pnas.org/content/114/36/9647

20 Zeebe R E, Zachos J C and Dickens G R, Carbon dioxide forcing alone insufficient to explain Paleocene-Eocene Thermal Maximum warming. *Nature Geoscience*, doi:10.1038/NGEO578, 2009. https://www.soest.hawaii.edu/oceanography/faculty/zeebe_files/Publications/ZeebeNGS09.pdf

21 Zeebe R E *et al.*, 2017. Anthropogenic carbon release rate unprecedented during the past 66 million years. *Nature Geoscience*, 2017. https://www.nature.com/articles/ngeo2681

22 Schellnhuber, J, 2009. *Warming Could Cut Population to 1 Billion*. *New York Times Dot.Earth*. https://dotearth.blogs.nytimes.com/2009/03/13/scientist-warming-could-cut-population-to-1-billion/

23 Cribb J H J, 2017. *Surviving the 21st Century*, Springer 2017; and Cribb J H J, 2014. *Poisoned Planet*. Allen & Unwin 2014. http://julian cribb813.wixsite.com/jca1/services

24 Landrigan P *et al.*, 2017. The Lancet Commission on Pollution and Health. *The Lancet*, October 19, 2017 https://www.thelancet.com/commissions/pollution-and-health

25 WHO, 2018. *NCD mortality and morbidity*. World Health Organisation, 2018. https://www.who.int/gho/ncd/mortality_morbidity/en/

26 Gilbert N, 2016. Global biodiversity report warns pollinators are under threat. *Nature*, February 26, 2016. https://www.nature.com/news/global-biodiversity-report-warns-pollinators-are-under-threat-1.19456

27 Wiekzorek A M *et al.*, 2018. Frequency of Microplastics in Mesopelagic Fishes from the Northwest Atlantic. *Front. Mar. Sci.*, 19 February 2018. https://www.frontiersin.org/articles/10.3389/fmars.2018.00039/full

28 WHO, 2018. Pandemic and epidemic diseases. http://www.who.int/emergencies/diseases/en/

29 Geisbert T, 2018. Emerging Viruses. *Virology Journal*, 2018. https://virologyj.biomedcentral.com/articles/sections/emerging-viruses

30 Di Bella S *et al.*, 2010. Selenium Deficiency and HIV Infection. Infectious Disease reports, 2010. https://www.ncbi.nlm.nih.gov/pmc/articles/PMC3892587/

31 Milner J J and Beck M A, 2014. Obesity and influenza infection severity. *Future Virology*, 9 (3), April 25, 2014. https://www.ncbi.nlm.nih.gov/pmc/articles/PMC3892587/

32 WHO, 2018. Noncommunicable diseases. http://www.who.int/news-room/fact-sheets/detail/noncommunicable-diseases

33 Radd S, 2016. *Food as Medicine*. http://foodasmedicine.cooking/

34 See for example https://www.ellenmacarthurfoundation.org/circular-economy

35 UN, 2015. Urban population growth. http://www.who.int/gho/urban_health/situation_trends/urban_population_growth/en/

36 Cribb J H J, 2015. The Nation State is on the Skids. MAHB, 2015. https://mahb.stanford.edu/blog/nation-state-on-the-skids/

Chapter 7

1 https://ejatlas.org/

2 World Economic Forum, 2016. War costs us $13.6 trillion. So why do we spend so little on peace? WEF, June 8, 2016. https://www.weforum.org/agenda/2016/06/the-world-continues-to-spend-enormous-amounts-on-violence-and-little-on-building-peace/

3 Rustad S A and Binningsbø H M, 2012. A price worth fighting for? Natural resources and conflict recurrence. *Journal of Peace Research* 49(4), 531–46.

4 FAO, 2017. The State of Food Security and Nutrition in the World. http://www.fao.org/3/a-I7695e.pdf

5 Carter J, 1999. First step to peace is eradicating hunger. *International Herald Tribune*, June 17, 1999.

6 De Soysa I and Gleditsch N P, 1999. To Cultivate Peace: agriculture in a world of conflict. PRIO, 1999. https://www.wilsoncenter.org/sites/default/files/feature2.pdf

7 Payne R A, 1998. The limits and promise of environmental conflict prevention: the case of the GEF. *Journal of Peace Research* 35(3), 363–80.

8 Ratner B, Gorsevski V *et al.*, 2018. Environmental security: dimensions and priorities. *GEF*, July 2018, p. 5.

9 Smith W D, 2018. The Connection Between Environment, Conflict and Security. Millennium Alliance for Humanity and the Biosphere,

May 1, 2018. http://mahb.stanford.edu/blog/environment-conflict-security/

10 UN, 2016. Environmental Cooperation for Peacebuilding Programme, final report 2016.

11 Stockholm International Peace Research Institute, 2018. Global military spending remains high at $1.7 trillion. SIPRI, May 2, 2018. https://www.sipri.org/media/press-release/2018/global-military-spending-remains-high-17-trillion

12 Pardey P *et al.*, 2016. Shifting Ground: Food and Agricultural R&D Spending Worldwide, 1960-2011. International Science and Technology Practice and Policy. Sept 2, 2016. http://www.instepp.umn.edu/sites/default/files/product/downloadable/Pardey%20et%20al%202016%20--%20Shifting%20Ground%20(2SEPT2016).pdf

13 GlobalFirepower, 2019. Defense Spending by Country. https://www.globalfirepower.com/defense-spending-budget.asp

14 Berkowitz B, 2003. *The New Face of War: How War Will Be Fought in the 21st Century*. New York: Free Press, 2003.

15 Hegre H *et al.*, 2011. Future of armed conflict: 2010–2050. http://folk.uio.no/hahegre/Papers/PredictionISQ_Final.pdf

16 Dyer G, 2011. *Climate Wars: the Fight for Survival as the World Overheats*. Oneworld; and Welzer H, 2012. Climate Wars: Why People Will Be Killed in the 21st Century. *Polity*, Jan 24, 2012.

17 Illing S, 2017. How climate change could lead to more wars in the 21st century. Vox.com, Nov 14, 2017. https://www.vox.com/world/2017/11/14/16589878/global-climate-change-conflict-environment

18 Author's comment.

19 For example, Bergen P, 2014. The Future of War (I): A New America project looking at 21st century conflict. *Foreign Policy*, 2014.

20 This day in history, 2018. Eisenhower warns of military-industrial complex: January 17, 1961. https://www.history.com/this-day-in-history/eisenhower-warns-of-military-industrial-complex

21 Barbut M, 2014. Land degradation – a security issue. UNCCD, 17 June 2015. https://www.unccd.int/news-events/land-degradation-growing-threat-global-security

22 Monks K, 2016. Can the Great Green Wall change direction? CNN, Sept 26, 2016. https://edition.cnn.com/2016/09/22/africa/great-green-wall-sahara/index.html

23 Laestadius L, 2017. Africa's got plans for a Great Green Wall: why the idea needs a rethink. *The Conversation*, June 18, 2017.

http://theconversation.com/africas-got-plans-for-a-great-green-wall-why-the-idea-needs-a-rethink-78627

24 Barbut M and Alexander S, 2017. *Land Degradation as a Security Threat Amplifier: The New Global Frontline. Land Restoration.* Academic Press. http://catalogue.unccd.int/761_Barbut_Alexander_2015_Chapter1.1_Elsevier_Land_Restoration.pdf

25 Ratner B D *et al.*, 2017. Addressing conflict through collective action in natural resource management. *International Journal of the Commons* 11(2), 877–906. https://www.thecommonsjournal.org/article/10.18352/ijc.768/

26 Ratner B, Gorsevski V *et al.*, 2018. Environmental security: dimensions and priorities. GEF, July 2018, p. 9.

27 GCOMS, 2018. http://demilitarize.org/wp-content/uploads/2018/05/GDAMS_Final_Statement_2018_Press_Confs_May2.pdf

28 Schmidhuber J *et al.*, 2009. *Capital requirements for agriculture in developing countries to 2050.* FAO, Jun 24, 2009. https://rrojasdatabank.info/ak974e00.pdf

29 Half Earth Project, 2018. https://www.half-earthproject.org/discover-half-earth/

30 Wilson E O, 2016. *The Global Solution to Extinction. New York Times,* March 12, 2016. http://eowilsonfoundation.org/e-o-wilson-op-ed-in-the-new-york-times-the-global-solution-to-extinction/

31 Conway G, 1997. *The Doubly Green Revolution: Food for all in the 21st Century.* Comstock Publishing Associates, 1997.

Chapter 8

1 UN, 2014. World Urbanization Prospects: the 2014 Revision. https://esa.un.org/unpd/wup/publications/files/wup2014-highlights.pdf

2 Rockstrom J *et al.*, 2009. Planetary Boundaries: Exploring the Safe Operating Space for Humanity. *Ecology and Society,* 2009. https://www.ecologyandsociety.org/vol14/iss2/art32/; and Steffen *et al.*, 2015. Planetary Boundaries: Guiding human development on a changing planet. *Science* 347 (6223), 1259855.

3 ABC, 2017. Fatberg 'as heavy as 11 double-decker buses' found in London sewer. Australian Broadcasting Corporation, Sept 14, 2017. http://www.abc.net.au/news/2017-09-13/a-total-monster-fatberg-clogging-london-sewer/8933254

4 Global Atlas of Excreta, Wastewater Sludge, and Biosolids Management, 2008. https://unhabitat.org/books/global-atlas-of-excreta-wastewater-sludge-and-biosolids-management/

5 Sutton M A *et al.*, 2013. Our Nutrient World. The challenge to produce more food and energy with less pollution. Global Partnership on Nutrient Management, 2013. http://nora.nerc.ac.uk/id/eprint/500700/1/N500700BK.pdf

6 Rodriguez O, 2009. *London Rooftop Agriculture: a preliminary estimate of London's productive potential.* Welsh School of Architecture, 2009.

7 Sokol K, 2018. Scientists pioneer a new way to turn sunlight into fuel. Cambridge University, September 6, 2018. https://www.cam.ac.uk/research/news/scientists-pioneer-a-new-way-to-turn-sunlight-into-fuel

8 Caputo S, 2018. How urban farmers are learning to grow food without soil or natural light. *The Conversation*, Feb 13, 2018. http://theconversation.com/how-urban-farmers-are-learning-to-grow-food-without-soil-or-natural-light-88720

9 Cribb J H J, 2017. *Surviving the 21st Century.* Springer 2017.

10 Caputo S, 2018. Op cit.

11 Caughill P, 2018. Why urban farming is changing the future of agriculture. WEF and Futurism, January 19 2018. https://t.co/w2mUdsbI3K

12 Judkis M, 2017. This shipping-container farm could someday solve the food desert problem. https://www.igrow.news/news/this-shipping-container-farm-could-someday-solve-the-food-desert-problem

13 Caughill P, 2018. Op cit.

14 Blue Smart Farms, 2018. http://www.bluesmartfarms.com/

15 Wong K, 2018. Paris to turn a third of its green space into urban farms. CNN, April 4, 2018. https://edition.cnn.com/style/amp/urban-farms-in-paris/index.html?__twitter_impression=true

16 Boeri S, 2018. Vertical Forest. https://www.stefanoboeriarchitetti.net/en/project/vertical-forest/

17 Cornu C, 2017. Vertical Forest is latest global trend. *Shanghai Daily*, October 15, 2017. https://www.shine.cn/archive/sunday/Vertical-Forest-is-latest-global-trend/shdaily.shtml

18 Hardman M, 2014. Look out behind the bus stop, here come guerrilla gardeners digging up an urban revolution. *The Conversation*,

July 17, 2014. http://theconversation.com/look-out-behind-the-bus-stop-here-come-guerrilla-gardeners-digging-up-an-urban-revolution-29225

19 Naidoo I, 2011. *The Edible Balcony*. http://theediblebalcony.com.au/book.html

20 Despommier D, 2010. *The Vertical Farm*. https://books.google.com.au/books/about/The_Vertical_Farm.html?id=0DxTK0jW35sC&printsec=frontcover&source=kp_read_button&redir_esc=y#v=onepage&q&f=false; and Cornell University, 2013. Visiting Professor at Cornell Encourages Vertical Farming in Buildings. Cornell University, April 25, 2013.

21 Plantagon, 2017. Urban Agriculture Just Got Serious. http://www.plantagon.com/

22 Hickman M, 2014. Agriculture-minded retirement community keeps greenthumbed residents happily occupied. MNN December 3, 2014. https://www.mnn.com/your-home/organic-farming-gardening/blogs/agriculture-minded-retirement-community-keeps-greenthumbed

23 Malek C, 2018. How does his garden grow? Sustainably, in the desert. *Arab News*, June 4, 2018. http://www.arabnews.com/node/1315006/saudi-arabia

24 CNN, 2018. The crops on this farm are grown vertically. http://money.cnn.com/video/news/2018/02/07/plenty-indoor-vertical-farming.cnnmoney/index.html

25 Cantieri J, 2018. Innovative Greenhouses Help Farmers Adapt to Climate Change. *National Geographic*, April 11, 2018. https://www.nationalgeographic.com/environment/future-of-food/telangana-india-agriculture-greenhouses/

26 Lufa Farms, 2018. Pure farms. https://montreal.lufa.com/en/farms

27 Cooke L, 2017. 6 urban farms feeding the world. *Inhabitat*, October 26, 2017. https://inhabitat.com/6-urban-farms-feeding-the-world/

28 Chow L, 2016. 3 Aquaponic Farms in Brooklyn Killing It. *Ecowatch*, June 17, 2016. https://www.ecowatch.com/3-aquaponic-farms-in-brooklyn-killing-it-1891176412.html

29 LivingGreen, 2018. https://livingreen.co.il/en/

30 CNN, 2018. 'World's largest vertical farm' to feed Middle East's high-fliers, CNN, July 11, 2018. https://edition.cnn.com/travel/article/dubai-vertical-farm-emirates-catering/?org=1364&lvl=100&ite=1910&lea=140666&ctr=0&par=1&trk

31 HumanHabitat, 2018. http://www.humanhabitat.dk/?portfolio=the-impact-farm&lang=en

32 Vuong L, 2018. 7 Offbeat Urban Farms Found Around the World. *Food52*, August 10, 2017. https://food52.com/blog/20185-7-offbeat-urban-farms-found-around-the-world

33 Kaplan D, 2017. Hospital Creates Largest Rooftop Farm In Boston. *GreenMatters*, December 2017. https://www.greenmatters.com/food/2017/11/02/fpayr/hospital-creates-largest-rooftop-farm-in-boston

34 HK Farm, 2018. Local Food. HK Farm website. http://www.hkfarm.org/local_food.html

35 Prinzessinnengarten, 2018. Nomadic Green and Princess Gardens. Website, 2018. http://prinzessinnengarten.net/about/

36 Nink E, 2015. Ten Unique Urban Agriculture Projects in Tokyo. *FoodTank*, 2015. https://foodtank.com/news/2015/02/tokyos-ten-most-notable-urban-agriculture-projects/

37 Cooke L, 2016. Belgian supermarket unveils plan to sell food grown on their own rooftop garden. *Inhabitat*, June 10, 2016. https://inhabitat.com/belgian-supermarket-unveils-plan-to-sell-food-grown-on-their-own-rooftop-garden/

38 Peters A, 2016. At This Supermarket, The Produce Section Grows Its Own Produce. *FastCompany* March 23, 2016. https://www.fastcompany.com/3058155/at-this-supermarket-the-produce-section-grows-its-own-produce

39 Cribb J H J, 2017. Solution to a looming global water crisis. Rolex Awards, April 4, 2017. http://blog.rolexawards.com/2017/04/solution-to-a-looming-global-water-crisis/

40 Holmgren D, 2018. About Permaculture. https://holmgren.com.au/about-permaculture/

41 Watts G, 2107. Critics of Permaculture. http://wattspermaculture.com.au/about-permaculture/critics-of-permaculture/

42 Sen A, 1962. An Aspect of Indian Agriculture. *Economic Weekly*, Vol. 14.

43 Falvey L, 2010. *Small Farmers Secure Food*. TSU Press, 2010.

44 Cribb J H J, 2012. Farm clearances at tipping point. *Sydney Morning Herald*, July 23, 2012. https://www.smh.com.au/politics/federal/farm-clearances-at-tipping-point-20120722-22hwp.html

45 Monbiot G, 2008. Small is Bountiful. Monbiot blog, June 10, 2008. http://www.monbiot.com/2008/06/10/small-is-bountiful/

46 Rolex, 2017. Anyone Can Change Everything. Also: http://www.rolexawards.com/

47 The Bonn Challenge, 2018. http://www.bonnchallenge.org/

48 Trillion Trees, 2018. A shared vision for more trees on our Planet. https://www.trilliontrees.org/

49 Vergara W *et al.*, 2016. The Economic Case for Landscape Restoration in Latin America. World Resources Institute, October 2016. http://www.wri.org/publication/economic-case-for-restoration-20x20

50 Poore J and Nemecek T, 2018. Reducing food's environmental impacts through producers and consumers. *Science*, June 1, 2018. http://science.sciencemag.org/content/360/6392/987

51 Alexander S, 2018. Stephanie Alexander Kitchen Garden Foundation. https://www.kitchengardenfoundation.org.au/content/pleasurable-food-education

52 Charas L, 2017. *Food Forever*. Feeding Good, Utrecht, Netherlands, 2017. http://www.feedinggood.com/food-forever

53 Radd S, 2016. *Food as Medicine*. http://foodasmedicine.cooking/

54 Bittman M, 2010. *The Food Matters Cookbook*. Simon Schuster, 2010. https://www.goodreads.com/book/show/7775632-the-food-matters-cookbook

55 Lappe A, 2010. *Diet for a Hot Planet*. Bloomsbury, USA, March 30, 2010. https://annalappe.com/portfolio/diet-for-a-hot-planet/

56 Oliver J, 2014. The next food revolution. https://ideas.ted.com/the-next-food-revolution/

Chapter 9

1 Ehrlich P and Harte J, 2015. Food security requires a new revolution. *International Journal of Environmental Studies*, 2015. https://www.tandfonline.com/doi/abs/10.1080/00207233.2015.1067468

2 Nierenberg D, 2018. We're a global community pushing for food system change. Food Tank – the thinktank for food. https://foodtank.com/

3 Foley J, 2013. Changing the Global Food Narrative. https://global ecoguy.org/changing-the-global-food-narrative-ae918e620b14

4 O'Neill D W *et al.*, 2018. A good life for all within planetary boundaries. *Nature Sustainability*, 88, 2018. http://go.nature.com/2nOPrSf

5 O'Neill D W, 2018. Living well, within planetary boundaries. *Natureresearch: Sustainability*. https://sustainabilitycommunity .nature.com/users/81832-daniel-o-neill/posts/29930-living-well-within-planetary-boundaries

6 Fan S, 2018. Innovations in food systems: The key to human and planetary health. IFPRI Blog, March 27, 2018. http://www.ifpri.org/blog/innovations-food-systems-key-human-and-planetary-health

7 See, for example, Kiley-Worthington M, 1981. Ecological agriculture. What it is and how it works. *Agriculture and Environment*, 6 (4), December 1981. https://www.sciencedirect.com/science/article/pii/0304113181900394

8 Moss D and Bittman M, 2018. Bringing Farming Back to Nature. *New York Times*, June 26, 2018. https://www.nytimes.com/2018/06/26/opinion/farming-organic-nature-movement.html

9 Moeller N and Pimbert M, 2018. We know how food production needs to change if crisis is to be avoided – so why isn't this happening? *The Conversation*, March 26, 2018. http://theconversation.com/we-know-how-food-production-needs-to-change-if-crisis-is-to-be-avoided-so-why-isnt-this-happening-92903

10 Da Silva J G, 2018. Agroecology: A Path to Sustainable Development. Foodtank, April 2018. https://foodtank.com/news/2018/04/jose-graziando-da-silva-agroecology-path-sustainable-development/amp/?_twitter_impression=true

11 Mann C, 2018. *The Wizard and the Prophet*. Penguin/Random House, 2018. https://www.penguinrandomhouse.com/books/220698/the-wizard-and-the-prophet-by-charles-c-mann/9780307961693/

12 C4 Rice Project, 2018. https://c4rice.com/the-project-2/project-goals/

13 Chory J, 2018. *Harnessing Planet for the Future*. Salk Institute, 2018. https://www.salk.edu/wp-content/uploads/2017/11/Harnessing-Plants.pdf

14 Stapper M, 2018. The Link Between Healthy Food and Biological Farming. *Future Directions International*, June 28, 2018. http://www.futuredirections.org.au/publication/dr-maarten-stapper-link-healthy-food-biological-farming-part-one/

15 Falvey, 2010. Op cit.

16 FAO, 2016. State of World Fisheries and Aquaculture (SOFIA) 2016. http://www.fao.org/3/a-i5798e.pdf

17 FAO, 2016. State of the World's Fisheries and Aquaculture, 2016. http://www.fao.org/3/a-i5555e.pdf

18 William M *et al.*, 2017. Cutting Out the Middle Fish: Marine Microalgae as the Next Sustainable Omega-3 Fatty Acids and Protein Source. *Industrial Biotechnology*, Oct 1, 2017. https://www.liebertpub.com/doi/10.1089/ind.2017.29102.wmo

19 Ajjawi I. et al. 2017. Lipid production in *Nannochloropsis gaditana* is doubled by decreasing expression of a single transcriptional regulator. *Nature Biotechnology*, 35, 647–52. DOI: 10.1038/nbt.3865. https://www.ncbi.nlm.nih.gov/pubmed/28628130

20 Sedayu B B, 2018. Seaweed, Indonesia's answer to the global plastic crisis. The Conversation/WEF, June 6, 2018. https://theconversation.com/seaweed-indonesias-answer-to-the-global-plastic-crisis-95587

21 Ullah K *et al.*, 2014. Algal biomass as a global source of transport fuels: Overview and development perspectives. *Progress in Natural Science*, Sept 2014. https://www.sciencedirect.com/science/article/pii/S1002007114000860

22 Jones R, 2017. *Aquaculture could feed the world and protect the planet - if we get it right.* The Nature Conservancy/WEF Oct 18, 2017. https://www.weforum.org/agenda/2017/10/how-aquaculture-can-feed-the-world-and-save-the-planet-at-the-same-time/?utm_content=buffer59662&utm_medium=social&utm_source=twitter.com&utm_campaign=buffer

23 Gunther M, 2018. Can Deepwater Aquaculture Avoid the Pitfalls of Coastal Fish Farms? YaleEnvironment360, Jan 25, 2018. https://e360.yale.edu/features/can-deepwater-aquaculture-avoid-the-pitfalls-of-coastal-fish-farms

24 Bush S *et al.*, 2018. *How fish farms are helping to fight hunger on a global level.* The Conversation/WEF. https://www.weforum.org/agenda/2018/03/let-them-eat-carp-fish-farms-are-helping-to-fight-hunger

25 FAO, 2018. Cities of despair - or opportunity? http://www.fao.org/ag/agp/greenercities/en/whyuph/index.html?utm_source=twitter&utm_medium=social+media&utm_campaign=faoknowledge

26 Wikipedia, 2018. Urban agriculture. https://en.wikipedia.org/wiki/Urban_agriculture

27 VFS, 2018. Advantages of Vertical Farms. http://www.verticalfarms.com.au/advantages-vertical-farming

28 Laird R, 2018. A National Security Perspective on Vertical Farming: Reducing Supply Chain Vulnerabilities. *DefenceInfo*, October 21, 2018. https://defense.info/featured-story/2018/10/a-national-security-perspective-on-vertical-farming-reducing-supply-chain-vulnerabilities/

29 Wikipedia, 2018. Hydroponics. https://en.wikipedia.org/wiki/Hydroponics

30 Permaculture News, 2018. What is aquaponics? https://perma
    culturenews.org/2016/05/30/what-is-aquaponics-and-how-does-it-work/
31 Aerofarms, 2018. Our technology. http://aerofarms.com/technology/
32 Wikipedia, 2018. Insect farming. https://en.wikipedia.org/wiki/
    Insect_farming
33 ICARDA, 2018. Protected agriculture: productive use of marginal
    land. https://www.icarda.org/tools/protected-agriculture
34 Chow L, 2015. Giant Solar Floating Farm Could Produce 8,000 Tons
    of Vegetables Annually. *Ecowatch*, May 26, 2015. https://www
    .ecowatch.com/giant-solar-floating-farm-could-produce-8-000-tons-
    of-vegetables-annua-1882045025.html
35 Hirschberg C *et al.*, 2016. The changing market for food delivery.
    McKinsey & Company, November, 2016. https://www.mckinsey
    .com/industries/high-tech/our-insights/the-changing-market-for-
    food-delivery
36 Post M, 2018. *Cultured meat.* Maastricht University, 2018. https://
    culturedbeef.org/
37 Tuomisto H L and Teixeira de Mattos M J, 2011. Environmental
    Impacts of Cultured Meat Production. *Environ. Sci. Technol.*, 45,
    6117–23. DOI: 10.1021/es200130u.
38 UN GEF, 2018. Novel entities: GEF STAP Report. GEF, June 25, 2018
    https://www.thegef.org/publications/novel-entities-and-gef
39 Peters A, 2018. Lab-Grown Meat Is Getting Cheap Enough For
    Anyone To Buy. FastCompany, March 5, 2018. https://
    www.fastcompany.com/40565582/lab-grown-meat-is-getting-cheap-
    enough-for-anyone-to-buy
40 Rorheim A, 2016. Cultured Meat: An Ethical Alternative To
    Industrial Animal Farming. https://sentience-politics.org/files/
    cultured-meat-revision.pdf
41 Mattick C, 2018. Cellular agriculture: The coming revolution in food
    production. Bulletin of the Atomic Scientists, January 8, 2018. https://
    www.tandfonline.com/doi/full/10.1080/00963402.2017.1413059
42 Stephens N *et al.*, 2018. Bringing cultured meat to market:
    Technical, socio-political, and regulatory challenges in Cellular
    Agriculture. *Trends in Food Science & Technology*, https://doi.org/
    10.1016/j.tifs.2018.04.010
43 Chadwick J, 2017. Here's how 3D food printers are changing what we
    eat. *TechRepublic*, November 7, 2017. https://www.techrepublic.com/
    article/heres-how-3d-food-printers-are-changing-the-way-we-cook/

44 Proffitt C, 2017. Top 10 3D Printing Companies to Watch in the
    Food Industry. *Disruptor Daily*, May 31, 2017. https://www.disruptor
    daily.com/3d-printing-watch-food-industry/
45 http://foodplantsinternational.com/plants/
46 Food Plant Solutions, 2018. https://foodplantsolutions.org/about-us/
    A history of the project is here: https://foodplantsolutions.org/
47 Fuangchain A *et al.*, 2011. Hypoglycemic effect of bitter melon
    compared with metformin in newly diagnosed type 2 diabetes
    patients. *J. Ethnoparmacol.*, March 24, 2011. https://www.ncbi.nlm
    .nih.gov/pubmed/21211558

INDEX